Becoming a Constant Object in Psychotherapy with the Borderline Patient

COMMENTARY

"This volume sets forth in a down-to-earth fashion the clinical applicability of such mystical-sounding terms as *holding* and *containing*. The book includes an abundance of compelling clinical vignettes that describe the verbatim dialogues between patient and therapist, guiding the reader with a commentary describing effective and mistaken interventions. Therapists at all levels of experience have known the difficulty of keeping the borderline patient in treatment, given his or her urgent need for a quick cure. A special feature of this book is that the authors advocate a therapeutic position termed *standing still* that helps that patient develop a realistic time sense and the patience and frustration tolerance to withstand the duration and trials and tribulations of treatment." —**Jeffrey Seinfeld, Ph.D.**

"This book focuses on how the therapist deals with the basis deficit in the capacity for object constancy during the initial, 'preconstancy' stage of treatment, when an attachment between patient and therapist must be formed. Cohen and Sherwood are especially sensitive to the effect of the therapist's interventions and silences on the therapeutic relationship. They advocate that the therapist say little and stand still in order to create an atmosphere in which the patient's sense of time is broadened and within which the patient can form an attachment to the therapist and develop object constancy." —**Andrew Druck, Ph.D.**

"This book provides an approach to the borderline patient organized around the key issues of abandonment fears, intolerance of separation, and difficulties with affect taming. The authors describe a method for expanding the patient's time sense, which affects the way he experiences affects and in turn can lead gradually to increased object constancy. Also recommended is a therapeutic posture correlated with the phase of treatment and the status of object constancy. Clarity of presentation, illustrative clinical vignettes, and good organization are especially noteworthy in this dynamically based account that is clinically focused." —**Marvin Hurvich, Ph.D.**

"Highly specific in focus, Cohen and Sherwood set out to present a thoughtful, informed, practical approach for conceptualizing and handling the opening phase of treatment with the borderline patient. The authors have achieved this and a great deal more. All therapists, regardless of discipline, level of training and experience, and theoretical persuasion, will find this book extraordinarily useful—an important reference to return to over and again." —**Paul Lerner, Ed.D.**

Becoming a Constant Object in Psychotherapy with the Borderline Patient

Charles P. Cohen, Ph.D., and
Vance R. Sherwood, Ph.D.

𝒜

JASON ARONSON INC.
Northvale, New Jersey
London

Production and interior design: *Gloria L. Jordan*
Editorial Director: *Muriel Jorgensen*

This book was set in 12/14 Garamond
by Alpha Graphics in Pittsfield, New Hampshire
and printed and bound by Haddon Craftsmen in Scranton,
Pennsylvania

Library of Congress Cataloging-in-Publication Data

Cohen, Charles P.
  Becoming a constant object in psychotherapy with the borderline
patient / Charles P. Cohen and Vance R. Sherwood.
    p.m.
  Includes bibliographical references and index.
  ISBN 0-87668-613-7
  1. Borderline personality disorder—Treatment. 2. Object
constancy (Psychoanalysis) 3. Psychotherapist and patient.
4. Psychotherapy. I. Sherwood, Vance R. II. Title.
  [DNLM: 1. Borderline Personality Disorder—therapy. 2. Object
Attachment. 3. Psychotherapy. WM 190 C678b]
RC569.5.B67C64   1991
616.85'852—dc20
DNLM/DLC
for Library of Congress   90-14556

Manufactured in the United States of America. Jason Aronson Inc. offers books and cassettes. For information and catalog write to Jason Aronson Inc., 230 Livingston Street, Northvale, New Jersey 07647.

To Lee and Alma

Contents

Acknowledgment

We offer our heartfelt appreciation to Jason Aronson, whose encouragement and guidance made this book possible.

We also thank the *Bulletin of the Menninger Foundation* for their kind permission to use portions of our paper, "Becoming a Constant Object for the Borderline Patient." And we acknowledge the help of Mark Horner, of the University of Tennessee, who supplied portions of the clinical material in this work.

We warmly thank Dr. Donna Walter Sherwood for her help in untangling tangled sentences and for wisely knowing when not to offer more help.

Finally, thanks to Gerald Sundal, for being a constant object.

Introduction

This book, like most events in the world, may be said to have
had multiple determinants. As practicing clinicians, we wanted
to understand and work more effectively with borderline patients. In studying the subject, we found that, with rare exceptions, the clinical literature relied heavily on hypothetical constructs borrowed from psychoanalytic metapsychology. While
that language has undeniably been rich and also useful in many
ways, we found it was a difficult language for describing the
experience of the patient and, to a slightly lesser extent, the
experience of the clinician. Constructs gleaned from psychoanalytic metapsychology tend to be somewhat arid and detached;
such terms as *unneutralized aggression* and *primitive defense*
sound inanimate or bloodless. It is hard to use such a language
to capture life as it is lived. Additionally, this language comes
from the observer's point of view. When hearing, for example,
that a patient has engaged in *projective identification*, one may
still have very little idea how the patient actually behaved, what
he or she experienced at the time, or how the patient organized
the interpersonal situation at that moment.

An additional incentive came from our experiences training
clinical students and consulting with fellow professionals. We
have found it frustrating to refer students and peers to the

clinical literature only to discover that they could not always make the leap from the theoretical constructs used there to actual clinical encounters—much less know what to do with the patient. We have too often worked with clinicians who were trying hard to do good therapy but who simply had no clear rationale for what they were doing with borderline patients. What often seemed missing was a capacity to see the world through the eyes of the patient, letting this guide one's therapeutic approach.

We do not imagine that this book is somehow the cure for all of these ills. It is certainly not a substitute for a solid intellectual foundation in the principles of personality development, psychopathology, and psychotherapy. Neither is it a substitute for undergoing one's own therapy nor for the ongoing consultation that should be part of one's professional career. Nevertheless, we believe there is value in trying to present a more descriptive, "experience-near" way of discussing the borderline patient.

This book focuses on the first stage of therapy with borderline patients, what we term the "preconstancy" stage, or the time during which a constant attachment must be formed between patient and therapist. Even though this is the first phase of treatment, it is neither quick nor easy to resolve. We believe therapists should expect the preconstancy phase to last at least a year and likely longer. This book is an effort to trace the issues facing the therapist during that time—quite probably a very stormy time.

We describe a treatment approach that calls for considerable restraint and discipline. Psychoanalytic technique and the techniques of the dynamic psychotherapies are all disciplined, of course, but we believe that most of the techniques and interventions taught by those schools of thought will not be helpful during the preconstancy stage of treatment. We propose a treatment approach built around broadening the patient's time sense. This may seem ironic, since we complain that classical metapsychology is too abstracted from actual experience, and since no category is more abstract than that of time. However, we think the patient's experience of self and other can be better grasped using such temporal categories as urgency and crisis, and emphasizing the "now is forever" quality to these patients' experience of affect. A treatment approach aimed at changing the time sense requires patience from the therapist, and a willingness to endure the frustrations of a process that is very gradual indeed.

The first chapter outlines our position. There we describe how we think the therapeutic task is different with borderline patients than with those suffering less severe disturbances, and we describe the importance of object constancy as an organizing factor in the personality. We trace a therapeutic posture we call standing still that, we believe, contributes to achieving constancy. It may be well to state here that there is nothing radical or utterly new in what we advocate. To the extent that we say anything different from what is readily found in other clinical works it is that we believe there is a particular frame of mind the clinician must assume, one in which therapists must be willing to *take their time*. This may be simple to say; it is not, unfortunately, simple to do.

The second chapter reviews some of the historical and current literature as it relates to the early stages of treatment. In this chapter we find the origins of two subtypes of borderline patient: the noisy, histrionic, and excessively dramatic type; and a quieter, as-if group, who present a false-self kind of compliance. This dichotomy is used throughout the book; we believe it helps in highlighting different etiologies and different tasks facing the therapist.

Chapter 3 continues themes begun in Chapter 2 but with a view on highlighting specific treatment issues likely to arise during the first stage of therapy. In addition to comparing the positions of leading writers in the field, we add our own approach to these issues. This is a relatively brief chapter and serves chiefly to sharpen the focus of discussion before heading into the next three chapters.

Chapters 4, 5, and 6 are the guts of the book. Each is built around a critical aspect of borderline pathology: Chapter 4 addresses the patient's perpetual concern with abandonment, Chapter 5 the patient's inability to modulate affect, and Chapter 6 the borderline individual's intolerance of separateness and autonomy. We believe these issues will dominate treatment for most of the preconstancy stage and will challenge both the therapist's skill and patience. However, these issues will arise in different ways for the noisy type of patient versus the quieter, as-if patient; therapists must be alert to this, using different approaches with each type of patient. We believe therapists can think through these problems by relating them to the patient's overly narrow time sense, and that is our approach in each chapter. We argue that standing still addresses these aspects of pathology by broadening the time sense. These chapters are practice-oriented; they carry many clinical vignettes, and each chapter ends with a transcript and commentary.

Chapters 7, 8, and 9 constitute the third and last section of the book. These chapters address changes in the patient and also in the therapy relationship the therapist is likely to see during the final months of the preconstancy stage. Chapter 7 deals with the creation of a secure and reliable ambience that we term the adaptive matrix. Here we address a variety of topics, ranging from therapy's physical setting to the (in our view often misunderstood) role of empathy. Chapter 8, titled "Differentiating Constancy," addresses the patient's gradually unfolding ability to differentiate among separate feelings near the end of the preconstancy stage and the attendant capacity to tolerate self-other differentiation. In Chapter 9, "Reparation Constancy," we deal with the final issue of the preconstancy stage, learning to repair broken relationships. Borderline patients have gone through their lives expecting relationships to end abruptly when there is a disagreement or when a flaw is discovered in self or other. We believe this changes near the conclusion of the preconstancy stage and that the discovery that relationships can be durable and reliable effectively ends the preconstancy stage.

In the last three chapters we advocate changes in the therapist's technique. It is too simple to say that the therapist must become more active, and yet this is true. After having cautioned therapists to show considerable patience during most of the preconstancy stage, we suggest ways in which the therapist must actively respond to changes in the relationship as a constant attachment is achieved. By the conclusion of the reparation constancy phase, therapists will essentially be handling the case as they would a normal therapy case, reclaiming the techniques and interventions that, we argue, are ineffective with borderline patients before object constancy is achieved.

We wrote this book with the hope of clarifying various issues borderline patients face in their daily life and also the attendant treatment dilemmas therapists face. Throughout we have tried to avoid, as much as possible, language and categories that are too abstracted from life as it is lived or therapy as it is actually experienced. To the extent that we have been successful, the book is missing metapsychological concepts and developmental discussions that are often part and parcel of this sort of work. This is not to say that we think such categories are without merit, however, and in fact we hope that readers will be stimulated enough by some of our ideas to become more familiar with the broader literature that is available today, especially those works written from a psychoanalytic perspective. Most of all, we have wanted to offer therapists a starting point for engaging this troubled and troublesome population, and if we have done this, we are content.

Part I

THE THERAPEUTIC TASK

1

Standing Still

The Changing Nature of the Therapeutic
  Task
Object Constancy
Standing Still
Using Time as a Vehicle for Change

The Changing Nature of the Therapeutic Task

The case examples of the early psychoanalysts are amazing to the modern reader; as the Dutch phenomenologist Van den Berg (1961) said, they read like novels. There seems some thread that runs through the symptom picture, some clue to be tracked down, and, eventually, some secret to be learned when the thread is followed to its end. Unlike the plots of most novels, however, the secret was hidden not only from the detective who was following the train of clues; it was also hidden from the "guilty parties," from the patients themselves. The early psychoanalytic patients wanted to keep their secrets from themselves more than from anyone else. Their secret thoughts, wishes, and fantasies took them places their Victorian values and the standards of their day would not let them travel. They were willing to suffer rather than face the products of their hidden wishes, and in time their suffering could become substantial.

Some of this is hard to imagine today; the cultural differences between then and now are jarring. Both the rigid social structure and a morality that seems heavily oppressive by present standards are foreign to late-twentieth-century Western society. It can be difficult to grasp how important it was to these early patients to conform to the structures and institutions of their day. They seemed to prefer being miserable to accepting their guilt. And yet their own ability to repress was not as great as that of their society. Freud (Breuer and Freud 1895) said his patients suffered reminiscences, meaning that their attempts to forget their unacceptable wishes were not completely successful. What was hidden was not entirely hidden, and that is what the early analyst figured out.

As is well known now, Freud found that his patient's symptoms were distorted expressions of these unacceptable impulses. Thus the art of the early therapist lay in deciphering a confusing symptom picture by laying bare the unthinkable wishes behind the symptom. The key to unraveling the confusion was making connections between events or fantasies from the past and the symptoms dogging the patient in the present. As Spence (1987) noted, the Freudian enterprise was built on a kind of peeling back of layers akin to the task of the archaeologist (cf. Gay 1988). The therapist sought to explore progressively deeper levels until an event or wish was uncovered that could be regarded as the core of the problem. Presumably the event was so traumatic or the wish so conflict-laden that normal development was arrested. The early analysts found they could cure much of this simply by learning their patients' secrets and by saying aloud what their patients had, to that point, not even dared think.

Today, of course, there seems precious little that remains unthinkable. If Victorian men and women were burdened by their values, the same could hardly be said of us today—we tend to travel light when it comes to principles. Wheelis (1958) saw this some time ago and made a good point when he said this shift may be necessary in a fluid society. A culture accustomed to rapid change favors those who adapt smoothly to new circumstances. In such a context, an individual who preserves a firm and unyielding value system runs the risk of being obsolete, of being unable to adjust to change. Where values and institutions are no longer absolute, there is little that need remain latent, and there is a corresponding decline in what must be kept out of consciousness, or repressed.

These changes raise the question of whether the therapeutic task has not also been changed. The factors that lent coherence to the early patients' personalities are increasingly missing today. Particularly remarkable about those early psychoanalytic cases is that in spite of outrageously confusing symptoms, a coherent picture of the case was possible and was usually gained fairly early. A coherent picture was possible because there was some underlying coherence in these patients' personalities or sense of self. This phenomenon is not surprising because their families mirrored a society in which roles were well differentiated, choices of action clear-cut, and consequences relevant for the future. These patients did not ask questions about their identities; rather, they felt blocked in expressing their identities or in becoming who they felt they were supposed to be. Their symptoms (and beyond them, their unthinkable wishes) lay in the way. But they *knew* who they were supposed to be.

While early analytic patients were trying to conform to values taken to be absolute and therefore unquestioned, today's patients are more likely simply to be reacting to their life circumstances, which are hardly absolute and tend to be transient. Such fluidity makes it harder to achieve either psychological or moral integrity. Of course, it is indisputable that some overarching integration remains with most persons even in a time of anomie and rapid change. And yet it is also indisputable that increasing numbers of patients seem to caricature the fluidity and reactivity of contemporary life. We refer chiefly to borderline individuals, and we believe the therapeutic task is much different with these patients than it was with the Victorian patients on whom our craft was forged.

In its early days psychotherapy became associated with discovering what was hidden, with making manifest what was latent. The analyst was a detective who pursued clues and hints until they added up to understandable sequences and patterns. To this day the dynamic psychotherapies are built around the search for such phenomena. Therapists are taught to seek out patterns or converging themes and meanings that will become the focus of interventions. For example, Basch (1980) writes of the "patterns of expectation" and "contradictory and unknown pattern[s] of motivation" that unconsciously determine behavior and must be uncovered in therapy (p. 35). Langs (1973) says, "The session begins with the patient talking about whatever is on his mind, thereby developing the major theme of the hour" (p. 279) and "In each session the therapist must search for the central issues and problems in the patient's current life" (p. 282). In both cases the therapist is advised to look for a coherent structure in the patient's productions: The "patterns of expectation and motivation," "major themes," and "central issues and problems" may be used by the therapist as guidelines for organizing what the patient presents.

We do not believe such principles of treatment can be used successfully with borderline patients. These principles presume much more coherence and organization than borderline patients are capable of. The personal lives of these patients—and their symptom pictures—seem always in flux. The well-known "stable instability" (Grinker et al. 1968, Schmideberg 1959) of borderline patients implies the shifting, fluid nature of their inner and interpersonal experience. There can be an amorphous, hard-to-get-hold-of quality to what ails borderline patients, who may complain of nothing more delineated than a generalized feeling of inner emptiness or a vague despair about their lives. Of course, others present florid symptom pictures in stormy, dramatic sessions. Yet even when there are flagrant and well-defined symptoms, these tend to come and go and to alternate with other, seemingly interchangeable problems. The clinician may well feel bewildered and at a loss to determine how to organize such apparent chaos.

Lacking a coherent experience of self and other, borderline patients cannot present themselves in a focused or integrated manner in the therapy hour, nor for that matter will they experience their therapists in integrated and focused ways. Therapists will be frustrated if they try to address a particular theme or symptom cluster or if they listen for converging meanings and issues. Borderline patients are simply not able to offer themselves to another person in such a way.

This lack of coherence changes the therapeutic task with these patients. Beyond the basic human tendency to seek meaning in events, our training as therapists predisposes us to organize what we hear and see with our patients. It is a mistake, however, to try to do this at the outset of treatment with borderline patients and can only be accomplished by superimposing the therapist's own meanings and organizations onto the inchoate and fluid productions of the patient. As such, the attempt to organize the borderline patient's poorly focused material early in treatment is a form of countertransference: The therapist attempts to allay his or her anxiety over both the disorganization of the patient's material and the therapist's own strongly felt need to "understand" it.

It can sometimes be terribly hard, moreover, even to pretend that one understands. Early sessions with the borderline patient can be like walking through a house of mirrors in search of someone. As we have described elsewhere (Cohen and Sherwood 1989), there is a "now you see it, now you don't" quality to what the patient is trying to communicate. Borderline patients may change subjects frequently—often several times within a session—and their presentations will be laced with lapses and silences, premature conclusions, and the unexpected intrusion of unrelated issues. Therapists may have to endure a confusing variety of complaints (many about the therapist), alternating with rapid changes of affect and repeated reversals by the patient on important subjects. There is little to get hold of with any certainty in such sessions, and after several months of this therapists may come to question whether these sessions can hold any meaning for such a patient.

The answer is no if therapists approach borderline patients with the same interventions and techniques they would use with less disturbed individuals. To work with this population, therapists will have to surrender for a time many of their most cherished notions of what constitutes proper treatment. Effective therapy with borderline patients will not depend at first on confrontations, interpretations, empathic mirroring, or the other major tools of the dynamic psychotherapies, though these may become useful at a later stage in therapy. Until there is greater coherence, borderline patients cannot make use of traditional therapeutic interventions.

We believe that the key to integration with borderline patients lies in the achievement of object constancy, an achievement that was certainly not at issue for the early analytic patients but that certainly is at issue today. Therapy will have the best chance of success if therapists apply themselves to the task of becoming constant objects for their borderline patients, and that, of course, is the subject of this book. In the following sections of this chapter we will, first, present our understanding of the constancy concept and then describe a therapeutic stance offering an opportunity for the achievement of constancy and, indirectly, the personality integration needed to return to the interventions and techniques used with less disturbed patients.

Object Constancy

In recent years there has been increasing attention given to object constancy as a process that helps to organize the personality. For example, Mahler and her co-workers (McDevitt 1975, Mahler et al. 1975) pointed to constancy as a foundation for identity formation. Rinsley (1982) described the organizing properties of object constancy as factors that help move individuals past such primitive psychological phenomena as entitlement, perpetual fear of abandonment, and magical thinking. Adler (1985) emphasized the same process—though using such terms as "holding introjects" rather than object constancy—as the basis for a coherent sense of self. While the definitive statement on constancy has probably not yet been made, the process seems to be seen as crucial to the child's growing ability to experience self and others in whole, realistic, and healthy ways.

Object constancy usually refers to the child's capacity to

remain attached to the mother even in her physical absence, when there is no instinctual need of her, or even when the child is angry with her. If the child can feel continuously connected to the mother under these circumstances, then the relationship between mother and child is constant indeed. Most writers (e.g., Burgner and Edgcumbe 1972, Mahler and Furer 1968) refer to an internalized image of the mother that comforts the child much as the actual mother did earlier in life. Constancy is said to be firmly established when the child can evoke a comforting inner image of the mother and when such an image is not deteriorated by the mother's absences or by the child's occasional strong feelings against her.

Contemporary writers on constancy place its consolidation no earlier than between 24 and 30 months (e.g., Leon 1987, Mahler et al. 1975). While the child may be able to evoke the maternal image by 18 months, the well-known turmoil of Mahler's rapprochement subphase appears to interrupt the child's ability to make comforting use of that image. Bergman (personal communication) speculates that rapid cognitive advances during the second year of life may enable children to represent their separateness from the mother at increasingly realistic levels. The resulting, somewhat sudden realization that Mother is a separate person then interferes with the comfort that can be taken from her remembered image. Since children are rapidly becoming more autonomous during this time, the sudden appreciation of separateness may not be welcome and may make their growing independence from the mother frightening. Most children do not want to exchange independence for a comforting enmeshment, and yet they do not want independence to come at the cost of being utterly alone. Object constancy is attained when children achieve the sense that even when they are separate, they are not alone; the mother is felt to be constantly available.

Independence from the mother, therefore, is the context within which constancy is pursued. Object constancy is often discussed in a related but different context, the child's fear of abandonment by the mother. We do not believe this is an accurate statement of the child's predicament. We believe the problem for the child is not whether the mother will leave, but *whether she will still be there if the child moves away.* The question children must answer is whether it is all right to leave the mother by becoming less dependent on her (Sherwood 1989). If children can gradually muster a sense of constant connectedness with the mother, they can pursue their individual identities without overwhelming distress at their separateness.

Kaplan (1978) has described object constancy as an illusion through which children maintain a delicate balance between a past that offered safety and a future yet to be discovered. Constancy can be seen as a kind of emotional home base from which children may venture forth to confront the larger world. Object constancy stabilizes this enlarged world through the illusion that a familiar presence sees, defines, and validates the child's strivings and feelings. This illusion serves as an emotional bridge for children: They may travel forward to explore and be challenged by the unknown, or return for a time-out from the strains of reconciling the familiar and the strange, the hopes and disappointments, the loving and the hating.

The child develops confidence that the mother is continuously available through repeated experiences of successfully separating and reuniting with her. The well-known game of "peekaboo" is a metaphor of the process. In this game, losing the other and being reunited are placed in a benevolent context. Parent and child share the experience of being lost to each other, gradually draw out the tension in a playful manner, and then celebrate the joy of reunion. The benevolence of this experience comes from the child's being allowed to participate actively in the process rather than restricted to the role of victim. Additionally, the tension is kept at a level the child can tolerate.

These are key elements in the overall mother–child relationship. Children must not only learn that the mother can disappear and return but that they, too, must be able to leave and come back. Once the child has moved away—either through a period of independence or perhaps through being angry—it is crucial that the mother be available when reunion is sought. When children seek refueling after independence, or reparation after anger, but find the mother unavailable, the tension may be more than they can manage, and the experience is destructive. The child comes to feel that leaving is not safe, that home base may not be there to return to.

The lesson the child gleans from such experiences is that unless others are clung to, they may disappear and leave the child terrifyingly alone. This impermanence to important relationships compromises the child's ability to express anger. Winnicott (1960) used the term "holding environment" to describe the way parents provide a stable and patient response to their child's intense emotions and destructive impulses, enabling children to learn that the world can maintain itself in the face of their rage. Without such a holding environment, children fear that anger can destroy an attachment. They are then left with untenable choices when angry: They may either underreact to frustration and thereby risk exploitation by others, or risk feeling overwhelmed with guilt if they do behave angrily— and then make some masochistic submission to undo the "damage" and magically restore the relationship.

While most theorists speak of the child's forming an internalized representation of the mother, it is at least as true that the mother also becomes a representation of the child (Sherwood 1989). On their own, young children cannot readily organize the mass of tensions and urges they experience. The mother's responses, however, if empathically attuned, will help children tolerate tension, organize inner chaos, and define discrete affects, thereby bringing a growing order to the inner life (Stern 1985). By consistently mirroring the child's inner strivings and feelings, the mother makes herself a representation of the child for the child to see. This is the mother who is internalized as a constant object—the mother in her mirroring role. Consequently, when children internalize the mother, they also internalize the sense of being seen, defined, and validated. Object constancy is the sense that the mother is constantly available in her mirroring function; children who feel that the mother who sees them is always available may pursue independent functioning with security.

By contrast, children who lack the sense that the mirroring mother is constantly available will have trouble becoming their own persons and will be forced to build their identities upon staying close. If the child needs the mother to feel safe, and if the mother cannot be counted on to be available when the child moves off, then the child will not move off. Clinging dependency replaces object constancy as the chief source of security, and identity must then be built around having some other who offers definition, not around pursuit of the child's own intentions and initiatives.

The borderline patient lacks object constancy. Those interpersonal and psychological achievements that are built on constancy are consequently missing, including the capacity for mature attachments, the ability to tolerate being alone, and a sense of sameness or continuity with self across time. In their place, borderline patients bring these convictions to treatment: Their important relationships are tenuous, and abandonment is inevitable; they cannot demand that their own needs be met in a relationship without losing the other person; anger and independent strivings will destroy a relationship; aloneness equals loss of self.

Patients with such convictions cannot approach the therapist as their ally in a difficult task any more than they can approach other relationships with confidence and hope. Rather, they come to treatment eager to find someone who will take care of them but assuming at the same time that the therapist will eventually grow tired of them, betray them, or throw them out of the office. Before borderline patients can make full use of the treatment they certainly need, their therapist must become a constant object; these patients must fashion the illusion that their therapists are always available to know them and to "hold" them. Before anything else is addressed, the therapist must create a context in which the slow processes of attachment and growth can take place.

Standing Still

Forming an attachment with the borderline patient will not come about through what the therapist says or does. In fact, therapists should take care to say and do relatively little during the first stage of treatment with the borderline patient. The basic therapeutic stance during the preconstancy stage of treatment is essentially that of waiting for attachment to unfold over time. There are interventions that will aid the formation of a constant attachment, and these will be discussed throughout this book. But in general the therapist's interventions are much less important than the ability to wait.

We describe the therapist's restrained and patient approach by the phrase "standing still." We mean to capture in this phrase the way in which therapists must avoid responding and intervening as they would with most patients and, instead, become practiced in the art of not intervening even when the patient virtually demands some help or relief. It is essential that therapists surrender their hopes of "getting something done," "making progress," and even "helping" the patient.

The closest analogy to the structure of therapy with the borderline patient is the experience of being with someone who is seriously ill. Those who have had occasion to spend time with a sick friend or relative know that little can be done by the visitor to make the seriously ill person feel better. Indeed, the visitor should accept the patient's discomfort and not demand that the patient feel better for the visitor's sake. The visitor's task is to spend time without feeling compelled to change or improve the patient's condition, simply sharing the experience of enduring pain and waiting for what comes next.

Therapy with borderline patients is similar: One must not attempt to *do* therapy with the borderline patient. Rather, therapists must be prepared to endure the tension and uncertainty of a slowly developing process without the reassurance that can be gained by seeing "progress," feeling "helpful," or sharing "meaningful dialogues." The therapist is trying to create a context in which a particular type of object tie can be experienced, and this is a different process from trying to change or directly influence the patient. The therapist's first task is not to help the patient but to establish that he or she is capable of being present without being intrusive.

In fact, it is crucial for the development of constancy that therapists *not* try to change or "help" the patient. Basic therapeutic techniques that would lead to change or progress in less disturbed patients will simply interfere with the process of becoming a constant object. The therapist's attempts to change the patient or to engineer "progress" are usually intended to meet the therapist's needs more than the patient's, and such attempts with borderline patients will eventually be experienced as intrusive demands the therapist places on the patient. This merely duplicates the patient's experience with most other people, including, most probably, the relationship with early caretakers.

Consequently, it is important that therapists make few interventions in the first months of treatment. Our rule of thumb is that therapists should offer occasional empathic reflections of their patient's state of mind, show a persistent curiosity or interest in the patient's life, and demonstrate awareness of the patient's difficulties. Little beyond this should be done or said. These relatively few responses are intended to allow the patient to feel heard, or to give the sense that "my therapist understands." This sense enables the patient to feel connected to the therapist and furthers the development of constancy. Such interventions, however, will not change or "help" the patient, nor are they intended to do so.

This is not to say that patients will welcome the therapist's restraint. Certainly most borderline patients will not feel helped by this stance. A therapist who does not react immediately and yet clearly remains attentive will initially confuse and probably frustrate these patients, who do not tolerate tension well and who expect the therapist to give some relief when they are upset. Borderline patients experience time in a distorted way that taxes their ability to endure tension or painful affect. Lacking object constancy, they lack self-constancy as well and thereby cannot build a sense of continuity with self across time. Thus, in a sense, the borderline patient's experience of affect is perpetually frozen in the present. There is no readily accessible, broader context of a remembered past and anticipated future against which to weigh current feelings. These patients consequently have trouble imagining that they will ever feel differently than at the moment.

Painful affect thereby becomes a difficult problem for these patients. They lack the perspective that would allow them to remember having felt badly before and gotten over it or to muster a sense of "This, too, shall pass." In the absence of such perspective, painful affect can seem almost unbearable, and there is an urgency to get rid of unwanted feelings. These patients will want the therapist to work fast and can be expected to place enormous pressures on the therapist to take some action to make them feel better.

Borderline patients' desperate urgency when upset makes it hard for them to feel connected with someone showing patience and restraint. These patients expect the therapist to share in and feel their distress and sense of "something must be done." They are unlikely to appreciate the therapist's ability to remain calm in the face of anxiety, and they may interpret the calm as a sign that the therapist does not care about them. As a result, the preconstancy state of treatment can grow stormy, dominated by what is usually regarded as negative transference while patients express their frustration with the therapist's restraint.

Although the borderline patient will experience the therapist as inactive and unresponsive, in fact the therapist's restraint addresses key aspects of borderline pathology, including the inability to experience gradations of feelings, difficulty accepting separateness, and perpetual concern with abandonment. The way in which these aspects of pathology are addressed and in part corrected by the therapist's restraint is the subject of Part II of this book and so need not be explored further here. The point here is that even though patients may not feel helped by their therapist's restraint, such restraint in fact is determined by and aimed at important dimensions of borderline pathology.

The therapist needs to remember this. In the midst of a troubled session in which the therapist is under attack for letting the patient down, it can be easy to give in to the urge to make some intervention, defend oneself, or at least explain to the patient the purpose of one's restraint. It is harder for therapists to stand still, allow the patient to push them away, and maintain enough confidence in their own potential meaning for another person that they can have faith the patient will return. It is probably only after seeing the constancy process through with several patients that therapists can allow it to unfold without undue anxiety and fear.

In the meantime, therapists must set their sights on the task of becoming a constant object, not allowing themselves to be governed by the inconstancy of the patient's inner and interpersonal life. Therapists must focus on presenting themselves as objects who can be approached, clung to, pushed away and left, and returned to. In the time spent with the therapist, the borderline patient must discover

1. an atmosphere of caring without the implicit demand that it be reciprocated

2. a person who listens and sees without offering prescriptions for action

3. a model of steady continuity in the face of the patient's despair, elation, rage, or silence—that is, a dependable attachment that can be experienced as nonfragile, nonengulfing, and self-sufficient

4. a person who mirrors positive feelings about coming together, thereby allowing patients to develop a belief in their own significance for another person.

Using Time as a Vehicle for Change

Becoming a constant object requires considerable patience and restraint by the therapist. The therapist is called on to be attentive, yet not immediately reactive, and to maintain this discipline for a fairly long time. While it could be argued that any psychodynamic approach requires these traits, we believe there is a major difference when working with borderline patients. The techniques, strategies, and interventions taught by the major schools of therapy are the vehicles for change when working with less disturbed patients. But we have already observed that such techniques are unlikely to produce much effect on borderline patients. With these patients, therapists must use time as the basic vehicle for change.

Such a therapeutic approach as we describe faces obstacles from two directions, however. First, the borderline patient's time distortions and attendant sense of urgency will reduce tolerance for a slowly developing process. Borderline patients tend to equate attachment with meeting one another's needs and relieving tension. They will measure the therapist's concern for them by actions the therapist takes to ease their distress during times of upset. Since enduring tension or painful affect is a difficult problem for these patients, they can place enormous pressure on their therapists to deliver quickly and in "package form" what is essentially a gradually unfolding process, namely a sense of interiority and the capacity for a genuine tie to a significant other.

If therapists are not practiced and disciplined in their response to such pressure, they will be constantly stampeded into interventions that are basically meaningless. Even if the therapist succeeds in providing some relief to the patient's distress, nothing really has been accomplished. The patient's tolerance of painful affect is not increased, and the patient will expect similar relief from the next upset. Moreover, most therapeutic interventions will not provide the kind of substantial relief the borderline patient seeks. The patient then has the experience early in therapy of seeing the therapist try but fail. Most treatments with borderline patients cannot succeed under such a burden.

Even if therapists endure their patient's demands for quick relief, they face a second, sociocultural obstacle related to time. Our cultural experience of time has become distorted in a way that curiously parallels the borderline patient's time distortions (cf. Chessick 1977). The fluidity and instancy of Western life evoke the expectation that we ought to be able to address problems speedily and offer instant solutions. The pressures of a society that emphasizes and expects rapid change subtly influence our conceptions of therapy. Unless therapists are aware of these influences and are able to resist them, the paradoxical nature of becoming a constant object will be missed, namely that *the therapist produces change in the borderline patient chiefly by standing still.*

Kroll (1988) has recently described the pressures faced by

those who believe that long-term therapy is the treatment of choice for many patients, including most borderline patients. Biological psychiatry and third-party payers are among the most obvious challengers to practitioners who seek to take their time as they work with seriously disturbed patients. Under such pressure, therapists may well feel both personal and cultural pressure to resort to one of the strategic, problem-solving therapies in which cases are approached by targeting certain changes to be achieved and specifying the techniques for inducing them.

While working with borderline patients, however, therapists should avoid such types of therapy. They presuppose a specificity of complaint and level of development that are simply not relevant for these patients. If, under the influence of cultural pressures, therapists set their sights at the outset on goals, progress, or even a particular treatment outcome, the result is likely to be a treatment impasse. Most borderline patients will not grasp what is being requested even by the ordinary question "How may I be of help to you?" Genuine self-disclosure can be a difficult matter even for healthy people; it is truly confusing for borderline patients. They will want to comply with the authority of the therapist by articulating an overriding problem to work on; borderline patients cannot, however, consistently differentiate between what is and what is not important to bring up. From session to session and even within sessions they will change subjects or run out of things to talk about altogether, reflecting the lack of cohesiveness in their experience of self and other. If the therapist keeps returning to an agreed-upon focus of treatment, the therapy will break down. There will be growing irritation by the patient, who keeps saying, "I (or you) don't understand"; the final stage is likely to be a premature termination from what is mistakenly viewed as the patient's resistance to treatment.

The failure of active, problem-solving approaches with borderline patients does not mean that principally empathic, mir-

roring approaches are necessarily more effective. In our opinion, these approaches have more of a place in the treatment of
borderline patients than do problem-solving therapies, but
empathic treatments are vulnerable to a different version of
the cultural emphasis on rapid results, namely the illusion of
instant intimacy. The therapist's empathic reflections of the
patient's inner states can tempt both patient and therapist to
feel connected and engaged in a deeply meaningful interaction,
when in fact they have had neither the time nor the shared
experiences on which to build a genuine tie. Moreover, borderline patients have had years of practice at appearing to be
connected while actually remaining watchful and distant (Gunderson and Singer 1975). The therapist's sensitive responses,
even if correct, will not quickly create genuine ties any more
than targeting problem behaviors will lead to lasting change.

The therapist will need time to work effectively with borderline patients. The hardest task will be adopting an attitude of
restraint that resists most interventions but finds ways to
maintain emotional contact with the patient. Yet the task will
be easier if therapists keep in mind that time is their best ally
and a sense of urgency their worst enemy. Just as baking bread
requires patiently waiting for the dough to rise, so therapists
must wait patiently and with restraint while a genuine tie
develops.

2

The State of the Art

Introduction

Over fifty years have passed since the borderline concept first appeared in the psychoanalytic literature. During this period there have been a variety of changes in how the concept has been defined and the criteria for its use as a diagnosis. The past two decades in particular have seen an explosive growth in its popularity even as the ambiguity of the term continues to plague clinicians. Questions persist as to whether we are dealing with a distinct syndrome, personality disorder, or a level of pathology that includes a variety of syndromes (Stone 1987). Furthermore, in this era of health insurance administrators dictating which services will be reimbursed, are we to focus on the affective disorder (which is often treated with chemotherapy), or is there necessity for including cognitive dysfunctions if the borderline concept is to remain viable (Kroll 1988)? Answers to these questions have been as diverse as the theoretical orientations and goals of the clinicians who have formulated them.

To appreciate the complexity of this subject one need only examine the growing number of reviews of the concept's history and the issues involved with its definition and etiology (e.g., Chatham 1985, Dorr et al. 1983, Gunderson 1984, Leichtman 1989, Meissner 1984, Wong 1980). Our intention in this chapter is to highlight some of the conceptual changes and their impact on ideas about treatment. Following this brief historical overview, we will deal in the next chapter with the issues currently associated with the psychotherapy of the borderline patient.

Early Theorists: Stern and Deutsch

Treatment of the borderline patient has long been recognized as a formidable and, at times, emotionally draining challenge. In her comprehensive review of the early literature, Chatham (1985) noted that the term "borderline" originally reflected the frustration of psychoanalysts who were unable to treat the condition or even to explain its confounding characteristics. Indeed, when Stern (1938) introduced the term, it was to describe a strange mixture of healthy functions coexisting with neurotic, psychotic, and character disturbances all in the same patient. These patients were subject to intense affect, with rapid shifts between paranoidlike rage and masochistic withdrawal, idealization and devaluation of the other, and somatic insecurity along with impulsive and potentially self-destructive behavior. They displayed an aggressive dependency in the form of making demands for relief of their tension and a readiness to leave therapy at the slightest frustration.

Presented with this dizzying array of symptoms, Stern could not categorize these patients neatly into psychotic or psychoneurotic groups. He thus came to the conclusion that they were on the border of schizophrenia, a view that was shared by Deutsch (1942), who described a quieter subtype of borderline patients, using the term "as-if" personality. While appearing to function at a higher level, these patients lacked any sense of an inner self or cohesive identity, and relied on social cues to imitate appropriate actions and feelings. They were emotionally detached and presented vague complaints of inner emptiness and a profound sense of aloneness, along with a diffuse sexual identity. All the while, they maintained what appeared to be fairly intact reality testing in nonintimate social situations. In the face of such puzzling behavior in both groups, it is not surprising that many clinicians came to the same conclusion as Stern, who had said that "this borderline group of patients is extremely difficult to handle effectively by any psychotherapeutic method" (p. 467).

During this period and the decade that followed, many clinicians recommended that treatment be limited to supportive interventions, since it was assumed that these patients could not tolerate any intensive exploratory approaches. Trying to improve social role performance and crisis management was emphasized. Zetzel (1971) went so far as to advocate strict limits on the frequency of contact between patient and therapist to limit the potential for unworkable, regressive transference reactions. The chief motivation for these treatment strategies seems to have been the desire to limit or contain the patient's pathology. In hindsight, we wonder if there was also a desire to protect therapists from *their* potential for extreme countertransference reactions.

Ego Psychology

With the flourishing of ego psychology in the 1950s a new concept emerged called pseudoneurotic schizophrenia (Hoch and Polatin 1949). These people were seen to function with ego defenses and character styles that were slightly more advanced than schizophrenics and at times could present a social facade that seemed at best normal and at worst neurotic. However, under stress these fragile defenses would fail, and schizophrenic features became evident. We can see here an attempt to locate the borderline concept along a continuum from normal to neurotic to schizophrenic.

In 1953 Knight proposed a different sort of continuum. He argued that the borderline state reflected uneven development of ego functions along a hypothetical line ranging from ego weakness to ego strength. Instead of searching for particular psychosexual fixations (a vertical continuum), Knight saw the borderline individual along a horizontal line. Thus in the borderline state some ego functions (e.g., integration, realistic planning, maintenance of object relations) tended to be severely weakened, while others (e.g., superficial adaptation to the environment, memory, calculation) seemed relatively unimpaired. Functions might further be weakened or strengthened with changes in the level of stress the individual faced at any given time.

The idea of uneven development of ego functions along a continuum meant that borderline conditions could be treated as a stable level of character pathology between psychoses and neuroses. Supportive treatment was given a new impetus and could then be conceived as an attempt to maintain defenses that furthered adaptation to the environment and increased the patient's frustration tolerance. This school of thought produced the well-known phrase "stable instability" (Grinker et al. 1968, Schmideberg 1959) to describe the uneven development of ego functions. A clinical picture was emerging of a fragmented and often chaotic personality structure that nonetheless possessed sufficient adaptive capacity to avoid subtotal regression.

Object Relations Theory

A move toward more intensive treatment of severe character pathology gained significant impetus from the British school of object relations. Members of this group (Fairbairn 1952, Guntrip 1968, Klein 1975a,b, Winnicott 1960) emphasized the importance of private, inner images ("phantasies") of ourselves and others that are begun early in life. These internalized object relations serve to organize experience of self and other and to govern interpersonal relationships. Emphasis on early object relations shifted the focus of psychopathology from Freud's oedipal child to the first three years of life. In effect, borderline problems could be seen to involve distortions in the development of a core sense of identity, occurring long before the Oedipus stage.

With the focus on preoedipal issues, the borderline patient's heretofore chaotic patterns of behavior were understood in terms of primitive conflicts and anxieties. As such, the defenses would also be primitive and would take such forms as splitting, idealization, and desire for fusion; devaluation; and fears of engulfment, along with archaic forms of projection and denial. Some of these defensive configurations also occur at later stages of life, of course, but they do not have the same raw quality in healthier individuals, nor does one find such rapid fluctuations as with borderline patients.

Transference

In terms of treatment, the borderline patient's shifting patterns of behavior were now conceptualized as arising out of pathological internalized object relations. More particularly, these patients' chaotic dealings with others—including the therapist—were thought to reflect a distorted sense of self and others, based on disturbances in early object relations. These intense transference reactions have generated much disagreement among clinicians about how to understand and deal with them. A central question is whether these reactions originate entirely in the patient's actual relationships with primary caretakers, or whether they arise chiefly from the patient's defensive distortions of these early relationships. Related to this question is whether therapists are to interpret these reactions or, by contrast, to withstand the intense affects and provide a holding environment (Winnicott 1960).

This latter term has taken on many meanings in recent years, and it might be of value to the reader to know what Winnicott himself had in mind when he coined the phrase. He was referring to the good-enough mother whose reliable holding includes fulfillment of the baby's actual physical need and the ego support she is able to provide to the immature ego of the infant. For purposes of our discussion the essential meaning of a holding environment in therapy is equivalent to the idea that when the mother's ego support is reliable, the infant becomes able to take it for granted and to be, for periods of time, unintegrated without threat to his or her personal continuity. The precise functions the mother carries out are not at all as important as the atmosphere or ambience she creates through her empathy and attunement to the child. This atmosphere allows the baby to go on being in the presence of the mother.

Whether interpretation and holding environment should be cast as a dichotomy is itself an interesting question. For certain kinds of borderline patients interpretations can be seen as one form of holding environment, thereby blurring the presumed distinctions between the terms. As we shall see later, the implications of this question are far-reaching; the position taken will determine the nature of the therapist's interventions and how the therapist conceives his or her task.

Countertransference

Object relations theory also sheds light on the therapist's countertransference reactions during the treatment process. Borderline patients often show unusually keen sensitivity to potential areas of vulnerability in the therapist and make these the focus of rebuke or attack. Thus, for example, an angry patient's devaluation of the therapist might well be aimed at a soft spot, an area of self-doubt for the therapist, leaving the therapist to struggle with whether the attack might in fact be justified rather than an expression of pathology. Shapiro (1978) noted that "this intuitive sensitivity allows for a powerful coercive use of projective identification because there is often some degree of perceptual accuracy in the projection that touches a conflicted area of the recipient" (p. 1308). If the therapist comes to feel intensely guilty or angry, borderline patients may well sense this, and they may then complain that they can't trust someone who lacks confidence or who is angry with them. The treatment process may well then be at an impasse because it is unclear whose issues are being addressed. With this blurring of boundaries, borderline patients may lose their tenuous sense of self, and as Shapiro noted, "experience the therapist as a reincarnation of the fantasied early frustrating parent" (p. 1308).

Countertransference reactions have been described in vivid terms by various clinicians, but unfortunately it is often impossible to capture the intensity of these reactions by reading a transcript of a session; the words of the therapists do not reflect the tension in their voice or what is being experienced at the moment. Those who have worked with borderline patients can attest to the sudden and pervasive tension that fills the room. Winnicott (1947), for example, spoke of therapists' needing to manage both their own "hatred" and need to retaliate when dealing with the anxiety evoked by the patient's rage and threatened disruption of the relationship. At the other end of the spectrum, Kernberg (1975) suggested that even sophisticated therapists may at times experience an "almost masochistic submission to some of the patient's aggression, disproportionate doubts in their own capacity, and exaggerated fears of criticisms by third parties" (p. 61). From a more experiential vantage point, Searles (1979) has poignantly described the analyst's sense of threatened identity and his own core experience of being an unwanted little child in relation to the patient.

Therapists will often find themselves momentarily in a no-win situation with borderline patients. We believe it is inevitable that therapists will find themselves from time to time intensely angry with these patients and then flooded with self-criticism for having evoked the patient's complaints and criticisms or for having responded badly to them. These experiences leave most therapists full of doubt over their capacities as healers, often struggling to suppress a rising sense that what they have to offer as human beings is simply not good enough. It may be helpful for therapists to remember that all of these momentary feelings are variations on what the borderline patient has grown up feeling daily.

The Influence of Mahler's Work

Mahler's observational studies of mother–child interactions (Mahler 1968, 1971, Mahler et al. 1970, 1975) offered a comprehensive genetic-dynamic understanding of the borderline syndrome that continues to exert considerable influence on clinical thought. Several factors underlie her ongoing influence. First, Mahler spoke in more operational and less ambiguous language than those writers relying heavily on hypothetical intrapsychic processes. Second, in contrast to much previous psychoanalytic theorizing that was based on work with adult patients, Mahler and her colleagues made direct observations of normal and disturbed infant and toddler behavior. Third, Mahler's perspectives on human behavior put much greater emphasis on the *mother's* actual behavior in relation to that of her child. In this regard, it is probably more than coincidence that both Mahler and Winnicott began their careers as pediatricians and thus came to appreciate from direct observation the importance of the way mothers and their babies interact. Finally, Mahler was able to organize her observations into a specific developmental timetable that spoke to such key clinical issues as self–other differentiation and the evolving sense of identity in the young child.

Mahler (1971) described complementary intrapsychic processes that unfold over the first thirty-six months of life, which she called separation and individuation. The phases of development that they encompass were later subdivided into four subphases (Mahler et al. 1975); our particular interest here will be on the rapprochement subphase. Many clinicians view the failure to negotiate the challenges of this period of development as the original basis for borderline symptoms. Roughly covering the period between 18 and 30 months, rapprochement is the time when the child's conflict between autonomy and reunion is most visible. There is a general tendency to have tantrums, be negativistic (the "terrible twos"), and display rapid mood swings and ambivalence. It is a time when the toddler is both engaged in seeking more independence and yet shows a constant concern with the mother's presence. We see here in stark terms the perpetual existential dilemma in which normal growth creates both loneliness and at the same time the urge to explore the world and become more autonomous. Mahler (1971) noted the appearance of two normal patterns here: One involved shadowing the mother, while the other involved darting away, with the apparent expectation of being swept up in the mother's arms. Mahler inferred from these patterns that the child feels both a wish for reunion and a fear of engulfment.

This can often be a difficult time for the mother. She is alternately rejected by the child and then sought after in a clinging manner. Not only must she be able to resist the desire to retaliate or withdraw, but she must also tolerate her own conflicted wishes for dependency and autonomy and be able to empathize with those of her child. The interaction between mother and child is critical at this point, since the mother's response can either support or undermine the child's developmental move toward autonomy.

Masterson and Rinsley (1975) proposed that borderline pathology results from the "mother's withdrawal of her libidinal availability . . . during the rapprochement subphase" (p. 167). They contend that the mother of the future borderline individual "is available if the child clings and behaves regressively, but withdraws if he attempts to separate and individuate" (p. 167). In this scenario the child learns early that independence and autonomy lead to abandonment and that consistent support can only be had by remaining symbiotically dependent.

The strain on such a child can be enormous; frustration builds, and feelings of rage and guilt become intertwined, with no clear sense of a self that is differentiated from the world. Failing to develop adequate frustration tolerance or an ability to live with ambivalence, borderline patients display from early in life an all-or-none philosophy. As adults they continue to see others as all good or all bad, depending on whether they are gratifying or withholding. This kind of splitting has been associated with the child's inability to evoke an image of a caring, mirroring mother when the mother is physically absent (Sherwood 1989). This inability suggests that the child lacks faith in the mother's reappearance, and this, in turn, leads to excessive reliance on her actual presence.

Mahler and colleagues (1970) observed two kinds of maternal empathic failure during rapprochement that contribute to the child's sense of anxiety and helpless rage. One group of mothers who had difficulties tolerating their own dependency responded with hurt and anger to their child's clinging when the child attempted to return after a time of independence. This type of rejecting mother will evoke anxiety in the child regarding dependency needs and wishes for nurturance. They can be seen as instilling guilt in the child for abandoning the mother, after which the child must face a "deserved punishment." A second group of mothers showed conflicts over autonomy and could be seen as threatening abandonment whenever the child dared to make autonomous moves. This group seemed focused on undermining the child's grandiose fantasies inherent in the freedom to explore and evoked a sense of humiliation over the continuing need for support. Such a child would be prone to the reactive fantasy "If I grow up, I'll be all alone."

The outcome of these patterns reflects problems seen clinically. The first type of interaction appears related to quiet borderline patients, those who are excessively compliant, insecure, and resemble Deutsch's (1942) as-if personalities. The second type of interaction appears related to the noisy type of borderline patient, those who behave with a sense of entitlement and seem constantly testing the limits of the therapy situation. This is almost an example of the repetition compulsion, particularly with noisy patients, who push limits to see whether the therapist will humiliate them and who fairly often try in turn to humiliate the therapist.

Kernberg's View

A prolific writer, Kernberg (Kernberg 1967, 1968, 1975, 1976, 1977, 1980, 1984, 1987, Kernberg et al. 1989) has been a major influence in establishing the position that borderline functioning represents a stable personality organization rather than a clinical syndrome. The reader will remember that this view was originally proposed by Knight (1953) from the vantage point of ego psychology. Unlike Knight, Kernberg does not view this form of experience as a weakness of defenses along a hypothetical continuum but rather as the operation of more primitive, Kleinian defenses. In particular he focuses on splitting and the related processes of projective identification, primitive idealization, and omnipotence. Kernberg has taken the controversial position that these processes are *specific* to borderline and psychotic patients, in contrast to neurotic patients, for whom defenses are organized around repression.

Kernberg views the borderline patient's reliance on splitting as an attempt to defend against excessive aggression, which he believes may either be constitutional in origin or the result of excessive early childhood frustration. In either case, excessive pregenital aggression is the fundamental difficulty for the borderline individual and becomes most problematic during Mahler's rapprochement subphase. At that time splitting is designed to keep separated contradictory images of self and others, so that positive, libidinally colored introjects will not be overwhelmed by negative, aggressively toned introjects.

The failure to integrate positive and negative affective experiences results in an unstable internal structure in which aggression is not neutralized (modified or channeled) and the individual's feelings are experienced out of context and in intense, extreme forms. For example, Druck (1989) noted that borderline patients tend to feel hatred more often than irritation or mild annoyance; conversely, they feel intense love more often than affection or simple liking. Feelings can shift fluidly from one extreme to another, and since positive and negative feelings are not integrated, patients often show what Druck described as a surprising *la belle indifférence* attitude when asked about these shifts. Druck went on to describe this phenomenon in a poignant way, saying, "Experience is sequential. When the patient experiences one group of feelings . . . it is as if the other never existed in the past and never will again. The patient either has no recollection of them or, if he has some recollection, it simply has no impact or relevance for him" (pp. 200–201). In sum, splitting affects the continuity of experience, allowing sudden, dramatic shifts in feelings, thoughts, memories, and behavior, and perpetuating a fragmented sense of self.

Kernberg believes that the early stages of therapy require confrontation of splitting. This defense is inherently weakening to the ego, and a positive therapeutic relationship is precluded as long as the patient views the therapist as a fantasy-dominated part object. Kernberg is also most emphatic that negative aspects of the transference must be immediately interpreted; he contends that such interpretation is the basis for helping the patient feel understood and accepted by the therapist.

One important aspect of this negative transference is projective identification (cf. Ogden 1982). This is typically manifested as intense distrust and fear of the therapist, who is experienced as attacking the patient. At these times patients experience themselves as frightened children, and the therapist is experienced in light of primitive, sadistic-parent images. It is characteristic of the borderline patient's fluidity that this may shift only a few moments later, with the patient feeling like the sadistic parent and experiencing the therapist as a guilty, frightened child. Kernberg (1975) states that these sorts of processes must be interpreted immediately; otherwise there is either the danger that the negative transference will become concealed and keep the relationship at a relatively superficial level, or the possibility that tension will build up and lead to serious acting out or premature termination.

As Druck (1989) pointed out, "Kernberg focuses on patients whose anger is prominent, who devalue or overly idealize the therapist, and in whom dependency is generally ego-alien" (p. 7), the sort of patient we earlier described as the noisy borderline patient. While Kernberg advocates a position of technical neutrality within a psychoanalytic framework, he does impose firm limits on the patient's expression of primitive aggression when it reaches the point of yelling at the therapist session after session (Kernberg 1975). Consistent with this line of thought is the article by Selzer and colleagues (1987) that proposes establishing an initial contract with the borderline patient. In the contract the patient agrees beforehand to inhibit certain expressions of anger and other intense affects. Selzer and colleagues believe that such a contract is "valuable for stabilizing the initial phase of treatment and providing a frame of reference for the ongoing examination of threats to the continuity of the treatment" (p. 930).

Kernberg believes in the primacy of interpretation and the other classical psychoanalytic interventions as the agents of change with borderline patients. While the therapist should be concerned for the patient, no supportive remarks or cues are to be offered. Working from a conflict model of pathology, Kernberg is rather critical of therapists who offer empathic understanding rather than carefully thought-out interpretations. As he sees it, empathy is a prerequisite for any meaningful intervention and is therefore not a replacement for interpretation; that is, empathy may be better understood as a form of observation than as a mode of interaction.

In summary, Kernberg's approach to the early stages of treatment focuses on splitting in hopes of neutralizing primitive, conflicting drives (particularly aggression) and helping patients achieve more moderated, realistic, and comprehensive self and object representations. Early interpretation of negative transference is considered absolutely necessary. In contrast to positions that emphasize structural deficits, Kernberg's is a traditional, conflict model of personality, and the interventions he proposes are consistent with that model. (Readers interested in learning more about Kernberg's approach to borderline patients are referred to the fine discussions presented by Chatham 1985 and Druck 1989.)

Masterson's View

More than any other writer, Masterson has emphasized the mother's role in the development of borderline pathology. While Kernberg stresses a fantasy basis for the patient's transference, Masterson (Masterson 1972, 1976, Masterson and Rinsley 1975) focuses on the realistic basis and has gone so far as to propose that the mother of every borderline patient is herself a borderline individual. (This view has been challenged by Shapiro et al. 1975 and Singer 1977, who found significant variability in parental psychopathology.)

As noted earlier, Masterson and Rinsley (1975) see the borderline patient's core problem to be fear of abandonment derived from the mother's libidinal unavailability during rapprochement. Extrapolating from child development, they believe that borderline pathology grows from an excruciating conflict: fear of engulfment if a move is made toward the object, versus fear of abandonment if a move is made toward individuation.

A key concept for Masterson and Rinsley (1975) is that "the borderline child has a mother with whom there is a unique and uninterrupted interaction with a specific relational focus, i.e., Reward for Regression, Withdrawal for Separation-Individuation . . ." (p. 56). This pattern is internalized and leads to two distinct ego states, each of which carries a self-image, a complementary object image, and a linking affect state. The first ego state comes from interaction with a mother who offers support for clinging, regressive behavior. Coinciding with this object image is the self-image of a good child who may also feel special. This "rewarding part object relation unit (RORU)" is chiefly invested with libidinal energy (Chatham 1985).

The second ego state derives from the opposite pattern of mother–child interaction. The object image is an angry and critical mother, withdrawing in the face of her child's assertiveness. The corresponding self-image is an inadequate, guilty bad boy (or girl), and the interaction is colored with abandonment depression. This withdrawing part object relation unit (WORU) is fueled primarily with aggressive energy.

These partial self and object images cannot be integrated with one another because of the intensity of aggression embedded in the WORU. Thus even if an individual is aware of each pattern, neither pattern of interaction can influence the other. The same patient may be clinging and compliant, seeing the therapist in idealized terms at one moment (a pattern of interaction governed by the RORU), but may become angry and withdrawn the next moment, experiencing the therapist as having been attacking and humiliating. These sudden and extreme shifts may occur when fantasies of fusion with the therapist are interrupted, or when the patient makes a move toward individuation and thereby inevitably triggers abandonment depression.

Masterson believes that the therapist is placed in the role of a transference object from the very outset of therapy. Consistent with his understanding of the etiology of borderline pathology, he believes the transference consists of alternately activating and projecting onto the therapist each of the part object relations units. When a patient projects the withdrawing unit onto interaction with the therapist, the patient experiences therapy as "necessarily leading to feelings of abandonment, denies the reality of therapeutic benefit and activates the rewarding part unit as a defense" (Masterson 1978, p. 131). Projecting the rewarding unit onto the therapist, with its reunion fantasy, leads the patient to feel good, although the patient is typically behaving in a regressive, self-defeating manner. Other object relations part units are seen as forms of transference acting out, with the primary goal of defending against abandonment depression.

For Masterson, the therapist's first task is to control acting out by confronting its self-destructive nature. Masterson uses confrontation in the classical psychoanalytic sense, the correction of a reality distortion. The therapist is not challenging the patient but rather "bringing to the attention of the patient's observing ego the denied realistically destructive aspects of his defense mechanisms" (Masterson 1978, p. 132). Since the therapeutic alliance is tenuous and can be shattered each time the withdrawing object relations unit is activated, the therapist must make the same confrontation repeatedly. Masterson (1976, 1978) speaks of an alliance between the child's rewarding maternal part unit and the pathological (pleasure) ego; he sees the therapist's repeated confrontations as the means of rendering this alliance ego-alien. A circular process begins, including resistance, clarification of reality, and working through feelings of abandonment (from the withdrawing part unit), followed by further resistance, further reality clarification, and further working through.

When the circular working-through process is successful, an alliance develops, formed through the patient's having internalized the therapist as a positive object who approves of separation–individuation. During this second phase of work—

through the pathological mourning associated with separation from the mother—a new intrapsychic structure is formed based on whole object relations. Curiously, as patients begin to experience themselves as more individuated, they often experience a talionic impulse, or deep hostility toward their parents for having thwarted them as children. Masterson (1981) has noted that patients can have such intense desires for revenge that they are willing to stop their own growth and to maintain symptoms as a way of punishing their parents. The talionic impulse must be worked through and the attendant desire for revenge given up. Masterson puts it well: "The patient must make a choice between getting back or getting better. He cannot have both. . . . He must give up the idea of revenge . . . and free his aggression to be used to support his self-image, rather than to attack it" (p. 188). Eventually the raging desire for revenge is partly discharged during therapy sessions and partly discharged through sublimation. In this way, underlying aggression is freed for use in constructive, assertive efforts at coping and adaptation.

Another major aspect of working through is what Masterson (1976) has called communicative matching. This entails the therapist's expressing approval of the patient's individuation by discussing the latter's new feelings and new interests, such as career plans, hobbies, the stock market, or dating. Working from Mahler's (1968) idea of empathic mutual cuing, Masterson posits that this developmentally appropriate experience during rapprochement was sorely lacking for the borderline patient. It thereby becomes the therapist's responsibility to provide a responsive, sharing experience, using the therapist's own knowledge in a self-disclosing, educative manner to help the patient develop and reality-test new interests. Occurring in the latter stages of treatment, this process supports the patient's emerging sense of self and furthers the process of differentiation while compensating for the defect left by the mother's withdrawal.

In summary, Masterson, like Kernberg, works from a conflict model. The primary issue in Masterson's schema is the borderline patient's need to defend against abandonment depression. The patient is vulnerable to such depression because of the mother's withdrawal during rapprochement when the child takes steps toward autonomy but still needs to return at times for emotional refueling. Masterson describes borderline pathology as the development of split object relations units through which the patient is rewarded for clinging, regressive behavior and punished with feelings of abandonment and rejection for moves toward independence. The first task of therapy is to confront the self-destructive nature of the patient's regressive behaviors.

Masterson agrees with Kernberg that negative transference must be addressed early in treatment, but Masterson stresses the role of confrontation rather than interpretation. Also in contrast to Kernberg, Masterson views the transference as a reflection of the patient's actual early experiences; he places relatively little emphasis on the fantasied aspects of early object relations. There is an obvious similarity between what Kernberg terms splitting and Masterson's rewarding and withdrawing object relations units, which must be kept apart to preserve the illusion of symbiosis while defending against abandonment depression. Masterson—again, like Kernberg—sees verbal intervention as the most powerful tool for producing insight and change.

In terms of style, Masterson (1976) is sometimes openly supportive. He does not seem to adhere to the principle of interpreting from a position of neutrality as closely as Kernberg does. Masterson believes that the therapist must recognize and support the patient's moves toward individuation, actively encouraging such efforts, and sometimes congratulating patients on their achievements. Masterson appears to see the therapist's task, in part, as creating a better parenting experience for the patient and thereby providing the basis for new, healthier introjects. This is certainly a contrast to Kernberg, who stresses a focus on negative transference and conflict.

Adler and Buie's View

Adler and Buie (1979) believe that the core of borderline pathology is the failure to develop the type of mental representation that captures positive experiences with nurturant caretakers. These representations are called holding or soothing introjects, and their absence results in a pervasive experience of aloneness that can appear in the context of important dyadic relationships, including psychotherapy. Adler and Buie focus on this sense of aloneness as a core feature of the borderline patient's experience and describe it as "an experience of isolation and emptiness occasionally turning into panic and desperation" (p. 434). Borderline patients defend against this catastrophic sense of inner isolation by projecting it into the environment; as a result, the world and life itself are experienced as empty and without purpose.

Working from this deficit model—which is heavily influenced by Kohut's (1971) self psychology—Buie and Adler focus on specific vulnerabilities in the borderline patient. These include intense longings to be held and nurtured by idealized objects, which leave the patient perpetually susceptible to intense separation anxiety. Additionally, these idealizations of the other and the attendant pressure of the patient's enormous demands inevitably lead to disappointments with other people and increasing anger. During periods of intense anger the sense of aloneness is felt more keenly, along with an inability to maintain positive images and memories.

Buie and Adler differ from Kernberg on the meaning of the patient's anger. Kernberg uses a conflict model and views excessive instinctual aggression toward both real and fantasied objects as the problem. In his view, the excessive aggressive energies are more than the child can defend against, and sadistic energies threaten to corrode the child's positive experiences. The problem is one of drive and (inadequate) defense. By contrast, Buie and Adler (1972) view the borderline patient's anger as narcissistic rage stemming from the frustration of the patient's *legitimate* needs for a self-object type of relationship. In effect, Buie and Adler believe that a healthy need has been frustrated and that anger is an appropriate reaction. Over the course of time, this originally healthy need becomes distorted, evolving into unrealistic demands that lead to still more frustration and to increasing anger.

In discussing the inability to maintain positive introjects, Adler and Buie (1979) make an important point about the loss of evocative memory and its distinction from recognition memory. They note that under stress borderline patients "can lose evocative memory capacity for important libidinally invested objects and regress to recognition memory capacity or even earlier in relation to them" (p. 447). The stress referred to is the patient's growing rage as unrealistic demands are not met. Adler and Buie divide this rage into two categories: recognition memory rage and diffuse, primitive rage. They believe that both forms stem from a failure of good-enough mothering at all early levels of development, though most significantly at the rapprochement subphase.

There are clinical implications from these two forms of rage. Patients who are experiencing recognition memory rage can still recognize and experience the therapist's presence while they are with the therapist. They cannot, however, remember what the therapist looks like between appointments. Adler and Buie (1979) suggest that therapists should express "empathic understanding of how empty, alone, helpless and frightened the patient feels when not in the presence of the therapist" (p. 444). They believe that establishing and supporting the collaborative nature of the therapy process can alleviate the intensity of the patient's aloneness and lay a foundation for exploring it. They further believe that an important therapeutic task is finding ways to help patients establish and maintain evocative memory between sessions. Adler and Buie are willing to make themselves available via telephone contacts between sessions, and they use such transitional objects as a tape recording of a session or a postcard while on vacation.

When patients regress to diffuse, primitive rage, they experience panic, intense anger, despair, and some cognitive disorganization. They become unable to recognize the therapist's presence affectively even while in the office with the therapist. Adler and Buie (1979) emphasize "that this affective nonrecognition prevails even though the patient may be able to perceive intellectually that the therapist is in the same room with him" (p. 438). Active intervention by the therapist is needed at such times. At the least the therapist should offer firm definition of the patient's overwhelming emotions and try to share responsibility for the experience. At times this will not be enough, and hospitalization may be necessary. Inpatient care may offer the patient a chance to feel cared for and protected while offering a holding environment.

Since Adler and Buie believe that the core of borderline pathology is a failure in the development of holding and soothing introjects, they argue that the early stages of therapy must offer patients the experience of being empathically held. Their reliance on the concepts of holding environment, good-enough mothering, and transitional object all reflect Winnicott's influence and an attendant emphasis on developmental failure rather than intrapsychic conflict. Thus the therapist is seen as someone who is available to be used as a holding self-object, performing the holding and soothing functions that patients cannot provide on their own. The idea of providing a holding environment has long been recognized as part of the overall psychoanalytic process. Adler and Buie, however, have extended this concept; in their schema the therapist actually functions as a stable, holding self-object for the patient.

As already noted, Adler and Buie's desire to foster evocative memory leads them to recommend various forms of contact between sessions. Presumably this contact is part of what it means to serve as a self-object. Adler and Buie (1979) recognize the potential problems that can arise, saying that the therapist "must carefully evaluate countertransference issues, the correct assessment of the patient's needs, and his own realistic personal limits" (p. 445). Needless to say, this admonition may be hard to follow. As with many techniques developed over the years, there is an obvious danger of misapplication, especially by neophytes in the profession and by those who unwittingly serve their own desire to be important to the patient.

There are several clear differences between Buie and Adler and Kernberg on treatment technique. First, Buie and Adler do not believe that interpretative content per se is the curative factor with borderline patients. Rather, they emphasize the therapist's coming to be seen as a stable, consistent, and caring person who survives the patient's rage. They argue that this holding function repairs deficits and enables new experiences to make a curative impact.

Second, there is a crucial difference in how the therapist is

advised to respond to the patient's idealized self-object transference. Kernberg would confront an early idealization by interpreting the patient's underlying hostility. By contrast, Adler
(1979) is concerned that early interpretation of any hostile
feelings will be heard as criticism by the patient. In turn this
would disrupt the patient's sense of being empathically held by
the therapist and destroy motivation for treatment. Additionally, Buie and Adler do not emphasize the hostility hidden
behind idealization; rather, they acknowledge the patient's
longings for a perfect caregiver and the importance of allowing
positive feelings for the therapist to emerge. Buie and Adler
only use confrontation and interpretation early in treatment in
ways that will help create and maintain a holding environment.
They regard the patient's hostility as secondary in importance
to idealization.

Buie and Adler (1982) follow Kohut (1971) in believing that
the proper working through of an unrealistic, positive transference comes through optimal disillusionment. Over time, patients begin to notice discrepancies between the idealized holding introject and the actual holding qualities of the therapist.
When these disappointments with the therapist are optimal
(viz., not overwhelming), patients gradually develop insight
into the unrealistic aspects of their positive feelings for the
therapist. Ultimately the therapist is accepted realistically
without undermining the holding introjects. The therapist's
task during this phase of treatment is to stay with the patient
empathically, providing clarifications and interpretations of
the dynamic bases for the disappointments but avoiding any
intervention that would intensify them.

In summary, Buie and Adler define the therapist's task to be
providing a real experience of good, parental caretaking, as a
substitute for presumed poor experiences in the patient's early
years. Like Masterson, they also emphasize providing the patient with new experiences during the later phases of treatment. This includes highlighting the patient's positive qualities

by showing appropriate subtle expressions of esteem when positive experiences are reported. Buie and Adler (1982) believe that such highlighting makes the qualities seem more real to the patient; additionally, through identification, the patient gains some capacity for self-validation and for autonomous self-esteem. The process they call validation emerges from their proposition that "the capacities to know, esteem, and love oneself can be developed only when there is adequate experience of being known, esteemed, and loved by significant others" (p. 77).

There are certainly many more writers who could be included in a review of the literature. We believe that those authors we have discussed are a good sample, however. Kernberg and Masterson represent the conflict theorists, while Adler and Buie represent the deficit camp and the Kohutians. Moreover, among conflict-oriented theorists, Kernberg emphasizes instinctual elements, while Masterson pays more attention to the impact of actual patterns of interaction with the parents. Thus the major positions have been covered, and we can move now to the question of how therapists address specific problems during the early stages of treatment.

3

Major Issues in Treatment of the Borderline Patient

The Initial Contract

In this chapter we review several issues that currently figure prominently in the clinical literature on treatment of borderline patients. We have selected those issues that seem to have the most relevance for the early stages of treatment, although some pertain to later stages as well. Using the previous chapter as background, we will attempt to compare different theoretical positions and highlight the contrasts. In the process we will add some of our own opinions to the discussion, since these particular issues will be with us for the remainder of the book.

Everyone agrees that it is necessary to establish a stable framework for treatment. A stable framework includes setting regular appointment times, providing a consistent boundary for beginning and ending sessions, agreeing on the necessity of keeping regular appointments, and agreeing on a basis for the payment of fees. In a recent publication Kernberg and colleagues (1989) are quite explicit about the importance of placing this stable framework on as firm a foundation as possible. They advocate an explicit, initial contract between therapist and patient and view the process of setting up the contract as crucial to the entire course of treatment. They believe that any deviation from the agreed-upon contract (e.g., a missed appointment, failure to pay fees) should be actively and fully explored in the therapy session.

Setting limits is an important part of the initial contract. Many therapists have difficulty in this area, handicapped perhaps by their own fantasies of omnipotence, desires to be admired, or conflicts over being sadistic. Such issues may make the therapist wary of provoking the patient's rage and devaluation early in treatment and may thereby keep the therapist from setting proper limits through an initial contract. Since borderline patients are prone to testing the limits in such areas as their desire for fusion, need to have omnipotent control of the other, or fear of being separate, the failure to set limits early in treatment will invariably undermine therapy.

The therapist will be hard pressed to weather the storm of the patient's chaotic feelings and demanding behavior without the framework of a clearly established contract. The therapist may well end up feeling confused and/or abused, with no basis for providing the stability needed by the patient. As Kernberg and colleagues (1989) have succinctly put it, "The major goal of setting up the initial contract is to protect the treatment structure from the patient's destructive actions while permitting a discussion of the patient's controlling and destructive fantasies toward the therapist" (p. 39). Additionally, the contract establishes the therapist as someone who is beyond the patient's omnipotent control and makes explicit that the patient is jointly responsible for treatment.

When taken at face value, the notion of an initial contract certainly has an inherent logic. There is wide agreement that the issues already mentioned—rules regarding appointments and fees—should be included. Most therapists would also likely include an inhibition on physical aggression and damaging the office. We do question the proposal of Selzer and colleagues (1987) that patients should contract not to yell or be verbally abusive toward the therapist. Those who endorse this idea might point out that such an agreement begins to develop the observing function of the ego and thereby supports other ego functions. Patients who might otherwise yield to aggressive impulse may be helped to back off from what they feel and delay acting on the impulse.

We believe, however, that such a ground rule does not protect the treatment setting as much as it protects the therapist's pride; working with seriously disturbed patients sometimes entails being yelled at, and it is important for the patient to see that the relationship can weather such attacks. We are not advocating that the patient be given carte blanche in the therapy session, particularly if therapists begin to fear for their physical safety. We are saying, however, that each situation requires the exercise of professional judgment. As we shall note later, even the difference in treatment settings (inpatient versus outpatient) can be an important factor in the therapist's evaluation of an appropriate response to an extremely angry patient. Suffice to say at this point, we believe that the initial contract has to be viewed as a general framework for therapy. Viewing the contract as a cover for all contingencies is at best an illusion that provides a false sense of security for the therapist. At worst it leaves the therapist not knowing how to respond to a deviation and prevents the therapeutic relationship from evolving.

Anyone working effectively with borderline patients will be subjected to intense negative affect from the patient. We believe that the therapist will do the patient more good by enduring and surviving these attacks than by insisting that they be expressed in a particular way. In addition, a restriction at the outset of treatment on verbal aggression could adversely affect the therapist's ability to reach important aspects of the patient's pathology. Quiet, as-if types of borderline patients could hear the restriction as a demand that they continue to be compliant, or as an injunction designed to produce guilt over any move away from the therapist. Such a reading of the restriction would simply reinforce the quiet patient's pathology, since it duplicates messages heard from the mother. Further, many noisy borderline patients might be able to cooperate with the restriction only by remaining superficial and uninvolved. These patients are frequently simply unable to modulate affect when upset. A demand that they do so at the start of treatment almost amounts to a demand that they be healthier than they are and could well be experienced by patients as an attempt to humiliate them for being weak. This in turn also comes very close to duplicating early patterns of interaction with the mother.

Finally, it is worth noting that many of the writers who work with borderline patients specify a minimum of two sessions per week and sometimes as many as four or five sessions per week. We believe it is not possible for most therapies to be conducted on such a basis. Economic factors alone will force most patients to limit themselves to one session weekly. While this may not be ideal, we believe that treatment can usually be successful on that basis, particularly with the quiet, as-if type of patient.

Countertransference

All writers agree that countertransference-based feelings must be monitored throughout treatment. Chessick (1977) noted that two of the most difficult problems in this regard are chronic, raging verbal assaults on the therapist and instances of erotization of the therapy or attempts to seduce the therapist. The former challenge the therapist's narcissism, while the latter may appeal to it. In both instances it appears important for therapists to examine how the patient's behavior is an attempt to avoid some painful aspect of his or her reality and how the therapist is being invited to collude in the attempt. Everyone agrees that therapists will be able to deal with these and other issues better if they have themselves undergone intensive therapy or analysis and/or if they seek out a good consultant.

It seems especially important for therapists to be aware of what they are feeling. The better the therapist's understanding of what feelings the patient evokes, the greater the chance that the situation can be confronted honestly and directly. As Chessick (1977) observed, "It is the therapist's attitude toward countertransference and what he does with it that determines whether it will be a tremendous hindrance, even destroying the psychotherapy, or it can even be helpful in obtaining more insight about the patient and oneself" (p. 217). Searles (1979) makes a similar point, saying, "The countertransference provides the analyst with his most reliable approach to the understanding of borderline [as well as other] patients" (p. 343). In the same vein he also says, "I find it particularly helpful when a 'personal,' 'private' feeling-response within myself, a feeling which I have been experiencing as fully or at least predominantly my 'own,' becomes revealed as being a still deeper layer of reaction to a newly-revealed aspect of the patient's transference to me" (p. 333).

The question of how to deal with countertransference-based feelings is far from settled. For instance, Masterson disagrees strongly with Searles' (quoted in Masterson 1978) position that "the feelings that the therapist is having are of the very essence of what the treating of such a patient is about" (p. 151). Masterson claims that if the therapist has "more or less successfully resolved his more primitive developmental conflicts, they have been transformed into intrapsychic structures and are therefore no longer available to appear in the countertransference except under extreme stress and regression" (pp. 158–159). Aside from the rather sanctimonious tone of this statement, we are frankly puzzled by Masterson's ability to present himself in such a detached (or, as Searles put it, dispassionate) manner when speaking about work with the borderline patient. Given the nature of this population, we find it hard to believe that even Masterson, with his wealth of clinical experience, would not find that various personal feelings are evoked in the course of his work and that these would be relevant to his understanding of the patient as well as to his understanding of himself.

At the same time, we agree with Masterson's concern that young therapists need to be well trained (have extensive knowledge of personality development, psychopathology, and therapy) and be sufficiently free from pathology that they can apply what they know. Without the "safeguards" of intensive training and an intensive personal therapy, the young therapist "could be unduly vulnerable to going astray and using the therapy for his own emotional needs rather than those of the patient" (p. 159). We might add the cautionary note that these "safeguards" offer no guarantee that the therapist will not go "astray." Rather, these constitute a foundation for developing one's professional judgment with increased experience.

Chessick (1977) has also made a cogent observation on the potential abuse of therapy techniques by poorly trained and/or untreated therapists: "Good, sound theroretical models which have been carefully thought out and worked over by highly respected and very excellent authors, psychoanalysts, and thinkers can be used by the untrained and untreated to *rationalize just about anything they want to do*" (p. 210, emphasis added). To this we can only add that working with borderline patients requires even greater attention to this potential pitfall.

Addressing Self-Destructive Behaviors

Another area of widespread agreement among clinicians is dealing with such self-destructive behaviors as drug use, promiscuity, and threats of or actual attempts at suicide. It is well known that borderline patients can act impulsively, often seeking simply to discharge tension and reduce anxiety, with little awareness of immediate or long-term consequences. These patients may make suicidal gestures without any real sense of their potential finality. In such cases, their desire is often more to be rescued and controlled than to die.

The clinical literature basically advocates the use of confrontation as the response to self-destructive behaviors. In its classical psychoanalytic sense, confrontation is an intervention designed to correct a reality distortion. In the case of the borderline patient's self-destructive actions, the therapist's confrontations must repeatedly and consistently direct the patient's attention to the undesirable consequences of such actions, all the while ignoring the motives offered by the patient for these behaviors. In effect, the focus must be on the actual results of self-destructive behaviors, with some attention as well to the way in which these behaviors help the patient avoid or deny painful, uncomfortable realities.

Basically we do not believe that classical interventions are useful or effective during the preconstancy stage of treatment; however, we do advocate confrontation of self-destructive behaviors. Self-destructive patients have usually managed to create a cycle that begins when painful affect leads to reckless acting out. These reckless behaviors in turn create a mess that the therapist or someone else is then called on to solve. The final stage of the cycle is the patient's sense of relief over being rescued and, subsequently, a sense of resentment that it takes a crisis to make others show that they really care. Therapists must try to cut off this cycle by consistently pointing out to patients what they are doing to themselves and by declining the opportunity to resolve the crisis or otherwise to treat the patient as a victim.

Origins of Transference

Although writers agree that borderline patients exhibit a primitive type of transference that is notable for its intensity, there is disagreement on the origins of the transference. The most important area of disagreement is whether the patient's transference reflects real early experiences with an inadequate mother, or whether there is a fantasy basis to the transference that should be emphasized by the therapist. Kernberg (1975) has taken the latter position and sees the transference to the therapist as originating in fantasy-based distortions of early object relationships. These distortions stem from excessive aggressive energies that contaminate actual experiences, causing the world to seem more frustrating and dangerous than in fact it is. In effect the child *creates* an exaggerated image of the threatening parents, and with the primitive defenses at his or her disposal, actively contributes to the development of disturbed parent–child relationships.

Based on this scenario, actual caretakers can only be experienced in ways allowed by the defenses the ego uses to fend off aggressive and persecutory fantasies. Thus the more primitive the defense, the more distorted and fantastic any relationship will be. We can see here Kernberg's attempt to integrate a Kleinian model with an ego psychology orientation. The Kleinian contribution is the emphasis on fantasy (of threatening "monsters" besieging the small child) and the primitive defenses used by the immature ego to protect itself; the influence of ego psychology is readily seen in Kernberg's emphasis on levels and types of defense and resulting weaknesses in ego functioning.

By contrast, Masterson (1972, 1978) and Buie and Adler (1982) argue that the borderline patient's intense transference reactions reflect actual disturbances in his or her primary relationships. As already noted, Buie and Adler (1972) believe that the negative transference is rooted in maternal failure and that the attendant rage is the result of the frustration of legitimate needs. Masterson (1972, 1976) has gone even further with his proposal that the mother of every borderline patient herself suffered borderline pathology. These positions emphasize that the borderline patient has suffered actual, problematic relationships in early childhood.

The significance of this debate is that it bears heavily on how one actually works with patients. If the chief source of the problem lies in fantasy and extensive distortion of childhood experiences, along with instinctual aggression, then the actual relationship between therapist and patient becomes less important and less useful. Interpretation and the interventions that prepare the way for interpretation become the most relevant means of change. If, however, the therapist emphasizes real, early experiences as the basis for transference, then there is greater potential for using the patient's actual experiences with the therapist as the agent of change.

Our position is that this is an impossible distinction to make.

The therapist must work with the *patient's* experience of the parents, and it is irrelevant whether that experience is "real"; it is real for the patient. We recognize that patients will indeed carry fantasy-based distortions of object relations that interact with actual interactions. Nevertheless, we do not believe that interpretations in the early stages of therapy have much meaning to the borderline patient, and we will elaborate this further in the following three chapters. Therefore, in terms of actual practice we believe that one important feature of the early stage of treatment is establishing a particular type of relationship between patient and therapist, one in which the therapist becomes a constant object for the patient.

Two other aspects of this debate about the origins of transference should be noted here. First, we are concerned about the possibility of seeing or the temptation to see the borderline patient as simply a *victim* of early childhood experiences. This seems to relieve patients of all responsibility for their behavior and reinforces the victimization theme that is often presented in therapy. To ignore the fact that patients have also created their views of the world and themselves is to follow a deterministic philosophy that we do not accept. By this we mean that it is not inevitable that every person with the same inadequate mothering will automatically become a borderline personality. Thus, and second, we advocate caution in reifying the mother-child paradigm into a causal relationship. It is important to remain aware of a larger context, and we fully agree with Chessick (1977) and Rinsley (1982) that changes in our society, including a breakdown in stable social networks, may well contribute to the undermining of the parent's efforts to provide a relatively secure environment.

Confrontation, Interpretation, and Creation of a Holding Environment

Much has been written about the differences in technique among the different theorists we have discussed. Kernberg is usually understood to focus on the role of interpretation, Masterson on the uses of confrontation, and Adler and Buie on creating an empathic holding environment. Although these writers are quite different in their approaches, some of their differences are more apparent than real. No writer uses only one type of intervention to the exclusion of all others, and there are many variables that seem to influence the choice of treatment style.

Kernberg, for example, does not discount the need for confrontation. Although he plainly believes that "interpretation is the fundamental tool of expressive psychotherapy with borderline patients" (Kernberg et al. 1989, p. 15), he just as plainly sees a role for confrontation. The latter is a "precursor to

interpretation. Its aim is to make the patient aware of potentially conflictive and incongruous aspects of the material" (p.
17). The real question to be debated with Kernberg, then, may
not be whether confrontation (or any other type of intervention) has a role to play but rather whether the borderline
patient can "hear" the content of an interpretation early in
treatment without construing it as an attack or a sadistic attempt by the therapist to expose a deficiency.

We observed earlier that Kernberg seems to be focusing on
noisy or angry borderline patients. Given this focus, it is easy to
see his rationale for early interpretations of primitive defenses
and negative transference. In effect he is conveying to the
patient that he is not intimidated by the patient's rage and can
respond to it within the therapeutic frame. Additionally, a well-
formulated interpretation may communicate a sense of understanding, establishing a holding environment. Patients may
well come to feel that they are with someone who is strong
enough to withstand their destructive impulses and interested
enough to engage them even in their painful state. *Thus it may
not matter whether the patient can fully use the interpretation's content.* The process by which therapists show they
understand what is happening in the session and can link it to
earlier experiences can still serve an important organizing
function for patients overwhelmed with strong affect.

We should note that Kernberg's style of directly confronting
and interpreting the patient's anger early in treatment could be
distorted and abused by naive therapists acting out their own
sadistic or omnipotent fantasies. With this possibility in mind,
we can well appreciate the question raised by Stolorow and
Lachmann (1980) as to whether the aggression expressed by
the patient toward the therapist is indeed not a function of a
failure of empathy, specifically, "a failure to recognize the
arrested developmental aspects of the patient's psychopathology . . ." (p. 191).

To think this issue through, it may be useful to imagine a

continuum on the uses of interpretation early in treatment, with Kernberg anchoring one end of the continuum. We might conceive Chessick (1977, 1979) to occupy a middle position. On the one hand, he agrees with Kernberg that early negative transference makes treatment difficult and must be successfully managed for therapy to continue. He recommends that the patient be confronted with the discrepancy between the reality of the therapeutic situation and the patient's distorted experience of it. On the other hand, Chessick (1982) disagrees that it is useful to interpret such primitive defenses as splitting and projective identification early in treatment. On this point his writings appear to reflect Kohut's (1971) concern that borderline patients will feel too narcissistically wounded by early interpretations and that they should be left for the later stages of therapy. Chessick (1979) argues that interpretations are likely to make borderline patients feel humiliated by the fact that someone knows something about them they do not know about themselves. Additionally, the interpretation may destroy the patient's illusion of merging with a good self-object who can be idealized as an omnipotent protector and at the same time can be controlled.

Here we can see some of the fundamental differences between Kernberg and those whose ideas show the influence of Kohut's writings. The question is whether it is more helpful for borderline patients to be made aware early of their separateness from the therapist or to allow the early fantasies of fusion and idealization to satisfy unmet narcissistic needs. These alternatives appear to reflect the eternal paradox that we desire to be understood as a means of connecting with others, but we also fear being understood too much because of the control this gives others. Chessick seems aware of this dilemma, and his approach appears to be an attempt at reconciling the two sides. On the one hand, he (1979) acknowledges that therapists will have to interpret self-object transferences and that this will cause narcissistic wounds. On the other hand, he recommends that therapists also empathize with the patient's experience of the disruption in the transference and convey an understanding both of the anxieties this arouses and of the patient's deepest needs.

One of Chessick's major contributions in this thorny debate is that he takes into account the different levels of organization presented by each patient. He notes that lower-level borderline patients are usually unable to make use of the content of verbal interventions. As Chessick (1977) describes one such patient, who presented an endless series of complaints session after session, "She rarely seemed to be listening to anything I said, and yet she came regularly; she felt that the therapy was helping and her life was even improving" (p. 179). Chessick goes on to conclude, "When the kind of transference I am describing is in effect . . . it doesn't matter very much what we say! The patient is not interested in the words at all, any more than when the mother picks up the baby, the baby cares which lullaby the mother is singing" (p. 179). Chessick is emphasizing the importance of experiential factors; he believes the patient internalizes aspects of the therapist and the total ambience of the therapy setting (see Chapter 6) and accordingly plays down the importance of interpretation.

Further along the continuum there is Searles' (1978) position, which is very close to our own idea of "standing still." Searles elegantly states, "I surmise that in working with any patient of whatever diagnostic category, my silence is my most reliably effective therapeutic tool; surely this is the case in my work with borderline individuals" (p. 56). Searles observes that silence may have many meanings, and the therapist's silence should not be automatically equated with neutral, evenly hovering attention. In contrast to Kernberg, who intervenes actively from the beginning of treatment, Searles says, "Surely 90% of most analysts' time with most patients is spent with the analyst's being silent, and in the work with many a borderline patient, 98 to 99% of one's time involves one's being nonverbal with him" (p. 58).

Searles accepts the fact that interpretations have a significant role in the analyst's work with the borderline patient. He (1986) suggests that the patient's level of ego development and the particular stage of the therapy should influence the form the interpretation takes, its length, and the therapist's vocal inflections. He (1978) says that with borderline patients the role of interpretation is a "relatively minor one by contrast to that of the analyst's nonverbal participation with him" (p. 62). In Searles' opinion the patient cannot make good use of verbal interpretations until there is a stable, internalized image of the self and of the therapist.

Buie and Adler and others influenced by self psychology occupy the far end of the continuum away from Kernberg. Their focus tends to be on the experiential aspects of therapy. They believe that interpretations do not address intrapsychic conflicts with borderline patients as much as they simply highlight ego defects. Consequently they believe that early interpretations of negative transference will probably be experienced by the patient as criticisms and may undermine the motivation for treatment as a disruption of the holding environment, of patients' need for an empathic extension of themselves (a self-object) who accepts their idealizations, their rage, and their longings for a perfect caregiver. In this context interpretations can only serve a limited role, as adjuncts to the creation of a holding environment.

As we mentioned earlier and wish to emphasize again, our concern with this approach is that it seems to reinforce the view of the patient as a victim who is going through life with an empty self (Cushman 1990), needing empathic mirroring to be filled up. Although the language has changed, there is a quality reminiscent of a song from the musical *West Side Story*, where a delinquent explains his antisocial behavior by, "Officer

Krupke, I've got a social disease." The idea is that all problems have an external cause beyond the individual's control or responsibility. Similarly, self psychology sees the borderline patient's problems in terms of maternal failure to provide mirroring and empathic understanding. This approach suggests that these patients lack even the most basic competencies and places the therapist too close to the role of a perfect caregiver who will save the patient from the inadequate mother. We think it is very often realistic and necessary to help patients see clearly the ways in which their parents failed them; but it is not the therapist's task then to replace the mother.

Summary

The borderline concept has undergone several changes since its inception. Chessick (1982) observes that some of the disagreements among clinicians may reflect the variety of patients who have been given this diagnosis. Additionally, different authors may be emphasizing clinical phenomena visible at different phases of the treatment process. Curiously, there has been little discussion in the literature of the way in which treatment technique may be a function of treatment setting. For example, in an inpatient setting therapists might well decide to be more active and rely more heavily on verbal interventions, trusting the inpatient milieu to provide a holding environment. By the same token, much of the treatment in an inpatient setting may be done by unit staff, with whom patients will often act out their various issues. It may be worth emphasizing here that we are focusing in this book on outpatient therapy with borderline patients.

Despite the increasing popularity of the borderline diagnosis, many questions remain about what is being referred to and whether there has been significant gain in therapeutic technique. As scientifically oriented practitioners, we are concerned that this diagnosis not fall into the same morass described by U.S. Supreme Court Justice Potter Stewart, who said in relation to pornography, "I can't define it, but I know it when I see it." Additionally, we are particularly concerned that the term "borderline" is a spatial metaphor. This spatial reference implies that there are categories of functioning that are well demarcated. Unfortunately this does not do justice to the variability of ego functions in the borderline patient, nor does it reflect the fluidity (viz., the rapidity of change) in the borderline individual's behavior. In this sense we think it would be worthwhile to consider a concept that focuses on the individual's experience of time and self when alone and with others.

CRITICAL ASPECTS OF BORDERLINE PATHOLOGY

Introduction

The chapters in Part II basically cover most of the preconstancy stage of treatment. The issues discussed here will occupy the therapist's attention for many months and in fact probably for the first year and more of therapy. It would be foolish to say that these issues then disappear; of course they do not. But we believe they dominate treatment until late in the preconstancy stage, so it is important for therapists to be prepared to address them. Only after the patient can experience the therapeutic relationship as fairly stable and reliable will these issues become muted and less prominent in the patient's life and in sessions.

There are three chapters in Part II, each covering a key aspect of borderline pathology:

- perpetual concern with abandonment
- inability to modulate affect
- intolerance of separateness

We have chosen these particular themes because there is wide agreement in the literature about their importance and also because we believe therapists will have many opportunities to see them during therapy sessions. Each of these themes should arise very early in treatment, both in the patient's reports of events outside sessions and in the relationship with the therapist. It is the latter that is more troubling to deal with usually, since the way borderline patients bring these issues into treatment often causes intense countertransference reactions in therapists.

Given that these themes can be difficult to address, therapists should think through their stance beforehand. We have tried to apply seldom-used categories to this process, especially the category of time, which we referred to in Chapter 1. In brief, we repeatedly emphasize that these themes are closely related to the borderline patient's overly narrow, almost collapsed experience of time and that the best therapy of these issues is a therapy that broadens and expands the patient's time sense. We argue that standing still accomplishes this; in the following chapters we describe the way in which this basic therapeutic stance in itself begins to address and resolve the borderline patient's abandonment fears, tendencies toward extreme feeling states, and fear of separateness. We also tend to emphasize the interpersonal features of this process.

Each chapter has a similar structure. There is a broad description of the problem, some attention to etiology, and then discussion of how the problem is likely to arise in sessions and how therapists might think through their response. Each chapter concludes with a transcript from a session along with commentary. The transcripts are not intended to illustrate proper technique; indeed, they are presented with no attempt to disguise the flaws. Rather, the transcripts illustrate the way in which the issues we discuss make their appearance in sessions and the choices therapists must make.

4

Perpetual Fear
of Abandonment

The Roots of the Borderline Patient's Fear of Abandonment

Various theorists (Angyal 1965, Bakan 1966, Schachtel 1959) have described a dual trend in human life, namely a desire for individuality or autonomy on the one hand, and an equally persistent yearning for embeddedness or dependency on the other. Tension between these poles is known not only to psychologists but surely also to most reflective persons. There are common phenomena, such as wedding-day jitters, that imply the anxieties even healthy people may experience when they perceive some loss of autonomy or individuality. Similarly, the fearfulness many persons feel when called on to make a presentation to a large group is an everyday example of the other side of the coin, namely being too much on one's own. In all areas of life, but most especially in our close relationships, we seek a compromise between these dual motivations so that we can have times of closeness without fear of losing our separate identity, and times of independence without the fear of being left terrifyingly alone.

Perhaps the best-known developmental example of conflict between these poles is the ambivalence and upset of the senior toddler during Mahler's rapprochement subphase of the separation-individuation sequence. At that time children seem to feel torn between the familiar home base offered by the mother, and their desire to master the larger world. The conflict appears to stem from the child's recognition that mastery of the larger world entails some loss of dependency. Similarly, however, remaining close to the mother necessitates the surrender of what White (1960) called effectance motivation, or the innate pleasure of attaining competence over some hitherto unknown aspect of the world. The growing child must eventually manage some balance between the two poles, a balance to be renegotiated many times across the years.

The capacity to balance ourselves between individuality and embeddedness is built on object constancy, or the illusion of the mother's constant availability to the child. Constancy makes separateness and independence endurable; the larger world can be explored and the child's own burgeoning competence exercised if there is confidence that contact with the mother can be resumed as needed. Such confidence makes separation feel time-limited. Hence the anxiety of separation can be managed; children can risk aloneness if they know connectedness will again be available.

Lacking constancy, borderline individuals cannot negotiate this needed balance between autonomy and homonomy. Every step toward autonomy diminishes the borderline patient's sense of connectedness with others, and they are similarly threatened by the independence of loved ones. This tenuous sense of attachment with others reaches such extremes that it is accurate to say that the borderline patient is perpetually concerned with abandonment. Unlike schizoid patients, who have given up hope of a meaningful attachment, and unlike neurotic individuals, who maintain some realistic hope, border-line patients constantly struggle with what they feel is an inevitable abandonment by loved ones. This feature of border-line pathology is so central that we regard the diagnosis as highly questionable if patients fail to show such fear of abandonment.

For example, one 34-year-old married mother of two has wondered *daily* if her husband would come home from work or leave her. This woman grew up in a home in which both parents were alcoholic and fought constantly; neither parent was reliably available for her. Now she is constantly fearful of losing any important relationship. Not only does she worry that her husband will one day not come home, but she is also excessively fearful about her children. She is overprotective, as might be expected, and feels constant tension whenever they are out of sight. This patient has made one suicide attempt and suffers an endless variety of somatic complaints. She is sure that her husband is fed up over all the medical bills and is about to take the children and leave. It is a sad irony that her fear of abandonment keeps her from even hearing her husband's fear of losing her and having to "raise the kids by myself."

Another example is a 22-year-old man who moved away from his hometown for the first time when he went to gradu-ate school. He unexpectedly found himself desperately home-sick and practically unable to remain away more than three nights at a time without making the long trip back home. At first he thought it was his fiancée he missed, but even after they married he could not complete a full week without going home. Whenever he tried, he felt so depressed he could scarcely function and became obsessed with fears that his family— chiefly his mother—was in agony over his absence and even that they might kill themselves if he did not return. This patient also needed frequent contact with friends, and without it he became convinced they had forgotten him or, in the case of his wife, that she was falling in love with someone else.

These two cases illustrate different but related sides of the borderline patient's fear of abandonment. First, there is a fear the other will grow tired of the relationship, lose interest, or simply leave—that is, the patient fears not holding enough meaning or significance to make the relationship worthwhile to the other person. Second, many borderline patients also feel that they have abandoned the other person whenever they become more autonomous or independent themselves. They then feel guilty over this abandonment and fear the other will retaliate by abandoning them, or by not being available when they seek closeness. Thus borderline patients suffer first, the inevitable sense of imminent abandonment that attends unreliable attachments, and second, the guilt of having abandoned the other and brought retaliation on themselves.

Both forms of abandonment fear have their roots in the patient's interactions with caretakers during childhood. Most children have fears of being abandoned at one time or another, but they move beyond these fears. They consistently receive pleasing feedback from those around them that they are wanted. Even when their parents are angry with them, the rejection they feel is time-limited and supplanted by a predictable return to normal relations. Borderline patients who are afraid the other will grow tired of them, however, have typically not had a sense that they were wanted as children. They have more often had a sense that they were tolerated because they filled some function for the parent or because the caretaker was stuck with them and had no choice. In any event, their presence in the home seemed conditional and based on something they could neither control nor count on. Children growing up in such circumstances may understandably come to feel that attachments are unreliable and that it is only a matter of time before the other person leaves them.

The borderline patient's guilt over autonomy is similarly based on interactions with caretakers. Rinsley (1982) and Masterson (1981) have described a characteristic pattern of interaction with the mother; the experience of many borderline patients was that the mother would withdraw in anger or depression whenever the patient moved toward greater independence and maturity. The message from such interactions was that the mother desperately needed the child to stay dependent on her and that independence would bring the loss of the mother. As a consequence, borderline patients tend to be vulnerable to anxiety and abandonment depression whenever they make gains in competency and autonomy.

For example, the 22-year-old patient who found himself homesick remembered many episodes in which his mother became angrily withdrawn and depressed whenever he tried to leave the family for the larger world of friends and school. He would eventually give up such efforts rather than face her withdrawal. This patient remembered trying out for the football team in high school in a thinly veiled effort at establishing some aggressive, masculine identity. What he remembered most was how exhilarated he felt at his initial success in practice; this exuberance was short-lived, however, when he learned in his third week that his mother expected him to go shopping with her and miss practice. When he reminded her of his obligation to practice, she fell sullen and depressed, leading him to ask his coach to be excused from practice so that he could go shopping with his mother. This request drew the response from his coach and teammates one might expect, and he elected to attend practice rather than face continued scorn and abuse. However, he then fell into an agitated depression in which he was unable to sleep or do his homework, and he found himself considering suicide. He felt his only way out of his depressed state was to quit football, which he did. It is clear that this patient had experienced an abandonment depression upon trying to become more independent of his mother. He felt that if he needed his mother less, she would be crushed and therefore unavailable to him at all.

Most clinicians have had occasion to confirm this pattern of early object relations in their borderline patients. We want to emphasize two additional points. First, while these patients complain that they fear *being* abandoned by the other person, the therapist should listen closely for signs that they actually feel guilty over *having* abandoned the other. Given the message that the parent needs them to be clinging and dependent, they experience their own growth as a betrayal of the parent's needs. When these patients become afraid they will be abandoned, they are chiefly afraid others are about to punish them for having dared to be less needy.

Second, the most important feature in such interactions is the temporal factor; this factor will eventually guide the clinician's approach to the patient. The temporal factor is essentially this: children experience their own period of independence from the parent as brief and time-limited, but they experience the parent's retaliatory withdrawal as potentially eternal. The crucial factor is not just that the caretaker—usually the mother—withdraws her libidinal availability but also that she withdraws for an *undetermined* period of time. The child is not only distressed to find that she is not there when sought; a still greater source of distress is not knowing when, or if, she will be available again.

The problem is that the young child cannot impose a time frame on the mother's withdrawal. When the mother withdraws, the child cannot imagine when she will return; it feels as though the withdrawal will be forever. The child then falls confused over having done something that seemed ordinary at the time but having received an enormous punishment for it. There is no proportion between the child's own action and the other person's reaction, and the child comes to feel that the offense (of independence) must have been huge. The child, after all, made a time-limited move away from the parent; the period of independence ended when the child came back for refueling or closeness. But the parent's retaliatory withdrawal has no perceptible end, and the young child lacks the perspective to realize that it, too, will be time-limited.

The child is unlikely to develop such perspective as long as the parent tends to withdraw in retaliation for the child's burgeoning autonomy. Perspective is developed through learning that different actions draw different reactions from others, that there is a proportion between what one does versus what the world does in response. But the young child cannot experience a withdrawing parent in this way. The child simply does not know when the parent will come back emotionally, and so it seems that every brief abandonment by the child draws the same, potentially eternal retaliation from the parent.

This uncertainty contributes to the borderline patient's characteristic time distortions. These patients tend to experience affect in a perpetually frozen present, and they have trouble imagining that they will ever feel differently than at the present instant. Time perspectives cannot develop when tension remains unbounded and ambiguous. Most people can endure tension or conflict if they know it is clear-cut and that it will stop at some predictable point, and in most families there are rituals of reconciliation or reparation that serve to bind or limit times of tension. Such cycles of anger, tension, and reconciliation teach children that painful feelings are time-limited and that conflict with others can be repaired.

Borderline patients, however, report few experiences of reparation after an argument as they grew up. They typically report having been uncertain over how long love would be withheld and then having suddenly found that the argument was over—they knew not how. As children they found the tension suddenly, unaccountably gone, and yet they could not determine that they had done anything to produce the tension relief. Since they could not thereby feel they had caused the change, they remained powerless to effect a reconciliation during the next conflict and again experienced a tension reduction with no discernible cause. In such circumstances children can have no sense of how relationships are mended and certainly no sense of what they can do to make the other person libidinally available again. They can only learn to wait to see *if* the tension ends.

One patient remembered that his mother would grow terribly upset whenever he went out to play with other children in the neighborhood. When he returned, he would find her angry with him, and there would be an argument without her ever saying what it was she was angry about. In the midst of the argument, his mother would go to her bedroom and lock the door. Since his mother suffered very poor health, the boy truly suffered from a fear he might not see her again; he would knock at the door, calling out to her, but the mother would not answer him. Finally he would promise to be good, saying that he would never play outside again, even though he knew this was a lie. Only after his promise was the door unlocked; the mother would come out and quiz the child about whether he really meant his promise. By that time the child would have promised anything to make the mother reappear and did promise whatever the mother wanted, knowing all the while that he could not keep the promise. (Later, in therapy, it was decided that the healthiest part of this interaction was the child's lying.) In this case the child was forced to make a masochistic submission to the mother's sadism; without such a submission the child had no way to influence the mother and was in a situation in which waiting was intolerable.

Such a pattern of interaction builds a chaotic inner world as the child grows up. Children cannot attain a sense of mastery or interpersonal competence when their actions have no predictable impact on others. In place of an inner confidence that they can affect loved ones in desirable ways, such children internalize the uncertainty and unpredictability that attends closeness and dependency. They perpetuate with others the patterns of interaction they experienced with their parents, and so as adults repeatedly experience unsatisfying and unstable relation-ships in which they are constantly afraid of being abandoned.

Borderline patients will bring this pattern of object relations into therapy. It is important that these patients become able to experience the relationship with the therapist as nonfragile, as one that endures without demanding that the patient surrender autonomous strivings. Two things must be accomplished for this to occur. First, patients must learn that there is usually a proportion between their actions and the world's response to them; they must become confident that others will, for the most part, deal with them in predictable ways. Second, they must discover that arguments are usually time-limited and that there are ways to end conflicts without sacrificing pride.

Interpersonal Patterns Stemming
from Fear of Abandonment

Many borderline patients appear competent and capable in such contexts as work, community activities, school, and recreation. It is when they are alone or involved in close relationships that the problems emerge that bring these patients to treatment. In relationships, borderline patients seem forever involved in some crisis that precludes their feeling content or comfortable with the other person. When these crises are examined, it is often unclear whether the patient is suffering some abuse or injustice at the hands of the other or whether they are themselves creating tension and uncertainty where none need exist.

A pathetic yearning seems to pervade borderline patients' close relationships. These patients want to feel significant or important to themselves and to others. They cannot find such feelings within themselves, however, so they look all the more

urgently for evidence that they are significant to others. Borderline patients never quite trust any evidence or reassurance
the other person offers, though. These patients view relationships in terms of satisfying or frustrating some need or desire
of the moment; there is no sense that connectedness can be
maintained without a specific purpose or need to be met.
Patients therefore seek ways to be important to loved ones, and
they expect loved ones to do the same for them, leading—they
hope—to intimate exchanges in which the other person confirms their existence by being grateful for their sensitivity or
devotion.

In the absence of such encounters, borderline patients begin
to doubt their value to the other person and the other person's
love for them. Hence there is a perpetual testing of loved ones
to determine whether they really care. Interactions often have
the quality of being staged because they follow such a predictable sequence, one repeated across many relationships and
many years. The patient first presents to the other person
some problem that is depressing or anxiety-provoking. The
patient hopes to evoke reassurance or support from the other.
Second, if the other person fails to offer the desired response,
or if the patient feels the response was somehow questionable,
the patient makes some provocative action designed to devalue
or anger the other person. Third, the patient then makes a
pseudothreat to end the relationship. Often there is a paranoidlike quality to the threat; patients may say, for instance, that
they have been used sexually or financially. This is often followed by a depressive complaint that the other person does not
really love them. Finally, there is usually an emotional reconciliation in which the patient uses the emotion to generate fantasies of oneness and restore a sense of being in an ideal relationship.

These reconciliations often include a masochistic rapprochement by patients, who allow themselves to be exploited in
some fashion as the price of reunion. Patients who have just

attacked the other and threatened to end the relationship will suddenly reverse themselves and make a submissive, self-effacing, and humiliating gesture to the other person. The other person is then seen as a strong protector, and the patient feels fused with the other through this masochistic submission. In this attitude of fusion the patient feels cared for in the desired way, and the crisis ends.

There are obvious sadomasochistic features on both sides of such encounters, and it is never completely clear whether patients are actually being victimized or whether these crises are self-inflicted wounds. They are seldom entirely one or the other. Both parties may feel there is nothing they could have done that would have been right. Their choice seems to have been to reach out and feel rejected or to withdraw and feel abandoned. Whatever resolution was achieved was not a true resolution; there was no sense of closure, nor could there have been, since the encounter was essentially the result of the patient's yearning for an illusory oneness that can only be felt in the aftermath of great tension. The patient has managed to produce significant tension, resolve it, and—because of the reduction in tension—feel fed or cared for.

The parallel with very early mother–child interactions is obvious. During the so-called need-satisfying stage of early object relations (A. Freud 1952, 1965, Hartmann 1952), the child experiences rising tensions from hunger, difficulty with temperature regulation, or need for sleep. The mother serves to interdict these rising tensions before they overwhelm the child. Through feeding, clothing, and soothing, the mother reduces the child's tension, which in turn creates moments of mother–child closeness. The borderline patient re-creates such experiences through self-generated crises, their resulting tensions, and through a submission that reduces tension and produces an illusion of closeness.

The important feature for the therapist, however, is not that this cycle re-creates a feature of early life, but that, lacking

object constancy, the patient cannot feel secure in a relationship without the reassurance of these periodic crises and reconciliations. Unless there is some periodic moment of truth in
which borderline patients reexperience a return to closeness,
they cannot feel securely attached, and they come to fear abandonment by the other person. This is not necessarily because
they are in fact about to be abandoned; rather, these patients
are creating the uncertainty, projecting it onto the relationship
from their own inner world.

The Expression of Abandonment Fear
in the Therapy Session

Therapists are usually trained to look for signs of distress in their patients over such treatment interruptions as holidays, the therapist's vacation, or illnesses. The theory behind this is that patients become emotionally dependent on the therapist and experience a regression to early childhood separation anxiety when regular contact is interrupted. Given the excessive fear of abandonment shown by most borderline patients, it might be expected that they would have an especially hard time with separations from the therapist. It might also be thought that therapists ought to take special measures to deal with abandonment fear, such as giving borderline patients their pictures or vacation phone numbers.

We agree that borderline patients will find ways to express their fear of abandonment in therapy. We do not, however, believe that these patients will typically have a hard time with such routine, expectable separations from the therapist as vacations, holidays, trips, or even illnesses. We certainly do not believe that unusual interventions are necessary to calm or prepare the patient for these separations, and in our view it is a mistake to make these interventions. As long as events are relatively clear and unambiguous, borderline patients are not likely to interpret routine separations as abandonment.

Borderline patients can often distinguish the intent of the therapist when events are expectable or unambiguous and can therefore discern that the therapist intends to return after a trip or illness. For example, one therapist suffered an unexpected hospitalization for several weeks. When he returned to work, he asked one borderline patient whether he thought the therapist had abandoned him. The patient replied, "No, I knew where you were. I called the hospital, and you were there." Another therapist, suffering a bladder infection, had to leave a session several times. When he returned, he asked the patient, who had just been talking about her fear that her parents would never come back when they angrily withdrew from her, whether she feared he might not return when he left the session. The patient replied, "Oh, no. I knew you intended to return." We have had similar answers to inquiries on how borderline patients react to trips. Our impression is that borderline patients do not generally feel abandoned by routine separations. When push comes to shove, borderline patients can usually differentiate a necessary separation from abandonment.

Borderline patients will, however, fear abandonment by the therapist in ambiguous situations. When events are not clearcut or well defined, and the patient must account for the ambiguity, abandonment becomes a likely interpretation. If a session is unexpectedly late in starting, for instance, or if the therapist fails to understand the patient during a session, borderline patients are likely to feel insignificant, that the therapist had no real desire to know them, and ultimately that the therapist is about to terminate treatment. One patient found her therapist late in calling her from the waiting room. She began to think she must be there on the wrong day. After checking her calendar and finding the day was right, she then assumed she must be wrong about the time. Finally she decided the therapist must have found something more interesting to do or replaced her with a patient he liked better. She never assumed she had any right to be there or that the therapist had been held up by reasonable circumstances.

The way in which fear of abandonment arises in therapy is, therefore, not dramatic and often not very obvious. It is important to keep in mind that this fear is part of the borderline patient's everyday life. These patients are always on the alert for signs that the other person has lost interest and is about to leave. Any experience of tension or ambiguity is sufficient for them to read abandonment into the other person's intent.

Even when events are relatively unambiguous and tension-free, borderline patients will often create the uncertainty themselves. Not only is this self-inflicted wound a feature of the patient's interactions with loved ones, but it is also the most common way abandonment fear will arise in the therapy session. The sequence will be substantially the same as that described in the preceding section, as the patient presents some problem in hopes the therapist will prove he or she cares by trying urgently to solve it. If the therapist's response is not satisfying, the patient will often create a crisis, threaten to end treatment, and then make a masochistic submission of some sort, seeking a masochistic rapprochement and the accompanying illusion of oneness.

Finally, borderline patients typically complain to the therapist about events in their lives and seem perpetually dissatisfied with how things work out for them. It can be easy for the therapist to miss the fact that these complaints are attempts to ward off abandonment. These patients expect—on the basis of their own guilt over having abandoned the mother—that any revelation to the therapist of having made a successful move on their own will lead to a sadistic abandonment by the therapist. Consequently these patients cannot let themselves feel satisfied with what they have done; they carry a guilt for the times they functioned without complaining and feel guilty whenever they are satisfied for any action taken on their own initiative. The many complaints they make are a form of masochistic submission to a sadistic parent, whose image is projected onto the therapist. Behind the patients' many complaints and chronic dissatisfaction lies the conviction that they will be left out in the cold if they ever do anything successfully.

Therapy Implications

No matter which way patients express their fear of abandon-ment—by interpreting tension or ambiguity as a sign that the therapist has lost interest, by chronic dissatisfaction, or by creating a crisis to be resolved through a masochistic rap-prochement—the therapist's response should be the same. The basic intervention should be that of standing still, maintaining a calm and steady presence in the face of the patient's fear or urgency. There is no need for the therapist to interpret, con-front, or make some other verbal intervention regarding the patient's abandonment anxieties. Even an empathic reflection such as "I know you're afraid I will lose interest in you" should be weighed against the possibility that it will be experienced as an intrusion or a demand.

Therapists should think long and hard before making any comment aimed at reducing the patient's abandonment anx-iety. It is true that patients sometimes need reassurance when their fears are overwhelming. Such reassurance should take the form of an empathic comment that shows—by its accuracy—that the patient is being understood. Most persons can withstand emotional pain if they know they are not alone; being alone is what makes distress unbearable. A comment that gives the patient the sense that "My therapist understands" can therefore reduce anxiety or at least make it bearable. But even such an empathic reflection can be unwise. If it appears that the patient needs to be drawn closer, an empathic reflection should be made. However, borderline patients sometimes create tension within a session to reaffirm their separateness prior to a return to closeness. In this case the distance should be respected, and even an accurate empathic comment can be experienced as intrusive or as a demand that the patient stay close to the therapist. It is often hard to tell whether the patient's intention is to affirm distance or to express fear of abandonment, and even empathic reflections, therefore, should be used judiciously.

Therapists may not find it easy to resist an interpretation when the pattern of interaction is transparent. For instance, it is often obvious that borderline patients create uncertainty or evoke a crisis within sessions out of identification with their parents. In essence they are doing with the therapist what their parents did with them, namely, acting in such a way as to call the relationship into question and generating uncertainty in the therapist about the viability of the relationship. The patient generally stops this identification with the aggressor when tension and uncertainty have been created and then assumes the role he or she held as a child, trying to effect a reconciliation with the therapist, who is then experienced as the parent.

It can be tempting for therapists to interpret the patient's attempts to bring on a crisis, saying, for example, "You're trying to get me to dump you" or "You're doing to me what your parents did to you." Such interventions are not generally helpful in the early months of treatment, however. We believe the closest the therapist should come to an interpretation is to say something to the effect, "You're trying to check out what kind of relationship we can have here," or "You're not sure how safe it is here." Therapists may well feel they should say more, that it might contribute to the formation of a benevolent introject, for instance, to reassure the patient of the therapeutic relationship's dependability. Therapists might also want to be sure the patient understands they are different from the patient's parents. But verbal reassurance is superfluous: Patients who do not trust the therapist to stay with them are unlikely to trust reassurances that the therapist will do so.

Therapists often overvalue their words and attribute more power to them than is realistic, and they are particularly prone to do this when they are unsure what value they hold for the patient. They may seek to assure the borderline patient that good things are possible in therapy, hoping thereby to resolve tension in the sessions and establish their value for the patient. Patients, however, will have to wait and discover for themselves what is possible with the therapist, and patients often seem to appreciate this fact even when therapists do not. One borderline patient, for example, presented herself for her eighth outpatient treatment. Near the end of the first session she urgently asked the therapist if he believed he could help her. She was visibly relieved when he said he thought he could understand her but did not know whether he would be able to help. The patient said all of her previous therapists had assured her they could help, but did not, and she was, paradoxically, relieved to hear someone express doubts. Apparently her other therapists had thought to ease her anxiety by their assurances, as if by saying they could help might make it so.

It is unrealistic and grandiose to reassure patients directly about fears the therapist will abandon them. In fact, in a successful treatment the patient will feel abandoned many times. Patients will create situations in which they believe the therapist is threatening termination in spite of everything said or done to the contrary; or the therapist will make a mistake or do something else to indicate that the patient has been misunderstood, and this will cause the patient to feel abandoned. In these and many other ways patients will feel their therapists never really cared for them or were just looking for a chance to be rid of them. Not only can these experiences not be avoided, but also they ought not be avoided. Over time, the patient should have the chance to find that the relationship endures in spite of moments of tension and instances of being misunderstood. Patients cannot experience relationships as constant without first realizing that people do sometimes fall out with and fail one another, but that such disappointments do not destroy the relationship.

The psychological atmosphere of the session is more important to the creation of object constancy than specific interventions. The therapist is trying to create a psychological space (Kahn 1969) or a psychic cocoon (cf. Modell 1976), as it were, within which the patient can simply be—a setting of safety and belonging in which the patient need not do anything or fill any function to be welcome. At the very least patients must feel confident that the therapist is attentive and grasps what they are struggling with. It is particularly important for the quiet borderline patient to have the chance to feel important to the therapist while they are together, even though these patients may not let themselves believe they are important for a long time. These patients tend to fear that at any moment they may make the wrong move and be thrown out of treatment. They are not likely to fear this any less if the fear is interpreted or even if they are directly reassured; rather, the interpretation or reassurance is likely to be experienced as a demand that they stop feeling that way, which in turn prompts them to behave as if they no longer fear termination of the relationship. Over time, an atmosphere of safety and belonging will induce a sense of constancy more effectively than verbal interventions with the quiet borderline patient.

It is better for therapists to appear glad to see their border-line patients when they greet them in the waiting room or find other ways to express the sense that "It is good we are together today." At most, therapists might point out that the patient has trouble believing he or she is welcome. Since these patients often did not have the sense of being welcome as children, and more often felt that they were tolerated for some function they played, it is easy for them to fear that they have outlived their function for the therapist, who would presumably be glad to be rid of them. One borderline patient, for instance, became angry when her therapist said "Come in" as she walked through the doorway to his office. Since she was already in the doorway at the time she thought he must be mocking her and trying to start a fight so he could end the relationship. It did not occur to her that it was a greeting or meant that he was glad to see her. It was more useful with this patient for the therapist to say, "I'm glad you're here" when he invited her in. It took over a year for this patient to feel she was "at home" or welcome in the therapist's office.

Noisy borderline patients are slower to respond to the psy-chic cocoon the therapist is trying to create. These patients often expect the therapist to meet their needs, and they have trouble imagining a basis for a relationship apart from meeting needs or reducing tension. Focused on this, they will accuse the therapist of not caring or of being too uninvolved. In this case a verbal intervention can be useful, and the therapist must be ready to say, "I wouldn't be here if I didn't care." The purpose of saying this is *not* to reassure the patient but rather to bring into the open the patient's belief "If you cared, you would do what I want." This in turn allows the therapist to point out that is how the patient learned about caring while growing up but that the patient is in therapy to learn a better way.

In sum, the basic therapeutic posture of standing still ad-dresses the borderline patient's fear of abandonment. The ther-apist need not produce specific interventions to address this fear; the establishment of a constant relationship will address it. As a nonfragile, enduring relationship unfolds, patients begin to gain a sense of proportion between their actions and what reactions can be expected from others, and they learn that conflicts can be resolved without their making a humiliating submission.

Clinical Transcript

The following transcript, from the fifth month of treatment with a noisy borderline patient, illustrates the self-generated crises that borderline patients can create within a session out of their fear of abandonment.

> The patient is a bright, articulate 32-year-old married woman who taught at a small midwestern college. She came for therapy complaining of intense anger at her husband, who appeared to be an especially private, withdrawn, somewhat schizoid individual. The couple periodically had explosive arguments that usually began with the patient's trying to get something from her husband—affection, sex, help with the chores, or conversation—but quickly feeling he would not respond. She would escalate her attempts to evoke the desired response, eventually moving into a furious rage in which she often physically attacked the man. The husband would then have to subdue her, and the patient would dissolve into

helplessness and tears, crying and apologizing while the husband comforted her.

Sessions with this patient had frequently been volatile, with a wide range of intense affect. At times the patient wept hysterically and at other times had been so angry that the therapist expected to be attacked himself. The patient was sometimes so morbidly depressed by the session's conclusion that it was hard to get her to leave the office. There were also times in which the patient seemed hypomanic, frequently pacing the floor as she talked and once impulsively reaching out to grab the therapist's leg as she laughed. Many of these states occurred within single sessions, and the overall impression was of someone who could not easily distance herself from what she was feeling at any given moment.

In the third month of treatment the therapist had made the mistake of placing his arm across the patient's shoulder at the end of a difficult session. The patient was crying at the time and appeared unwilling to leave the office; the therapist did not think she was upset enough to justify extended time and hoped the gesture would ease the patient out of the room. When the patient subsequently asked for another hug at the end of the following session, the therapist knew he had made a mistake and said as much to the patient, adding that he did not think it was his role to offer physical contact. The patient, though angry, appeared to accept the therapist's stance. However, two months later, while leaving the office, the patient again asked to be hugged. The therapist refused and brought the subject up at the start of the next session.

T: I wanted to talk with you about how we, um, ended last week. At the door out there? You had said something to me about missing hugs or wanting hugs?

P: I said I didn't get my hug.

T: Yeah, I wanted to talk with you about that. You want me to hug you?

P: [*long pause*] Sometimes.

T: I wanted to talk with you about that, because you seemed to be asking me to hug you, and I wasn't exactly sure what you wanted or whether I wanted to do it, and I wanted to talk with you about what you expected.

P: [*pause*] Okay.

T: So what do you want? What were you asking me for?

P: I think contact.

T: Physical contact, you mean?

P: [*nonchalantly*] Yeah.

T: I'm not real comfortable with that.

P: I know you're not, and I'm not real comfortable without it.

T: Um, I'm not sure it's my job or role to provide that for you, though I don't discount its significance in somebody's life. And I wanted for us to be clear on what's going on.

P: It sounds like you think it's inappropriate.

T: I do. I think it crosses a boundary of what I should provide and what I shouldn't.

The therapist is trying to emphasize boundaries with this patient and throughout this exchange tries to differentiate his point of view from the patient's. In his focus on boundaries, however, he misses something of the structure of the exchange, namely that the patient is creating a problem where none need have existed. She already knew the therapist would not hug her before she asked; she is creating the tension by demanding something that is unavailable. The patient is trying to make the therapist prove he cares.

P: See like [*inaudible*] I think that's just your own personality and your own interpretation of your professional [*inaudible*]. I don't see that at all! People, all psychologists, are doing that now.

T: I certainly can't speak for all.

P: I know that. Nor can I, but I can speak for those I know. Anyhow, and um . . .

[*Silence for about 3 minutes*]

P: [*mumbles*] . . . [*sounding depressed*] I think it's unfortunate.

T: Does it sound like I'm criticizing you or putting you down or something?

The patient tends to feel criticized or rejected whenever the other person does not see things as she does. The therapist, still working on boundaries, wants to show the patient that she equates differences of opinion with being personally rejected. However, this is not the issue here, and the patient says as much.

P: [*cold, angry*] Well, I mean that I could take it that way but I think it's just a difference in how you want to be professionally and that I consider it appropriate.

T: However we decide that, I want to be clear that I'm not putting you down or criticizing you for wanting such a thing. I don't consciously intend any criticism of you.

P: But it does sound like you think I'm asking for something physical from you that I should get somewhere else. And either we have a relationship or we don't, and I just don't buy that. I mean, if we're having a relationship don't tell me that I can't have a squeeze or a hug or handshake from you! [*escalating and angry*] If I can't leave a note on your car because you're not your car [*a reference to an earlier issue*], then forget that! That doesn't hold water. You're uncomfortable! Fine! If you're uncomfortable, then there's nothing I can do about that. I mean all the hugs in the world from [*her husband*] are not going to change whether I need hugs from you because of our relationship.

T: Uh-huh.

P: You know I do think it's unfortunate, because if that has to be an issue for me, it's going to get in the way of our therapy. But if it's going to be an issue for you, it's going to get in the way, too. I don't stand to win much either way.

The tension level in the room is high by this point, and the patient is very angry and is growing depressed. The therapist is trying to keep in contact with the patient without moving to ease her distress or lower the tension. The patient's increasingly depressive stance re-creates many interactions in which her chronically depressed mother had arrived at an "I don't stand to win much either way" position with the patient. The therapist does not want to point this out, however, and is more interested in showing that the therapeutic relationship can endure this conflict.

[*silence—the patient is withdrawing emotionally*]

T: I can see it's important to you, and I'd rather keep talking it out with you and see what we can learn, rather than make it a hit-and-run subject where you wind up feeling misunderstood or disconnected.

[*silence for several more minutes*]

P: [*heavy sigh, weeping*]

T: What you look like is you look like somebody that's been rejected or lost something.

P: [*sullenly*] Well, I have.

T: Well, what do you feel like you've lost?

P: I can't have a hug when I need one and [*inaudible*].

T: What's the significance of that do you suppose?

P: It means I have to think about something. I have to be cautious. Not myself.

T: In that respect, yeah, it does.

P: [*inaudible*]

T: In that respect if being yourself means you have a right to a hug when you want one, then it does mean you can't be yourself in that respect with me.

P: Yeah! Well, that's a loss.

[*silence*]

P: So?

T: Well, I don't want to push you to say more if that's all there is to say, but you look real angry and upset.

P: Well, I feel upset [*inaudible*].

T: What you look like is that you have a right to this from me and that I'm being strange in not giving it. Kind of withholding.

[*silence*]

P: [*depressed and sullen*] I don't know. Kind of [*inaudible*].

[*silence for several minutes*]

P: [*still heavy and depressed*] I don't know because I don't know how important an issue it is to me right now.

T: I can only go on your response, and your response suggests it is a big issue and what you said earlier suggests you think if there's any significant relationship between us it's discounted if I don't hug you.

P: Well, it is to me.

T: Do you think there can be meaningful relationships without physical contact?

P: Uh-huh. It's not a part of me I consider in need of repair.

T: I wasn't suggesting you ought to repair it. I was suggesting I don't want to provide it.

P: It's not like you're providing it, though. I don't like the way you're saying that. It's a form of communication.

T: Then it's not a way I want to communicate

P: You're uncomfortable with it, and you know I can understand that, but it doesn't mean I have to like it.

T: I agree with that. You don't have to like it.

P: But it puts a burden on me. I don't always want to have to be concerned about it.

T: What's the burden?

P: That I have to be careful not to touch you. On the one hand, I mean, what did you say, that in therapy you can be a baby and a teenager and in therapy are the times you do something? Uh? Something about letting things go, or . . . Oh God, I can't remember it. [*silence*] But I have to, uh, you know, not express myself if I have to be concerned and cautious and careful. There are times it will interfere with what I have to deal with what happens, but that could be okay, uh . . . we've had a relationship for a long time. It's not going to undermine it . . . I don't think. [*silence*] If I decide I can't stand it I can always get out.

T: Uh-huh.

P: [*much softer tone of voice, almost seductive*] I didn't want to make you uncomfortable. It was not my intention.

T: I didn't understand it to be your intention.

P: [*pleasantly*] Well, to me a handshake is fine. To me that's a hug.

The patient sought to make the therapist prove he really cared by asking him to hug her, even though she knew he would not. Not getting what she wanted, she then escalated and threatened termination of the relationship, much as her mother would imply that she would not be around much longer whenever the patient was "selfish" as a young child. When the therapist still did not respond or try to lower her level of distress, the patient then became submissive and masochistic. She is now willing to say that she did not really want to be hugged and that a handshake would do, even though it is clearly not what she wanted. Moreover, she knows the therapist typically shakes her hand when she offers it at the end of a session and so settling for that is gaining nothing at all.

P: Well, I'm losing my composure [*starting to choke up again*].

T: Yes, you look upset.

P: It's understandable. It seems to me that what you're saying is that for several weeks you haven't been giving me a hug.

T: It's been a long time, more like a couple months.

P: But we've been shaking hands, and you're fine with that. And when I said "hug" last week, that threw you a curve.

T: Yeah. I wasn't aware you expected me to hug you.

P: Well, to me a handshake isn't any different than a hug. Because I wasn't aware that for two months I hadn't been getting a hug. To me they're the same thing.

T: To me they're different. Putting my arm around you, or you putting your arm around me crosses a line.

P: And I can understand that. There's a lot of people like you. Especially when in this kind of business you have to be careful, I would think. We have to be careful with our students [*inaudible*]. . . . It's just that . . . there seemed to be a misunderstanding.

T: That a hug and a handshake are the same? That you'd be as satisfied with one as the other?

P: Yeah.

The patient has given in and offers to accept much less than she asked for as a way of stopping the conflict. She even lets the therapist off the hook by saying, "in this kind of business you have to be careful," which is in contrast to her earlier claim that "people, all psychologists, are doing that now." (The therapist still does not realize this and has focused instead on keeping emotional contact with the patient without offering to relieve the tension.)

This sequence, while certainly not as dramatic as some, illustrates the borderline patient's ability to create a crisis in the process of making the other person prove he or she cares and then adopt a masochistic stance to resolve the conflict and make up, producing an illusion of closeness.

5

Inability to Modulate Affect

Urgency, Impatience, and Extreme Reactions

Borderline patients frequently seem to be "living on the edge," and it takes surprisingly little to prompt an extreme emotional response. Patients commonly experience exaggerated feeling states in situations that do not seem especially intense to an outside observer or may even sound rather commonplace to the patient's therapist. Borderline patients report sudden affective explosions in situations that clearly could have been handled in an even-tempered way, profound depressive reactions to seemingly minor frustrations, and rapid emotional involvements in relationships that are patently unpromising. The therapy session itself can provide opportunities to witness these extreme responses. Therapists are often surprised at the speed with which an apparently uneventful session can become charged with intense feeling. This is illustrated in some of the earliest literature on the borderline population, for example, Stern's

(1938) description of these patients as likely to leave treatment at slight frustrations.

The experience of feelings in extreme forms is a clue to the inner world of these patients. Borderline individuals cannot readily integrate good and bad experiences. There is, therefore, only a rudimentary framework for the gradation of feelings, or for experiencing affect in modulated ways. In addition, borderline individuals have not been able to develop effective time perspectives regarding what they feel. When aloneness is painful and attachments seem continually in doubt, the emotional atmosphere is too malignant for time perspectives to unfold. As a result there is little sense of how things might change and even little capacity to remember how they have changed in the past. In the absence of such perspective, exaggerated responses seem appropriate.

Such extreme reactions can resemble the theatrical stance frequently assumed by hysterics. The predicament of the borderline patient is very different from that of the hysteric patient, however. The crucial difference is that hysteric individuals use their emotional outbursts as ways of staying related to and influencing those around them, while borderline patients typically feel cut off from others during displays of extreme emotion. Hysteric individuals remain keenly aware of the other person's response to their affective display and in fact are using the display to control others without taking responsibility for the control. Consequently they are actually only drawing attention to the *appearance* of a feeling state, and these apparent feelings can change very quickly, depending upon the other's reaction.

By contrast, borderline patients are often oblivious to the response of the other and to the context in which they find themselves. Whereas hysterical individuals seek an audience whose response can be manipulated, borderline patients experience exaggerated feelings even—and especially—while alone. It is also worth mentioning that borderline patients do not feel less anxious because of their dramatic affective reactions, whereas hysterics tend to use their dramatic outbursts to avoid actual anxiety-provoking issues. Such outbursts are distractions for the hysteric, drawing attention away from what is genuinely anxiety-provoking and toward matters that are at best symbolically related to the real issue but often are of obscure significance. Thus the borderline patient's exaggerated responses should not be mistaken for more adaptive attempts to manipulate the other person and defend against anxiety.

We emphasize the difference between borderline and hysterical expressions of exaggerated affect to highlight the borderline patient's affective helplessness. These patients are truly unable to manage their feelings better or find more moderate affective expressions. Borderline individuals experience feelings on an all-or-none basis within a now-is-forever time frame. They do not *resort to* extreme feelings; rather they *lack* moderate ranges of affect, particularly when dealing with issues related to their most basic fears and/or primitive idealizations.

This failure to arrive at moderate ranges of affect results from the borderline patient's characteristically constricted sense of time. These patients tend to experience events as pressured and urgent, tightly compacted into intense moments, and begging for speedy resolution. They lack the capacity to wait or take their time, and they are constantly driven to precipitous action through either overestimating the danger or overvaluing the importance of what happens. For these persons, time feels like a raging current bearing them rapidly along to ruin unless they *do something now*.

Such a time contraction causes borderline patients to live in a perpetual state of alarm or concern. The emotional atmosphere is tension-laden for these patients, and there is a hovering sense of things about to go bad or opportunities about to be lost forever. Even slight ambiguity can feel almost unendurable, and the borderline patient desperately seeks closure to escape the tension. Persons with a less constricted time sense might well find the same events far less pressing. Normal persons can tolerate a certain amount of ambiguity and lack of closure through stepping back from the situation and seeing things from a larger perspective. This tolerance allows normal persons to show patience, bide their time, and see what happens next before taking action. By contrast, borderline individuals cannot step back from their situation to gain perspective. They are frozen by the tension they feel whenever a situation is unclear or ambiguous, and they seek rapid closure to relieve the tension. Whereas normal persons might expect ambiguity to be resolved with time and might therefore be willing to wait, borderline individuals feel as if their tension might last forever. Due to this urgency, they try to force closure themselves rather than wait on developments. Their responses are accordingly often impulsive and driven; these individuals take action long before most people would.

The borderline patient's ongoing sense that the ax is about to fall not only reflects the patient's inner world but also probably reflects accurately the behavior of others toward the patient during the growing-up years. Many borderline patients report growing up in extremely tense atmospheres. One patient, for example, said that he never had any idea how his mother would react to what he said or did. She sometimes seemed indifferent to his actions or even to accept them, while many other times she unexpectedly blew up at him and then lapsed into a withdrawn, sullen, depressed state that could last for days. Because she was so unpredictable and her reactions so extreme, the patient remembers constantly walking on eggshells around the house and yet knowing that no matter how careful he was, there would eventually be some explosion from his mother. Long after leaving home he experienced his relations with bosses, friends, and girlfriends as always on the verge of disruption, even when there was no good reason to think so. He consequently tended to overreact to interpersonal problems, plunging into morbid states over very minor rifts.

This patient's situation is not atypical; his perpetual sense of tension and alarm mirrored the pattern of interaction with a major figure in his life.

Such an atmosphere of tension during the growing-up years underlies the borderline patient's characteristic time contraction. To develop adequate time perspectives, the growing child must be able to relax, to take things for granted, and to find that the world is reliable even when it isn't being watched. There must, in other words, be a sense of constancy. When this is missing and the world seems volatile, the child learns to stay on guard, alert for signs that things are about to get out of hand. This distorts the cognitive focus: perspective becomes too tight and narrow, and the larger picture is missed. When perspective is so narrow, every problem becomes urgent, and no difficulty seems small. As one patient put the situation, "It's like I'm always seeing things through a zoom lens."

It is a mark of maturity to be able to distinguish those circumstances that can wait from those that require immediate action. This differentiation requires life experience, of course, but beyond that, it presupposes a capacity to ignore or filter out stimulation. It is probably impossible, for example, to carry on a lasting, meaningful relationship without ignoring a great deal of what the other person says and does, attending rather to the overall tone of interactions and trusting the constancy of the relationship. Yet a narrow cognitive focus and an attitude of being on guard for the next crisis scarcely allow the individual to let things pass without undue anxiety. Events are taken too seriously or experienced as far too pressing because there is no context or perspective for them—only a sense of this particular event, interpreted in light of basic fears or idealized fantasies.

The capacity to ignore an event for a time is essentially the capacity to put it in the background, allowing other matters to come forward, as it were, and become the focus of attention. In terms of sensory perception, recent research (Stern 1985) shows that newborns have a greater capacity for distinguishing figure from ground and for other elements of focal attention than had been thought; this appears to be a process that will unfold naturally unless interfered with. However, the young child will need help from the environment to learn what to attend to emotionally and to tolerate strong feelings without being overwhelmed by them. The infant needs someone to buffer or filter out strong affect at first; in this way infants are helped to take distance from what they feel.

Most mothers protect their babies from impinging and intrusive stimulation. They are usually sensitive to the child's level of excitement and stop the stimulation when they sense the baby cannot process it. Additionally, they soothe their upset children and give them many clues that the upset is not so bad and can be endured. These ministrations help to build what Buie and Adler (1982) call a holding introject, an inner structure through which the child comes to comfort himself or herself. The mother's soothing and comforting activities gradually inspire a kind of confidence in the growing child that he or she will not be swept away by strong affect, that someone will be there to help if needed.

Children who have been consistently shielded from overwhelming aversive stimulation develop different time perspectives from those who have not had such help, or who have had it erratically. The former need not always respond to tension immediately, because they have some sense that it will not go on forever. They gradually learn to step back emotionally to see if the situation will change. The development of an effective time perspective in itself alters the intensity of what is felt: Knowledge that things can change with time "flattens out" or moderates the level of distress or excitement. This simple truth can be seen at sports events, for instance, where a close contest usually generates more intense excitement late in the game than early, or in romantic relationships, where couples usually experience their early days together with more intensity and excitement than in the succeeding years.

Borderline patients lack the time perspectives and adequate cognitive focus that would lead to more modulated affective experience. As a rule they do not seem to have received the help they needed as children in filtering out impinging stimulation. Indeed, as noted, interactions with caretakers were themselves often the cause of tension, and so there was no reliable sense that someone might be available to soothe them or to buffer intense affect. Given this state of affairs, they never learned to "back off" or to relax in the face of uncertainty. Their attention was not only riveted by uncertainty and tension, but also they learned to be on guard for the next possible source of tension. People who do this cannot experience time as a benevolent process to which they can surrender themselves; rather, time is *this present moment*, with demands and risks that must be handled carefully, to be followed by yet another tense moment that is essentially unrelated to the first.

It is extremely difficult for someone with such a distorted sense of time to live through a conflict, or even merely an ambiguous situation, without feeling compelled to respond. Since, as a rule, no one reliably buffered them from intense affect, they have not learned to do this for themselves. As a result, intense feelings do not give way to more moderate affect states; rather, intense feeling remains intense and draws a response, usually an overreaction and often precipitous in nature. These individuals want a conclusion to the tension-producing situation.

The task of therapy is to produce a benign emotional atmosphere that will help the patient learn to wait without having to make a response. Feeling states can only become graded in a benevolent time frame. The patient must have the chance to step back from events and see that most things change with the passage of time, and this affects what action—if any—one takes. This is the condition under which patients learn to modulate their affective responses.

Speaking metaphorically, where time is a placid lake rather

than a raging stream, patients may learn that being bounced up and down is not a prelude to sinking or being thrown out of the water. The therapist functions as a reliable "North Star," allowing the patient to become oriented to these basic truths:

- It is in the nature of air and water to move boats about at times and at other times let them be still.
- Those in the boats can play a large role in how they are guided, no matter what the prevailing winds.
- Boats can be constructed with the intention of keeping them afloat, even if there are no guarantees that they will always remain so.

To continue the metaphor, one might say that it is faith in our seaworthiness that ultimately represents object constancy.

The Unhurried Treatment of Urgent Problems

It is well known that borderline patients can place enormous pressure on their therapists to "do something" when they are upset. Since these patients often experience even ordinary problems as major crises, they genuinely believe they need immediate help, and, not surprisingly, they expect the therapist to deliver it. We noted in Chapter 3 that borderline individuals tend to feel that the only basis for a relationship lies in meeting needs, relieving tensions, or performing some other function for the other person. They will therefore expect the therapist to meet their needs when they are upset, and they will define this as "making me feel better."

It is easy to understand a therapist's desire to offer some help. For one thing, experienced therapists know that borderline patients may leave treatment—especially in the early stages—if they fail to receive the relief they demand. Additionally, the therapist may see clearly that a patient is overreacting to a problem and may feel that the patient could come to see this with a little assistance; it is tempting to try to point out to the patient something that is so obvious to the therapist. Finally, borderline patients often make the therapist the focus of intense complaint when they think they are not receiving the help they deserve. These and other factors may lead the therapist to respond to the patient's exaggerated emotions, trying with some urgency to solve problems, induce a more balanced view of things or a more moderated affect, or uncover some underlying issue that can be taken as the "real" problem, thereby taking attention from the immediate problem.

We believe that these types of response are a mistake. In the first place, they are not likely to work. Borderline patients are not generally able to focus on and analyze a situation causing them anxiety. Doing this would require a capacity to step back from the situation and examine it from a different perspective; this, however, is the very thing borderline patients are usually unable to do. If encouraged to problem-solve by the therapist or to look for underlying issues, borderline patients may try to cooperate, but typically they will bog down quickly. They will fail to recognize the most relevant features of the situation they are analyzing, switch subjects unexpectedly, or become so over-whelmed by the intensity of what they feel that they are reduced to helplessness. The most likely result will be a re-newed conviction on the patient's part that the therapist must now do something. Even though borderline patients may be accomplished problem-solvers and analysts on their jobs, they are surprisingly unable to do this in their personal lives, even if helped by the therapist.

Additionally, even if the therapist's efforts were to succeed in helping the patient feel better or master the immediate prob-lem, no good work has actually been done. While it is true that patients will usually be satisfied if they come to feel better, the therapist must see the larger issue: the absence of longer time perspectives and the consequent narrowing of cognitive focus. The therapist should realize that most of the problems border-line patients present as urgent crises will in fact resolve themselves with more time. It is more beneficial to help patients experience the way time changes situations than to relieve their immediate tensions. Whatever response the therapist makes should address the borderline patient's distorted time sense and consequent inability to tolerate tension, not the immediate problem the patient is complaining about and the accompanying exaggerated affect.

The patient's constricted time sense will best be addressed by therapists who take their time. The patient's urgency ought not pressure therapists into delivering interventions aimed at easing the patient's discomfort. Rather, the therapist must learn to endure the patient's discomfort while finding ways to stay in emotional contact. Most persons can bear emotional pain if they feel they are not alone with the pain. The tragedy for borderline patients is that generally they feel alone or in imminent danger of being left by themselves, and they feel their aloneness even more keenly when they are in a state of discomfort: They take their discomfort as confirmation of their aloneness. Thus, the more they are upset, the more they feel cut off from others or in danger of being cut off from them. Borderline patients have little sense that people can simply be with one another during times of distress. Normal persons, by contrast, usually find some comfort in knowing that others are with them, even though they neither expect nor find that others are able to take away their pain. Borderline patients will be surprised to learn that the therapist wants to maintain contact with them even though he or she is not trying to perform some function or ease their distress.

Therapists maintain contact in these circumstances by making occasional empathic comments, showing persistent interest in what is happening, or pointing out features of the situation the patient had not noticed. These responses are not intended to help or change the patient, although it is possible they may have that effect at times. These responses are simply intended to make the patient feel heard or understood, thereby allowing the patient to feel connected with the therapist. (If the patient can feel connected even though the therapist is not trying to help, the patient may gradually come to believe that relationships may be founded on something other than tension relief or need satisfaction.)

In Chapter 1 we suggested that therapists ought to say or do relatively little during the preconstancy phase of treatment. It can be trying to put this suggestion into practice when patients are struggling with extreme affect states. On the one hand, the therapist wants the patient to feel heard; on the other hand, the therapist does not want to "buy into" the patient's distress. Unfortunately there can be no hard-and-fast rules concerning how much—or even precisely what—must be said to keep emotional contact with distraught patients. Therapists may find themselves saying much more with some patients than with others and never being quite sure whether they should have said less or perhaps should have said more.

In trying to decide whether to respond to a patient, it is probably more fruitful for therapists to focus on their motivation for responding rather than to focus on their response frequency. If therapists find themselves responding to patients out of tension, pressure, or a sense of urgency, then their intervention is most likely a mistake, since it reflects the very sense of crisis in the therapist that needs to be corrected in the patient. For example, therapists may feel that a patient will terminate treatment if they do not make just the right intervention and make it soon, or they may fear their patient is about to become psychotic or commit suicide without a proper intervention. Although we are not saying that such crises do not occur in treatment, we believe that therapists making responses out of fear that these or similar events are about to occur have probably, through projective identification, come to feel the patient's constricted time sense as their own.

The therapist's overall intention with the highly distraught borderline patient is to broaden the patient's constricted sense of time, the focus on *this instant* and attendant sense of crisis. Consequently, whenever therapists respond from their own inner urgency or tension, they are cooperating with the patient's pathology, not undermining it. The tension the therapist is feeling probably reflects precisely the patient's own inner world at that moment. Therefore the therapist has an opportunity to demonstrate the ability to handle the very situation the patient cannot; obviously it will not be particularly helpful for the therapist to be unable to endure the momentary crisis without feeling compelled to intervene. Therapists should aim at living through the crisis of the moment without trying to "do something" about it.

The therapist's decision to respond or keep silent should therefore be based on what will help the patient substitute a more normal, broader time perspective for his or her own, overly narrow time sense. If the therapist elects to keep quiet, this should reflect the therapist's confidence that there is nothing that needs to be done in this situation, an ability to wait and see what happens next. If the therapist determines to respond, this, too, should be with the intention of evening out the extremes in the patient's emotional reaction.

The following exchange illustrates an intervention intended to make a patient's experience of her situation less extreme and intense. The patient had been tense and on the verge of crying throughout the session. She was upset with a problem at work and with her own inability to handle it more calmly, having been labile and angry most of the preceding week.

P: [*crying*] I think I'm afraid I'm going to panic.

T: Umm, okay, and what then?

P: [*pause*] I'd feel defeated.

T: Okay, so you'd feel defeated. What would happen after that?

P: I don't want to feel defeated.

T: No one does, but it happens sometimes, you know.

P: I'd rather choose not to.

T: How we feel or react is not always something we can choose, in my experience.

At this point the patient calmed down. The problem she was struggling with had not been resolved by any means and continued to vex her for several more weeks. The sense of crisis, however, eased, and she was able to see the problem as something to be addressed *over time*.

The therapist's intent is to stand still in the face of the patient's urgency, modeling the capacity to step back and see a larger picture than just what is felt at the moment. The patient must be able to count on the therapist's calm, that the therapist will not panic. This allows the patient gradually to feel confident that someone is there who can contain and endure what the patient cannot. The therapist's ability to be with the patient and yet remain calm and steady serves over time to buffer the patient from tension. In turn this helps the patient develop more benevolent time perspectives.

When tension and urgency can be endured, they are changed into more moderated affects. The capacity to endure painful affect takes much of the fear out of the experience, and this in itself makes painful feelings less extreme. The therapist is trying to induce in the patient the ability to live through a problem without having to respond. Whether the therapist is quiet or makes some response, the idea is to inform the patient's capacity to wait, delay action, and see matters from an enlarged perspective. The therapist's basic response to the patient's urgent crises, therefore, should be to endure the urgency. The therapist's calm must communicate to the patient a sense of "This, too, shall pass."

The Patient's Response to the Therapist's Calm: Anger, Splitting, and Devaluation

At times a fairly simple empathic response from the therapist will alter the patient's experience of the "crisis" and make it more bearable. For instance, one patient complained of problems with being a single mother and having trouble finding baby-sitters when she wanted to go out on dates. Her way of handling this situation was to invite men to her home for the evening, which frequently led to her being taken advantage of sexually and yet feeling obligated to allow this to happen. She began one session by saying, "You've got to help me. I don't know what I'm going to do," and had gone on to press the therapist for a solution. Her therapist listened to her complaints, occasionally making a remark to the effect that many single mothers face the dilemma described by the patient and that it was indeed a hard one to solve. The patient (who was in the midst of an idealization of her therapist) then relaxed and said with a sigh, "I don't know how you do it. I feel so much better." The therapist's ability to console the patient had allowed him to buffer the patient from her own anxiety much as a mother soothes her infant. The patient then felt he had helped her, even though he had actually offered no solutions to her problem.

In the early months of treatment, however, the therapist's steady manner may very well not reassure the patient. The opposite effect can often be expected, as patients interpret the therapist's calm as a sign of unconcern. This in turn may lead the patient to feel abandoned by the therapist and may for a time heighten anxiety. One patient, for example, had been complaining during her third month of treatment that her husband was unresponsive and that she thought the marriage might be nearly over. The therapist knew that the patient periodically felt like this and that nothing was really new in the situation; it was a chronic problem that tended to get better after a while and not one that suggested an imminent divorce. The therapist was also aware of the parallel with the therapy setting, where he could be taken to be unresponsive and where the patient occasionally made vague threats of ending treatment. The therapist was nonetheless surprised by the vehemence of the patient's response to his bland remark that "I can see how that would be a hard thing for you to handle." The patient erupted with, "A hard thing for me to handle! What's that supposed to mean? Of course it's hard. That's why I'm telling you! I want you to tell me what's going on. You don't give me enough feedback!" These remarks and the attack that followed were all the more surprising since the patient had been praising the therapist in idealized tones in the previous session.

The borderline patient's outrage with the therapist in such circumstances illustrates one aspect of the absence of object constancy, the patient's experience of the therapist—and others in his or her life—as part objects, as either entirely gratifying or entirely frustrating. This is, of course, the well-known phenomenon of splitting, or the tendency to compartmentalize experience into all-or-none categories. While splitting avoids the experience of ambivalence and thereby preserves "good" experiences from the danger of contamination by hate, it also prevents the gradation of feelings by locking experience into extreme, all-good or all-bad groupings. Splitting is thus an underlying factor in the borderline patient's inability to modulate affect.

The therapist can see splitting during sessions in the patient's tendency to shift rapidly between the different sides of a conflict, apparently unaware of or unconcerned with the inconsistencies or contradictions. If the therapist confronts borderline patients with their double standards, they often seem genuinely puzzled and many even make a defense to the effect, "I see it, but I can't help it." Splitting allows patients to preserve a primitive idealization of the significant persons in their lives, experiencing them as powerful protectors in a dangerous world. At other times, however, borderline patients readily experience the same individual in light of the patient's own feelings of guilt and self-loathing; the other person then seems to be a harsh judge seeking to impose severe punishment on the patient. Borderline patients thus frequently shift between idealizing the other person, on the one hand, versus seeing them as the "wrath of God" on the other. This amounts to a kind of personalized courtroom drama, as these patients move through life experiencing a series of imminent disasters followed by temporary reprieves.

The clinical literature suggests ways in which the therapist can point out or interpret splitting (e.g., Kernberg 1968, Masterson 1976, Wells and Glickauf-Hughes 1986). The idea behind such interventions is to encourage a more complex experience of persons and situations, thereby making experience less disjointed, or broken into extreme fragments. It is an important achievement to be able to experience onself and others in complex, realistic ways, as composites of good and bad, and as neither ideal nor degraded. This achievement of whole or total object representations is generally equated with object constancy (e.g., Kernberg 1976, Leon 1984). Therefore, interventions designed to address splitting are designed to further constancy.

We do not advocate the interpretation of splitting, however. We believe that establishment of broader time perspectives will of itself begin to remedy splitting and that interpreting splitting may well interfere with establishing such perspectives. The patient may experience the interpretation as a demand to change or correct the all-or-none perceptions the therapist is pointing out. Of course, the patient cannot do this, and several responses to this "demand" are possible, none of which furthers development of less constricted time perspectives. First, the patient may feel inadequate and criticized by the therapist's intervention, in which case the therapist is experienced as a bad object who rejects the patient. This will only heighten the patient's sense of urgency. Second, the patient may see the therapist's point intellectually but be unable to let it affect his or her emotional life; in this case the quiet borderline patient will try to behave as if he or she benefited from the intervention. This only cements the patient's pathology. Finally, the most likely response—especially from the noisy patient—will be an attack on the therapist for having said something that did not "help." The patient's response to the intervention in this case will be something along the line of "So what?" followed by a series of devaluing complaints about the therapist's ineffectuality.

We believe that the patient's all-or-none distortions are better left uninterpreted during the preconstancy phase of treatment. Living through these situations with the patient will ultimately do more good than trying to intervene and correct the exaggerated perceptions and emotions the patient shows. This is especially important when the therapist is the subject of distortion; the patient's exaggerated experiences of the therapist are better endured than interpreted. The therapist must be willing to listen quietly and nondefensively to the patient's complaints, needs, and demands. As a rule, the therapist should not respond to the patient's outbursts except to acknowledge the specific emotions being expressed. What is needed in such a situation is the ability to respond in a calm, steady tone that conveys the knowledge that the patient will survive and that the crisis of the moment will not turn into a catastrophe.

The temptation to interpret such attacks may well be an expression of the therapist's desire to defend against the patient's unfair rebukes more than a desire to be therapeutic. Borderline patients are often adept at sensing the therapist's weak spots and focusing on these. It may seem to require the patience of Job to weather attacks by a patient who has accurately targeted the therapist's own personal issues and is now using them to rebuke the therapist for not trying to "help." Certainly it is human for the therapist to feel angry and unappreciated at such a time, and the desire to control the patient or retaliate may be very strong. A confrontation or interpretation may be a more or less sublimated expression of that desire. We believe the best course for the therapist is to endure the patient's attack, resisting the impulse to respond.

Withstanding the patient's attack furthers the development of more adequate time perspectives. When borderline patients make an attack on the therapist, they are essentially bringing their most difficult problem into the consulting room: They are giving the therapist the chance to handle the very problem they cannot, namely, the experience of tension. It is important that the therapist model some capacity to face tension without being forced into taking action. Not only does the therapist show the patient that tension can in fact be endured without urgent, desperate responses, but the therapist also shows that there are broader perspectives for experiencing a problem than the immediate crisis. When therapists contain and endure an attack by the patient, they show that they expect their relationship with the patient to survive the crisis of the moment, that the crisis can and should be experienced in light of their overall, ongoing relationship rather than in light of this particular tense moment.

Clinical Illustration of a Patient
Who Is Unable to Modulate Affect

The following transcript illustrates additional points to those
made in the preceding section, where we focused chiefly on the
handling of intense affect directed at the therapist. In this
transcript we see a patient recount frustration from daily life
and note her difficulty experiencing it in a balanced, moderate
way. In short, she overreacts and is much more angered than
the situation called for. She describes the problem to her therapist, who is faced with a series of choices regarding the best
response.

   The patient was a 28-year-old mother of three who had come
   to therapy complaining of marital conflicts. The origins of the
   marriage give some clues to the patient's personality. She was
   living in a West Coast resort community and met her future
   husband, a dentist, while he was vacationing there. He had

picked her up in a bar, they had a brief sexual liaison, and then he left. Before leaving, however, he had said to her that "It's a shame this has to end." She took this to be a proposal of marriage, and, after he left, she quit her job, sold her house, and traveled to the Maryland town where he lived. She literally showed up on his doorstep one morning, to his utter surprise and dismay. He allowed her to live in an apartment over his garage for a year and then, for reasons neither she nor her husband could really explain, they married. Not surprisingly, the marriage was conflict-ridden.

During therapy it became clear the woman was unable to manage her emotional responses. She could grow violently angry, throwing things around the house in great temper fits. In therapy, too, she became intensely angry at times, once storming out of an early session, yelling that the therapist didn't "know a fuckin' thing!"

By the time the following session took place, therapy was in its second year, and the therapist had a fairly durable relation- ship with the patient. The preconstancy stage was nearly com- pleted, and the therapist was more active than he would have been earlier in treatment. (Even so, the following transcript begins twenty-five minutes into the session, by which point the therapist has spoken a total of only fifteen words.) The patient, who is pregnant with her fourth child, has been rambling somewhat through the session, discussing a very wide variety of topics, all of which might be loosely grouped around the theme of whether she will give birth to something monstrous. Apart from this, there really has been no organizing theme, illustrat- ing the way borderline patients often lack coherence in their verbal productions, even after months of treatment.

The patient has just described several childhood interactions with her mother. She has emphasized the way in which her mother would one-up her complaints, saying to the patient, in effect, "You can't complain if you've got it bad, because I had it worse." The therapist is thinking of the way such experiences kept the patient from ever knowing what was an appropriate emotional response and kept her locked into extreme, flagrant, affective displays. He decides to become more active at this point, feeling he can probably produce a useful focus on the way the patient expresses anger. Earlier in treatment he would not have attempted this, and if he had, it would most likely have come to nothing. At this time, however, he thinks the patient can become organized enough to look at this topic.

Even at this point in the treatment, however, the therapist does not believe the patient can make consistent use of interpretations, and so he keeps his comments descriptive for the most part. Earlier in the session, for example, there were opportunities to interpret the patient's fears about the baby-monster growing in her womb, and later the patient describes interactions in which she may have experienced a sales clerk as though the clerk were her mother. The therapist avoids interpreting any of this, however, and simply tries to help the patient sort out what she experienced. Nonetheless, some comments during the session do have the character of interpretations.

The patient has just described her mother's habit of beating her and then saying, "Even if I am crazy and beat the shit out of you, most of the time it is because of what my parents did to me; your life isn't shit compared to what I went through—how dare you complain!" This has left the patient unsure whether she has the right to get angry, even though in fact she gets angry quickly and frequently. The patient is describing recent experiences that angered her.

P: Like yesterday—these are the—and I really got angry with myself for doing it, because as Donnie [*mumbles*] says, when you've gotten angry you've already lost the argument.

Donnie is her husband.

But you know I immediately [*mumbles*] anger. I bought these shoes and I—uh—we were buying school clothes or something for my daughter, and while we were at the mall there was a Sole Train store. Well, I have to buy her shoes at Sole Train because she has a duck foot—it's so wide—um—and she doesn't have an arch and no ankles, she takes after Donnie—I have ankles, but . . . So I thought, well, while we're here we'll go ahead, you know, and get her school shoes, those saddle Oxfords. So [we] got them there.

Well, she only wore them, wore 'em like the first couple of weeks of school and then she showed me how—she said it was because she fell on the rocks—but she showed me her shoe, and it was like where the crease of the shoe is right across here, the leather was separating or something; it had cracked, like somebody had taken a razor blade and just slit it open there [*inaudible*] like that with both shoes [*inaudible*]. And I said, I'm gonna take 'em back. We have a Sole Train store in Harriman, which is usually where I buy all of her shoes because it's the only shoe store in all of Harriman, Oak Ridge, or Knoxville [*laugh*] that sell[s] wide shoes. So I went there yesterday and took the shoes. Now all I said to her was I bought these shoes, and of course I had Ginger with me—there's no way I could lie—

Ginger is her daughter.

It turns out she did try to deceive the clerk, which made her anxious and defensive.

—and I said, uh, because I wasn't really sure whether they wrote down the shoe when you buy the shoe or not because they keep a card on everybody, and I wasn't really sure if they wrote down at the time that we buy the shoes or not, but they do, so they caught me on that, and said, I bought these shoes at the beginning of school. I don't remember if I bought 'em here or if I bought 'em at the store in Knoxville. So, of course, Ginger says, "You bought 'em in Mox, you bought 'em in Moxville, Mommy [*mumbling*], madder 'n' hell [*mumbling*], I said, "Aw, shut up!" So I said, "Okay, I bought 'em in Knoxville, I don't remember, but it was a Sole Train store, you know, I said, and obviously the shoes are defective or something because look what they're doing."

The somewhat disjointed style reflects the patient's tension and the way her anxiety interferes with clear thinking. Recounting the origins of her conflict with the sale clerk is making the patient so anxious that she is somewhat disorganized. Again, we see how rapidly she loses the capacity to back off and think when she starts to get upset. In turn, this increases the likelihood she will arrive at some extreme affect state.

So she looks at 'em and says, "Well, I don't think we have that. . . ." "No, no," she says, um, well, she's looking up in the file and asking me my name and everything, and she says, "Well, you didn't buy them here at this store." I said, "Well, irregardless, it's a Sole Train shoe, you know; isn't there any way . . ." And I don't think the guy even mentioned about exchanging the shoe at the time. . . . [*She describes more of the interaction, leading to an argument over whether they can exchange the shoe.*] I said, "I didn't [*mumbles*] say anything about a cash refund?" I said, "All I did was show you that there was something wrong with the shoe. I didn't say a goddamned word about the cash refund. All I want is an exchange of the shoe because this is obviously a defective shoe." I said, "I should not be penalized because I bought the thing in Knoxville and if Sole Train doesn't stand behind their shoe then that's fine. I just won't come here and shop anymore." I said, "I've bought shoes for this child since she was 6 months old exclusively at this store. I'm not some schmuck that comes in here off the street, and you're going to stand there and tell me you're not going to give me a cash refund when I didn't ask for a frickin' cash refund in the first place." And she says, uh, no, I said, "If you don't want to exchange the shoe, that's fine! Just give me Sole Train's address; I will mail the shoe back to them and have them give me a new shoe, which is what I wanted in the first place!"

The patient is quite angry as she describes all of this. At times she is yelling as she tells her story.

And she said, "Well, let me see if I have it in the back." You know, and I'm pissed [*giggles*] by this time, you know, you bitch!

With the clerk's agreement to look for new shoes, the patient feels she has won something. Her giggle shows she is pleased that she can be righteously indignant while having been untruthful.

I don't know if you think I'm just stupid or what but I guess it's because I feel like they, they group me in with all the rest of this town's bimbos, I don't know [*mumbles and then starts to talk fast*]. So, so then she comes back out with another shoe, and she says, "All I have it in is gray." And I said well, you know, well she tried it . . . no she said, "I don't even know what size it is because she's worn the size out." I said, "Well, I'm fairly sure its a 13 or 13½, but I'm not sure about the width—but I do know it's a wide width; it could be a DD or an E or something." So she tries on the other shoe, and it's way too tight. And she tries to tell me that's what the problem is; they fitted her with a shoe that was too tight, and it just split from the tension or something. And I said [*sounding briefly like she's weeping*], "I can't believe that, I'm sorry, but I can't believe that!" I said, "Listen, honey, I've worn tight shoes all my life, and believe me, my [*inaudible*] can account for it," and said, "Every single pair of shoes I've worn I've never had a

shoe split after 3 weeks of wear or because it was too tight.
I mean, get real."

*The patient is obviously quite excited and is virtually
reliving the experience at this point. The therapist is not
concerned about this and intends to let the patient have
her say. An intervention would have been experienced by
the patient as an attempt to get her calmed down. The
patient would then have felt guilty at being angry and
would have become defensive in an attempt to justify her
feelings. In short, she would have repeated the very pattern of interaction she is describing with the shoe clerk.*

   Well, what they did was fitted her with a size bigger than
she takes to make up for the width. And I'm going, "Uh!
Look, I'm really getting pissed off standing here trying to
talk to you people! I normally don't pay attention when I
take the child in to get her shoes fitted because I assume that
people know what they're doing!" I said, "But you're telling
me one thing; I see something else." I said, "I don't, I don't
think either one of you people know what the hell you're
talking about, you know." [*She continues this story for
several minutes more, sounding tense, angry, and agitated.*]

*The therapist senses that the patient's anger has run its
course. He wants to "unpack" some of this incident, feeling that the patient is not completely aware of why she got
angry. As long as this is so, she will be conflicted about
being angry, which, in turn, makes her anger even more
intense.*

T: Aside from her not wanting to give you what you
wanted, what do you think was pissing you off
[*inaudible*]?

P: Because she was treating me like I was, like I was a
moron, not a moron but I mean she wasn't even conde-

scending because I don't even think she knew that . . . but I guess just the fact that she was belittling my integrity, questioning my integrity . . .

T: Hmm.

P: Because that's the norm of this area [*inaudible*].

The patient did try to deceive the clerk but avoids facing this by belittling the community, which she regards as "hick."

T: It's the norm I think for most salespersons, unless you're in a pretty classy store.

The therapist wants to make the clerk's behavior seem more impersonal so the patient can take some emotional distance.

P: Well, I mean you figure the damn shoes, the markup must be at least 900 percent on the damn things. I mean, I paid $65 for those things, and when we go in there to buy shoes we don't buy just one pair of shoes. I mean, she got a card with a whole list of shoes that I buy her. And this is the only store we buy her shoes in because they have extra-wide sizes. You know, so just by looking at the card . . . she could see I don't . . . you know she remembered, thing was that one of them remembered when we were in there in August! Because I bought her a pair of, I bought her sneakers, and a pair of like the [*inaudible*] type shoes, brown canvas-type shoes. Now those damn things were $35; I pay more for her shoes than I do mine. I mean that bitch is going to stand there and say [*mimicking*], "I can't give you a cash refund." You know. Well, I found out another store sells wide shoes, too. So I'm going to tell them when I go back in, "The only reason I came to your fucking store is because you're the only ones that sold wide shoes, but if Caroline Carter can [*inaudible*]. That just, stand there and talk to me like I'm some kind of a fool to believe that's what happened to the shoe because this other salesman in Knoxville ill-fitted her shoes, then screw it! You know, I said, "[*inaudible*] this is a defective shoe, you know, just give it up." God, I'm so angry!

While the patient's material is a bit rambling and perhaps tedious, it is important for the therapist simply to listen. Experienced therapists will doubtless recognize the tone to this session; there is nothing dramatic going on, and there is a "he said-she said" quality. Yet with seriously disturbed patients, therapists must listen without discomfort at either the tedious content or the intense affect.

T: Hmm. I can appreciate you being pissed because several things kept hitting you at the same time. Well, you did try to hustle her [*laughing*] on where you bought them.

The patient feels guilty and angry. She tried to deceive the clerk and got caught. The therapist wants to bring this out, but to make it less conflict-ridden. So he refers to trying to hustle the clerk, knowing the patient can see this as clever rather than wrong.

P: Well, because I, no, because I didn't have my sales receipt, and I didn't know she was going to give me a hard time, and then I thought, well, even if she does, you know, Sole Train [*inaudible*], and then I kept debating with myself, "Well, should I just admit it?"

T: Right! 'Cause I can hear it when you first started telling me. "Should I play it straight with this place, or should I try to . . ."

P: [*talking at the same time*] Yeah, shoot no [*inaudible*]. So I said I don't remember if I bought it here or Knoxville; at least I said . . .

T: And then you got your little helper with you [*laughing*].

Using sarcasm to empathize with the patient's irritation with the child for telling the truth and thereby betraying her hustle.

P: Yeah! "They're from Moxville!"

T: And then the other thing is the way you [*inaudible*] a lie, that these people weren't really trying to hustle you personally. They were doing what anybody . . . now you could say, like you just did, "Who do they think I am, just anybody, that they could try this with?" Yes, that's who they think you are because they don't know any better, and there's no reason for them to individualize you from everybody else. They don't know you.

P: I know. I knew that.

T: I mean, you want to be pissed they don't know how to separate you from the masses? Fine, go ahead, but you should know it's gonna happen constantly. All of us get treated like the masses.

The therapist tries to undermine the patient's egocentricity. If the patient can experience the situation less personally, she will be less angry.

P: Ohh.

The patient is surprised to hear that everyone is relegated to anonymity.

[The patient talks in a more relaxed way for a few minutes, reviewing the shoe store incident and gradually starting to question her right to have gotten so upset.]

P: The whole thing was stupid to begin with. Maybe I shouldn't have been so . . . um . . . I don't know. Who am I to do that, anyway?

T: [*laughing*] Who are you?

P: Yeah, (mumbles) judging . . . but the thing . . .

T: [*still laughing*] Who do you need to be?

P: I don't know.

T: I've told you that story, didn't I? One time I got pissed at my youngest son, and I said to him, "Who do you think you are?" And he looked at me and said, "Who . . ."

P: "Who do I need to be?" Yeah, I wish I could be somebody else, but I don't know who.

The patient remembers the story—an achievement for this point in treatment. She adds her own humorous comment on identity problems.

The thing that I guess I get angry with myself about is that—um—I couldn't, I can't be condescending, what, I don't know about anybody else, but fries me more than anything when somebody comes across to me like that, you know, drives me crazy, but to keep very cool and calm but very sarcastic and to get your point across. Of course they're so stupid they wouldn't know when they're being insulted anyway.

T: Right. And usually I don't encourage people to go around being pissed, but did it ever dawn on you that in this situation it was maybe because you got pissed that you got the new pair of shoes?

The idea here is to make anger less conflict-ridden by focusing on its uses. This intervention essentially encourages a sublimation of aggression, placing anger in the service of competency.

P: Well, yeah.

T: Controlled anger is fine, nothing wrong with that.

P: Well . . .

T: You can't monitor yourself while it's happening.

P: I guess actually I didn't monitor myself, 'cause I went in there—there have been instances where I'm ready to fight when I go in. This wasn't the case. I didn't expect her to be this difficult, because I was more on the defensive because I was going in there lying!

T: Um-hmm!

P: You know, more like whatever they hand me, I'll take!

T: Right! But you did have reason to believe that since it's another Sole Train store it's all the same.

Again, trying to show there is some validity to the patient's expectations.

The session continued along the same themes and need not be followed further. What we see in this transcript is the way the patient's doubts over the legitimacy of her anger led her to become tense. The tension, in turn, made it impossible for her to experience the encounter at the shoe store as a simple frustration; instead, she became intensely angry and felt personally abused. The therapist did two things. First, he tolerated the patient's tension and anger as she told the story, and second he tried to reframe the experience in a larger, less personal context. The patient was willing to hear him out as he did this, largely because of the stability of the therapeutic relationship at that point. In the first year of treatment, this patient would not have tolerated the therapist's attempts at reframing the event and would have heard it as criticism.

6

Intolerance of Separateness

The Fear of Being Alone

All children gradually arrive at the awesome realization that they and the world are separate, though related. They discover the independent, and at times alien, nature of the world through repeatedly finding that the environment does not always submit to their wishes. From the moment of this realization, relationships develop against the backdrop of existential isolation: Periods of closeness with another eventually yield to the fact of aloneness. Schachtel (1959) noted that the human condition entails repeatedly emerging from embeddedness into individuation, attended by an anxiety that should not be considered pathological. In fact, in the temporary dissolution of unity children can master the anxiety that accompanies separateness, learning to replace embeddedness with loving communication and gaining confidence that the world can be managed, even if it cannot always be controlled.

The healthy child develops the capacity to be alone and may

find aloneness to be desirable at times. For such a child, aloneness offers respite from the demands of others, a contented solitude that allows quiet activity and pleasurable fantasy. Aloneness can carry such a positive valence because the healthy child is confident that isolation is temporary and will eventually be followed by a return to connectedness.

Borderline patients have not achieved the capacity to be alone. Burdened by a now-is-forever orientation, they either cannot imagine or are unable to maintain the idea of a temporary dissolution of unity. Being alone is experienced as remaining forever unconnected, even as being with others involves a tenuous state of embeddedness. There is no opportunity to achieve the sort of balance reflected in a well-known aphorism of Hillel, "If I am not for myself, who will be? And if I am only for myself, what am I?" (quoted in Buber 1970, p. 85).

Consequently, borderline patients tend to demand a degree of closeness and involvement that other persons may well find excessive. Both in and out of the therapy hour, borderline patients can be extraordinarily sensitive to any sign that they are more "on their own" than they wish. Finding such signs, they can place considerable pressure on the therapist or others in their lives to come closer. Especially with those they have idealized, borderline patients seem to be seeking a kind of emotional merger. As those who have worked with these patients know, the desire to be close can become so desperate that borderline individuals frequently hurl themselves headlong into patently unpromising and self-defeating relationships; their judgment is overwhelmed by their fear of being alone.

In a sense, we might say that borderline patients can't stand their own company. Their own reports are often of boredom when alone; this is not, however, the boredom most persons occasionally complain of, a slightly painful state of unstructured, empty time to kill. Rather, the borderline patient's boredom is hungry and restless. There is a driven quality to it, or, as one therapist said, "These people are walking responses looking for a stimulus." Borderline patients seek others for the stimulation they provide or, perhaps more accurately, for the distraction. The borderline patient's boredom can quickly turn into a subjective sense of emptiness that is painful and distressing. Thus the desire to be with others is often a desire to be distracted from inner emptiness.

Interpersonally, emptiness is experienced as loneliness, a state that often leads to panic in borderline individuals. Adler and Buie (1979) refer to the "experience of isolation and emptiness, occasionally turning into panic and desperation" when the patient not only feels cut off from others but also cannot even summon "the fantasy of any positive, sustaining relationship" (p. 434). The patient feels a growing desperation to be with someone and an escalating fear of never again being connected. A catastrophic reaction approaching panic ensues in which the patient simply cannot tolerate being alone. One patient, for example, found after his wife's death that he could not function during the day unless he had arranged to spend the evening with friends. He found he had to plan his days in advance so there was no prospect of having to pass time alone. After several weeks even this stopped working, however, and he could not function during the day either; he spent much of each day restlessly visiting one friend after another, barely suppressing a feeling of panic, as though he were about to dissolve. He eventually became suicidal, hoping to escape his almost constant distress and, possibly, rejoin his dead wife.

Borderline patients panic over aloneness because they cannot imagine their situation changing. They experience their loneliness as ongoing or unalterable, and they have no sense of how long their distress will last. Most persons can sustain themselves with memories and fantasies of comforting, nurturing interactions, and these can carry them through a period of loneliness. Borderline patients, however, seem impoverished of such memories and fantasies when they are in pain. Their ability to generate comforting fantasies—to hope—rests on their mood. When with an exciting, idealized other, they can become euphoric and unrealistically imagine a satisfied state of oneness that will last forever (although this euphoric state will give way in a relatively short time to fears of abandonment). When angry or disappointed, however, borderline patients appear to have no positive memories or fantasies at their disposal to counter their distress of the moment. Their painful feelings have swept positively colored fantasies away, and what pleasant memories they recall only serve to make them feel their current distress more keenly. Thus they are stuck in the present, vividly experiencing momentary loneliness as though it could never be different.

Curiously, borderline patients may know very well that their feelings are momentary and that they ought not panic. Yet knowing this abstractly does not help them very much. One borderline patient, who was in the second year of treatment and past the preconstancy stage, reported reading on this subject in a self-help book and realizing that she tended to feel things in an extreme fashion. Unfortunately, this information was only briefly of use to her. In the very next fight with her husband she quickly lost sight of this truth and ended the fight feeling utterly alone and as though the marriage were over. The patient had not been sustained by the abstract knowledge she had gained; to paraphrase Kierkegaard, it may have been true, but it was not the truth for her.

In the following therapy session the patient mournfully told her therapist that she believed the marriage was unworkable and that "this time it's really over." The therapist had heard this complaint several times before and replied, "You panic too quickly; I'll tell you when it sounds like the marriage is beyond repair." The patient was able to use this comment to calm herself not only during this session but also when she was at odds with her husband in the months that followed. This helped relieve her sense of aloneness during arguments and tended, in turn, to make the arguments less extreme. It is not uncommon for therapists to have this experience, of saying something the patient already knew but finding that what made the difference was the therapist's having said it. Such experiences suggest a basic truth, that the capacity to be alone is gained through certain types of interaction with another. Borderline patients lack the capacity to be alone because they have lacked the types of interaction that bring this possibility to life.

Winnicott (1958) argued that one particular type of experience was crucial and that "without a sufficiency of it the capacity to be alone does not come about; *this experience is that of being alone, as an infant and small child, in the presence of [the] mother.* Thus the basis of the capacity to be alone is a paradox; it is the experience of being alone while someone else is present" (p. 30). The mother's ability to be present yet nonimpinging creates a special type of relationship, one in which each person is separate, yet related. The infant, whose ability to manage self and the world is weak, draws on the stronger ego of the mother without having to surrender independence. The mother places herself in the position of being important to the child without demanding that the child be directly involved with her. She thus gives a kind of permission to grow up without the child's having to negate their relationship to do so.

According to Winnicott (1958, p. 34), the child's inner life can unfold when he or she is alone in the presence of the mother; the mother's presence gives the child confidence to forget the external environment, as it were, and simply "be," trusting that the world will still be there when the child returns from private interests, explorations, and fantasies. In such a setting the child's own impulses, wishes, and other "id experiences," as Winnicott terms them, feel real and are "truly a personal experience." These lay a foundation for an inner life by making children feel that their inner world, the personal and private self, has reality. Such children can respond confidently to their own directions, initiatives, and autonomous strivings. Without the assurance of personal reality, however, the child cannot forget the external world but must constantly watch it to make sure it won't go away. As Winnicott said, this leads to "a false life built on reactions to external stimuli." False self-compliance to the wishes of others then replaces the development of inward, autonomous strivings.

The nonintrusive yet reliable mother is introjected, or taken into the child's personality. This introject, or good internalized object, becomes the foundation for the capacity to be alone. Of course, we are describing object constancy here; achieving object constancy secures the ability to tolerate aloneness without undue fear (Sherwood 1989). Without using the term, Winnicott has captured the essence of the process leading to constancy, the mother's ability to let the child alone while yet remaining related. The available yet nonimpinging mother becomes part of the context of life (viz., an internalized object) for the child.

Being alone in the presence of the mother colors the child's experience of time. When the child can be alone with the mother in a comfortable way, there is a sense of what might be called *going on being*. Self and world can be counted on to continue without direct interaction or frequent feedback. The experience of time can be described as flowing: The present proceeds at its own pace, and the future is open for whatever unfolds. Such is not the situation, however, for the child who lacks the experience of being alone in the presence of the mother. For that child, being alone entails the loss of the future, and the present is experienced with panic and an urgent desire for change.

It is the different experience of time, as much as anything else, that determines the individual's ability to be alone without undue fearfulness. The individual who has internalized the unintrusive yet present mother experiences loneliness as time limited. Aloneness can thereby be endured with some equanimity even when the presence of others is wished for and may even be sought, since there is an inner confidence that it will not last forever. However, the borderline individual has not achieved that internalization and therefore lacks the sense of an open, potentially benign future. When such persons are alone, they feel trapped in that aloneness without confidence it will change. In this truly painful position aloneness becomes an overwhelming loneliness, and autonomy is gladly exchanged for the chance to merge with another person. This is the predicament of the borderline individual, who cannot tolerate separateness and who instead tends to pursue excessive dependency in relationships.

Intolerance of Separateness

Separateness is the psychological awareness of the freedom of the other, the awareness that you are not controlling the other. It can be difficult to reconcile the other's freedom with the desire to connect with him or her. Any connection necessarily involves a potential restriction on our freedom by the other person without the assurance that we can control the other person in the ways we wish. Presumably love involves granting the other person some power to control us, hence the vulnerability that is often associated with love. Of course, there are gradations of attachment, a continuum along which the desire to control the other yields to a willingness to accept the other's freedom.

Early theorists, such as Hartmann (1952) and Anna Freud (1965), described a brief continuum of object relations, marking two stages. The first, which they called need-satisfying object relations, describes a type of attachment in which the

166

other is experienced as an extension of our own needs. The other person exists simply to meet our needs—in the early months of life, mostly physical needs, but later in life, emotional needs as well. This sort of attachment rests on denying the freedom of the other, on controlling the other person utterly. Hartmann and Anna Freud theorized that in the need-satisfying type of attachment, the other person is not even felt to exist apart from our need of that person.

These theorists further postulated a later stage of object relations, which they called object constancy, though they did not use that phrase in the way it is used today (cf. Sherwood 1989). This second stage describes the growing child's ability to become attached to one particular person regardless of whether that person is actively involved in meeting the child's needs. This is clearly a more mature form of love, since it does not reduce the other to an extension of the child's needs and thereby accepts the other's freedom to a higher degree. However, the other's freedom is not welcome to the individual at this stage of object relations. Separation anxiety is often felt when the other leaves for a time, such anxiety indicating a desire to control the loved one and keep him or her physically near.

Most persons today think in terms of an expanded continuum of object relations. Mahler's (Mahler et al. 1975) separation-individuation sequence implies one such continuum, and, more recently, Daniel Stern's (1985) work implies a somewhat different continuum. No matter whose terms or categories one uses, the continuum generally implies a range of relationships in which utter control of the other is sought at one extreme and acceptance of the other's freedom is at the other. Most persons find themselves moving all along such a continuum most of their lives. It is a significant accomplishment to feel connected to other persons and at the same time accept their freedom, eschewing attempts to control them. Such an accomplishment, however, tends to be a fluid one.

While we might accept the other's freedom at one time, at another we might regress and seek greater control. Normal persons will find themselves repeatedly in conflict over how much to seek control of the other, and sometimes forced to accept the other's freedom from that control more than they might wish. Healthy persons, however, will be able for the most part to accept that freedom—if for no other reason than that they will want also to preserve their own.

There are, however, two types of persons who will have trouble being reconciled to the freedom of the other. The narcissistic individual will not be able to accept the other's freedom out of a desire to make the other an extension of his or her own wishes. Narcissists wish to preserve their own complete freedom, disregarding any independent needs or wishes the other may have. In such a case the freedom of the other is at best a matter of indifference and at worst an offense to the claims the narcissist places on the other.

The second type of person who will have trouble accepting the other's freedom is the person who does not feel free himself. Those who do not experience themselves as free and independent necessarily feel controlled by those who are important to them and will in turn try to control those significant others.

Borderline individuals fall in the latter group. Given their fragmented sense of self, they cannot experience themselves as free and therefore cannot readily accept the freedom of the other. If others are free, they become unpredictable; the borderline patient then has no way of knowing whether the other will attend to the patient's needs. Individuals can accept unpredictability only if there is a prior foundation of predictability; in the absence of object constancy, relationships are not experienced as founded in consistency or predictability. Without constancy, the future of the relationship is perpetually in doubt, all the more so if the other person is free.

Borderline patients cannot, therefore, tolerate separateness. They need others to structure time and organize experience.

Further, they need others to be present physically; they lack the comforting introjects, or inner confidence of the other person's ongoing interest in them, that would allow them to feel connected even when the loved one is physically absent. Consequently they tend to be clinging and smothering in relationships. They are like tourists in a strange land who want above all else to stay close to the tour guide for fear of being left behind. When others leave, even temporarily, the borderline patient is never confident they will reappear.

The patient's intolerance of separateness is therefore chiefly expressed in attempts to negate the freedom of the other. Somewhat paradoxically this very often takes the form of trying to force the other person to take away the patient's freedom, to force the other person to control them (cf. Kroll 1988). Borderline patients try to negate the freedom of the other through forcing others to attend to their needs. This is especially true of noisy patients, who may place themselves in dangerous situations to force loved ones to attend to them. For example, one young man whose wife had separated from him went to see her and began cutting his arm with a butcher knife to force her to spend the night with him. He reported that he had no intention of suicide; he "just didn't know what else to do to make her come home." This incident illustrates the borderline patient's refusal to accept the other person's freedom.

It often comes as a surprise to the borderline patient that others do not wish to be controlled. Having little sense of their own freedom, these patients tend to assume that others seek the same clinging, mergerlike relationships they themselves seek. Borderline patients usually have preconceived notions of how others should react to the offer of fusion. Specifically, they expect the other person to welcome it. When others seek to preserve their own freedom instead of rushing toward merger, the patient has little ability to understand the other's reservations and usually experiences the situation as a rejection.

Often this rejection leads to an emotional crisis for the patient.

When the patient offers a fusionlike closeness, the other's response becomes a moment of truth in which the patient's existence is about to be affirmed or negated. When others appear to tolerate the closeness, borderline patients experience a sense of well-being approaching euphoria. Additionally, they feel an overwhelming affection—approaching adoration—of the other person, even if in fact only minimal tolerance of the closeness was shown. The patient can be seen at these times to be projecting idealized fantasies onto the other person in an apparent attempt to live out the primitive narcissistic goal of oneness. By contrast, when the offer of closeness is refused, it feels to the borderline patient as though the jury has just returned with a guilty verdict. The patient typically feels enraged at the other person and consumed with self-hatred as well. These are the times borderline patients are most likely to commit some dangerous act, either hurting themselves or, less frequently, hurting the other.

The therapist will have many opportunities to observe the borderline patient's intolerance of separateness. Quiet and noisy patients tend to show this in different ways. The quiet or as-if type of patient gives the appearance of accepting the therapist's freedom, all the while fantasying that the therapist must feel especially close to such a mature patient. These patients can be exquisitely sensitive to what the therapist values or wants from patients, and they quietly set about trying to embody the therapist's desires. At times they seem to become caricatures of the therapist, matching the therapist's style of talking and way of thinking through problems. Since imitation is often the first step to identification, the therapist may believe that the patient is forming an introject. This, however, is not the case. These patients are not taking the therapist into themselves in any lasting way. If they change therapists, they can adopt the new therapist's style and adapt to his or her different expectations very quickly. Their purpose, after all, is not to internalize the therapist but to be part of the therapist's life, to sustain their fantasies of mergerlike closeness.

If quiet borderline patients become aware that the therapist is in fact not controlled by their compliance, they tend to become confused and experience a sudden fearfulness, often accompanied by a sense of having been found out. The therapist may be surprised to see a patient who had apparently been doing so well suddenly become so shaken. The patient often feels demoralized, alone, and depressed, with little hope that things will ever be the same again with the therapist. Premature termination is quite possible at this point no matter what the therapist does.

Noisy borderline patients typically seek fusion with the therapist by pressing for prompt action when they have a problem or for tension relief when they are upset. In pressing the therapist in these ways, they are asking the therapist to overidentify with their needs and feelings, something they themselves do in relationships. Indeed, these patients can hold a seductive appeal for others due to their seeming sensitivity and empathy. It usually becomes clear fairly quickly, however, that borderline patients are not being truly empathic—or temporarily taking the imagined position of the other—but are literally taking on the needs and feelings of the other. When allowed to do this, borderline patients may experience themselves and the other person as one fused entity sharing a common existence at that moment. Similarly, these patients are not asking the therapist to be empathic; they want the therapist to adopt the patient's own wishes and fears as though they were the therapist's own. They are asking that there be no boundaries with the therapist.

When patients press the therapist for help, it is not always apparent to the therapist that the issue is one of separateness. We noted in the first chapter that borderline patients panic in the face of painful affect, becoming desperate to be rid of "bad" feelings such as anger or depression. Psychic pain tends to make borderline patients feel isolated and cut off from others, and this is a key to understanding their complaints that the therapist must relieve their distress.

Borderline patients make two assumptions about relationships that are pertinent here. The first is that caring for someone entails a commitment to relieve their distress and that failure to do so—or at least failure to try very hard to do so—means that one does not truly care. There is, in other words, no sense that it is possible to care for others and to be able to tolerate their distress without taking action. The second assumption is that painful feelings isolate the patient from others. We mentioned in Chapter 4 that borderline patients believe relationships are founded on meeting the other's needs or otherwise performing some function for the other person and that if no function is performed the relationship becomes doubtful. Quiet or as-if patients are especially vulnerable to the fear that they cannot perform needed functions for others if they are down or upset and that relationships can thereby be lost if they become weak.

When the therapist does not seem to share the patient's distress or fails to take rapid action to "help," borderline patients become painfully aware of their separateness. Most persons can accept being separate and on their own—even when upset—if they are confident they will regain closeness later. The borderline patient's constricted time sense does not allow such confidence, and the feeling of being separate from others can suddenly become one of frightening isolation and loneliness. Hence patients can become urgent in their demands that the therapist make them feel better *now*. What they are asking is that the therapist not leave them alone, and it is important for the therapist to hear this issue underneath the demands for rapid relief.

Treating the Patient's Intolerance of Separateness

It may seem to require the patience of a saint to work with borderline patients who are demanding immediate help. These patients pressure the therapist in a variety of ways to alleviate their distress. The quiet, as-if type of patient may present a blank, virtually expressionless face when upset, similar to the empty and affectively vacant expressions observed by Spitz (1945) among institutionalized infants. Such patients also tend to sigh deeply after statements. The therapist may well experience a sudden sense of having lost contact and feel an almost desperate urge to reestablish connectedness. By contrast, noisy patients are far more open in making demands on the therapist; often they appear to feel entitled to relief simply because they have insisted on it. It is hard to convey to someone who has not experienced it the tension the noisy borderline patient can suddenly create. Either type of patient can be sorely trying to the therapist.

Our approach to such situations in the preconstancy stage is to hold still rather than try to interpret what is happening. Much of the time this means simply saying nothing. It may be appropriate with quiet, as-if borderline patients to offer a simple, empathic remark such as, "I can see this is not easy for you." The sound of the therapist's voice may foster a sense of connection at that moment, and it can be helpful for patients to know the therapist is aware of their distress. Even such a simple intervention, however, ought not be made more than two or three times a session. The more often such seemingly empathic remarks are made, the more likely they reflect the therapist's impatience rather than his or her empathy. Even if the therapist is not impatient, these interventions may well be experienced by the patient as demands to speak or otherwise perform. Many of these patients grew up believing they needed to meet their caretakers' needs. It is easy for them to assume they should become the sort of patient the therapist needs them to be as well, and they will be alert for clues on how the therapist wants them to behave. Empathic comments, if made very often, will sound to such patients as though the therapist were saying, "I understand, so you should move on now." It is important that quiet borderline patients adapt to the social world at their own, private pace; the therapist must take pains not to be experienced as intrusive or impinging.

With noisy borderline patients, *any* intervention seems to reinforce the patient's attempt to force an interaction on his or her own terms. This seems to hold no matter whether the therapist is attempting an interpretation or an empathic reflection. In either case the patient is likely to degrade the remark and devalue the therapist in some way and then shift to a new topic, inviting the therapist to try again, as it were. We believe that saying nothing can convey to the patient that the therapist is capable of withstanding such rage reactions and yet remain available. Such a response preserves boundaries by showing that the therapist does not share the patient's sense of urgency.

By thereby highlighting the question of just who is feeling the urgency, the therapist indirectly focuses on the question of separateness, even though nothing has actually been said.

When borderline patients become angry with the therapist's restraint and urgently demand help and relief, the therapist should realize that separateness is the unspoken issue. It is as though these patients were asking the therapist whether they must go through the difficult experience alone. Of course, the answers to this question are both yes and no: They must go through their upset as separate persons, and yet they are related to the therapist while they do. This is not something that can effectively be put into words, however; it is something that must be lived through over and over in the therapy hour. The therapist must endure the patient's pleas for help, rebukes and attacks for not helping, and threats to leave treatment. The therapist's restraint refuses the merger the patient is seeking; however, it creates an atmosphere in which the patient can learn to be alone in the presence of the therapist.

Additionally, the therapist's restraint furthers the attachment process. The patient's anger stems from fear that the therapist does not care. Since borderline patients assume that satisfaction of needs is the sole basis for attachment, they conclude that therapists who do not try to meet their needs do not care for them. The patient's angry complaints therefore always imply the question "Don't you care for me?" Patients assume the answer must be no, and they expect the therapist to terminate the relationship when the complaints start. The attachment process is furthered when—to the patient's great surprise—the therapist does not terminate treatment. The therapist accepts the patient's right to complain and accuse, and the patient makes the important discovery that the environment can maintain itself and its attentive attitude even in the face of anger.

The therapist's restraint violates a basic assumption borderline patients make in relationships, that frustration of either party inevitably leads to the end of the relationship. On the one hand, if patients are frustrated by loved ones, they believe they are bad for having made a demand in the first place, and termination is the punishment. On the other hand, if a loved one makes a demand, these patients assume (or project) a threatened termination if the demand is rejected. Borderline patients thus feel tremendous guilt when they thwart a loved one's wishes, and it becomes virtually impossible for them to impose a limit or frustration on a love object. If they do attempt some limit, the attendant guilt often leads to excessive efforts to undo or compensate for the momentary rupture in the relationship.

The therapist's ability to stand still and take no action in the face of the patient's demands for help and anger at not receiving it gradually teaches the patient that relationships need not end simply because one party is frustrated, that they will not be abandoned for having made a demand, and that it is possible for persons to refuse demands and stay connected. This puts separateness in a new light, for it suggests that events that leave the patient feeling alone do not necessarily mean loss of the other person, that the relationship may continue even though the patient feels alone. This discovery is an important part of the process that eventually allows the patient to feel alone in the presence of the therapist.

We do not mean to imply that it is easy or automatic for therapists to show restraint when patients are enraged over— as they see it—being left alone by the therapist. It is never an effortless and unemotional decision whether to intervene when patients are furious and attacking.

An example of the difficulties presented by such patients is a restaurant owner in his early thirties who had grown up with an emotionally withdrawn father and a dangerously volatile mother, whose rages included threatening the patient's life while bitterly complaining that his presence had caused her "nothing but grief and trouble." Occasional visits with his paternal grandmother were his only source of emotional warmth as he grew up. As an adult this patient had moved in and out of intense relationships with women over several years and eventually found himself considering suicide. He entered therapy at that point, saying he was "tired of feeling like an emotional yo-yo." He viewed all people, and especially women, as "a bunch of phonies who'll drop you in a minute for someone else," although he felt compelled to pursue them anyway.

The fluidity of the patient's emotional states and his readiness to see others as fraudulent could be seen in the therapy hour. This patient often became enraged while talking about feeling alone; he complained he could not stand it and demanded the therapist do something about it. Several times he would scream at the therapist, "You're absolutely worthless!" and "You're just another phony!" When the therapist remained silent, the patient would stare at him for a moment and then begin to talk about business in a relaxed tone as if that had been the topic of conversation the entire session. It is not easy to convey in words the terrible rage in this patient's eyes when he grew angry at the therapist; it took a long while for the therapist to believe that a physical assault would not follow. It was therefore all the more amazing that his mood could shift so quickly, like the passing of a thunderstorm.

The therapist considered several interventions during this patient's outbursts. The therapist thought of offering the interpretation that the patient's behavior with the therapist reflected exchanges with his mother while growing up. This option was rejected when the therapist became aware that his motivation was to gain control over the patient by exhibiting knowledge the patient did not have. Such an exhibition, in turn, would have been intended to quiet the patient down and prove that the therapist was not a "phony." This illustrates the countertransference issues the therapist must be aware of. In the midst of a difficult session it is often hard to keep focused on what *the patient* needs at that moment as opposed to what would be comforting to the therapist.

The therapist also considered confronting the patient on his inordinate anger at not getting what he wanted and the apparent entitlement this implied. The therapist rejected this intervention, too, however. Such a confrontation would simply have been provocative, and the patient might very well have felt he was being taunted. The therapist also thought about offering empathic remarks focused on the patient's distress and acknowledging the legitimacy of his anger. Such comments were also ruled out. The patient might have seen them as the first step in offering some prescription for action and would inevitably have felt disappointed that the therapist was not following through by producing such a prescription.

After ruling out these options, the therapist thought his best intervention was silence, and this became the response to the patient's attacks. Near the end of the first year of treatment the therapist modified his approach by commenting to the patient, "Have you ever noticed how quickly your feelings can change?" This intervention was useful. The patient came to see that his rapidly changing feelings could lead others to see him as unpredictable and that others might then prefer to avoid him, leaving the patient feeling isolated because, in fact, he was.

Clearly the therapeutic technique used in this case is not revolutionary or novel. Much of what we propose with borderline patients can be seen in the therapeutic process appropriate to many types of patients. At the same time there is a different ambience that must be recognized and addressed when working with borderline patients. The therapist must be much more sensitive to the vulnerabilities of the borderline patient and also to the intense countertransference feelings that are likely to be evoked. When dealing with the patient's intolerance of separateness, therapists must be willing to let the patient feel distress over separateness without trying to take either the distress or the separateness away. Additionally, they must be willing to withstand the attacks that are likely to follow without trying to justify their restraint to the patient or reestablish their competence in the patient's eyes. By their restraint, therapists communicate to the patient their own tolerance for distance and differences.

Quieter, as-if types of borderline patients may present quite different problems for therapists. As mentioned earlier, these patients tend to deny separateness by trying to intuit what the therapist wants them to be; they then set about trying to embody the therapist's imagined wishes. In seeking to become an extension of the therapist's wishes, the as-if type of patient is asking for the privilege of being a kind of Kohutian self-object for the therapist. In this way the patient avoids having to stand on his or her own by subtly merging with the therapist. Ironically, these patients make themselves more isolated or alone by refusing the actual relationship that is possible in favor of the fantasied relationship (of being what the therapist wants) they project onto the therapist. This leads to a paradox: In these cases, the therapist's job is not to confront the patient with separateness but to point the way to a relationship. The therapist must communicate to the patient—of course, without saying it—something to the effect, "No, you can't be an extension of me; you must be separate from me so that we can be related."

With such patients therapists may have to bypass seemingly rich material and deliberately seek out more mundane, less emotionally charged subjects. As-if types of patients may produce meaty subjects in the belief that this is what their therapist wants them to do. If the therapist addresses the meaty subject, he or she only confirms the patient's expectation that this is what the therapist expects. The patient then simply plays out the role of "good patient" by producing more such material (Sherwood 1987). However, the patient is merely playing a part, complying with fantasied expectations, and not engaged in anything meaningful with the therapist, no matter how weighty the subject matter. The therapeutic task is to maneuver the patient back into some position from which a relationship can be started. As long as patients merely act the role of a good therapy patient, they deny their separateness from the therapist; their compliance with what they believe the therapist wants from them, then, is in fact resistance to being alone.

An example of such a patient is a mental health care worker in her mid-twenties, who came for therapy with a variety of complaints, including a sense of inner emptiness, occasional depressive episodes in which the patient could not get out of bed for days at a time (usually occurring on a weekend), periods of binging on junk food, and a diffuse gender identity with accompanying body image concerns. This woman's parents were both professionals, and her older brother was the "star" of the family. His accomplishments were impressive—he was a National Merit scholar, lettered in two sports in high school, edited the high-school newspaper, and was immensely popular. The patient herself had been a good student but had not attained the brother's popularity and had not matched his many achievements. The patient had dated some but never really had any close relationships. She engaged in several sexual relationships in a mechanical fashion, feeling that sex was expected by the men she dated. In her work at a mental health clinic, she was highly regarded by her supervisors, who saw her as highly sensitive to her patients.

This material came out during the first three sessions, during which the patient talked rather mechanically, much like a computer programmed to produce the information. She began the fourth session by asking, "What else do you need to know?" When the therapist replied, "You can talk about whatever you'd like, or we can sit quietly together," the patient's whole manner changed. Her face contorted and her body became tense; she visibly tightened her grip on the arms of her chair, and tears welled up in her eyes. Then with a heavy sigh she began to cry more heavily and said, "I don't know what you want from me!" The therapist remained silent. The patient paused and then— in obvious distress—began to describe how as a teenager she would sneak into her brother's room and masturbate with one of his sports trophies, fantasying that she had a penis "bigger than my brother's." When she reached an orgasm, she would throw the trophy on the floor with disgust, beginning to experience "horrendous guilt." She would then wipe off the trophy carefully, replace it on the shelf, and pick up another trophy, which she would hug while thinking about her "wonderful brother." After relating this story the patient asked, "Is this the kind of self-disclosure you want?"

The therapist analyzed the situation. The patient was plainly upset and agitated, and at first glance it might appear that her distress was related to the material she produced, which contained many obvious id derivatives and might therefore be anxiety-producing to the patient as it entered conscious awareness. The therapist, however, did not believe that the material upset the patient. He noted that she had grown upset after his remark that she could talk of whatever she wished or that the two of them could sit quietly together. It appeared that the patient felt left alone by this remark and that her aloneness upset her. She tried to avoid her separateness through guessing at what the therapist wanted from her and then complying, hoping to become an extension of his wishes.

The therapist could think of no way to respond to the patient's question that would help her feel safer or more connected. To say nothing at all, however, would almost certainly leave the patient feeling she had failed and would evoke another attempt at the kind of self-disclosure she imagined the therapist wanted. The therapist therefore decided to switch topics and asked, "What do you find is the most interesting challenge in your job?" There was a startling change in the patient's demeanor. She brightened and without hesitation replied, "Dealing with incompetent people at other agencies." The patient's body visibly relaxed, and her voice was firm and steady; this suggested to the therapist that the patient felt on safer ground.

The therapist chose this approach because he felt more time was needed to form a secure attachment with the patient before moving into problematic material. He felt it would be a mistake to address either the content of the patient's report or the process that led her to produce it. Prior to the establishment of a firm relationship the patient could only have reported the story as a masochistic submission to the therapist, offering to expose herself in hopes he would not make her be alone while she was with him. No meaningful analysis of the material would have been possible under such circumstances. Interestingly, this material reemerged in the third year of treatment, and the patient remembered her sense of relief that the therapist had not "pounced on me" when she had first brought it up. She remembered leaving that early session feeling, "Maybe he doesn't think I'm totally crazy."

This case illustrates the way in which quiet, as-if borderline patients may demonstrate their intolerance of separateness through trying to become what they imagine the therapist wants them to become. In such cases the therapist's task is to steer the interaction in a direction that will allow a relationship gradually to unfold over time—in contrast to the patient's desire to be merely an extension of the therapist and to enter into such a fusion immediately.

Whether working with noisy or quiet borderline patients, therapists should think of separateness and connectedness as being in a figure-ground relation to one another, with first one and then the other being dominant. With an expanded time sense and the achievement of object constancy, patients may come to see that both separateness and connectedness will vary in their duration and intensity. Prior to these changes, however, borderline patients tend to focus only on separateness, which is intolerable for them. The therapist addresses this situation by allowing attachment to develop slowly over time, much like a baker waiting for the dough to rise. The therapeutic task is to help the patients manage their solitude in the quiet presence of the therapist.

Clinical Transcript

We include here a transcript of a session with a quiet, as-if type of borderline patient, along with comments on the therapist's technique and the way in which the patient's productions illustrate points made in this chapter about intolerance of aloneness. The patient is a single man in his mid-twenties who works in the technical sector. He came for therapy complaining of depressive feelings and a sense of emptiness when alone. He also complained that he was dissatisfied with his relationships, saying that most of them "don't offer much except as a way of filling up time."

This man was the second of four children, and he learned early in life that there was little point in making demands; his mother's attention was focused on his siblings, especially his sickly older brother. The patient was not close to his younger sisters, who seemed close to one another but not to him. The patient's father held a job that required travel, and he tended to be emotionally distant from the household. When he was home, he was treated more as a boarder than a member of the family; the patient could recall only a few exchanges with his father during his whole life.

This patient was originally diagnosed as obsessive-compulsive by his therapist. When the case failed to go well, however, the therapist began to have reservations about this diagnosis and sought consultation with one of the authors, who suggested that the patient's dynamics might be clearer to the therapist if he asked the patient to sit facing the wall during the next session. The idea behind this suggestion was to create a situation that would bring into focus both the patient's discomfort with aloneness and also his need to watch the therapist for clues on how to behave. This transcript is of the next session, the fourteenth of the treatment.

P: I'm at a loss for what to say.

T: Is that uncomfortable?

P: Um-hm. Yeah.

T: Can you describe how it's uncomfortable?

P: I feel kinda anxious. I feel I should be talking about something.

T: The "shoulds" come in again.

P: Um.

T: You often seem to be caught between different "shoulds."

The first four comments by the therapist seem unnecessary. The therapist appears to be telling the patient—in a subtle way—to talk. It would be better to communicate a willingness to let the session unfold at the patient's own pace. The comments about "shoulds" seem especially misplaced. While they are presented as observations, the second comment refers to nothing the patient has yet said, and so it is at best premature.

P: Hm. [*pause*]

T: Would you be willing to spin around and face the wall?

P: Sure. [*turns chair around*] Now what?

T: Just sit there for a minute and tell me what you notice.

P: [*long pause*] Almost immediately I feel less anxious. But then . . . then I started to get anxious again pretty quickly.

T: Can you put words to the anxiety?

In inviting the patient to "put words to the anxiety," the therapist invites the patient to gain cognitive control.

P: I . . . think . . . that when I was turned around the other way, the anxiety was more, um, had to do with the interaction between you and I, I think. So by turning around I was aware that, that that happened right away, too, that that's why I . . . it relieved it, because it kinda broke the interaction that we were having. But then, thinking about that, um, brought on a different kind of anxiety, that was more of an anxiety about why that interaction that we were having was so uncomfortable.

T: Um-hm.

P: And it scares me that just sitting in the room with you, um, is hard for me.

T: What's scary about that?

P: [*pause*] Well, I think it's because it's . . . it's intimate.

T: What's scary about intimacy?

P: I don't know. [*pause*] I guess intimacy involves trust, and it involves exposure, and it involves showing you who I am and being responsible for who I am. It involves being responsive to who you are. And it's one-on-one; there's no one else around to hide behind or rely on to fill in the quiet, um, segments when I don't have anything to share or say. Then I get uncomfortable with it. [*pause*]

T: What do you think the quiet segments mean?

P: [*pause*] I don't know. It doesn't, I mean, they really don't mean that much, uh . . . Although as I think about it, till I put the "shoulds" in there, you know, it's like, well, I should be talking. And so when it's like I don't have anything to say, and it gets quiet, then I get anxious, because, you know, then the quiet segments . . . if you get rid of that "should" then the quiet segments would be as important as, or even maybe more important than, when I am talking and saying things. It's uncomfortable.

T: Well, what is the purpose of continuing to talk? You say you feel like you should do that. Why do you feel that way?

Given what the patient has just said, it is not clear why the therapist is making an intervention here. If the therapist

*felt an intervention was needed, he could have commented
instead on the remark "It's uncomfortable" with a question
refocusing the patient on his responsibility for what he's
doing to make himself uncomfortable. An example would
be asking, "What happens between us when you don't want
to say anything or have nothing to say?" The therapist's
final question appears to create a situation in which the
patient can continue talking on the therapist's terms.*

P: [*pause*] I don't know.
[*pause*]

T: Does it feel like a demand from me, an expectation?

P: Yeah. I think so. And I think, you know, I want, I
wanna please you. I think that's important to me.

*The patient indentifies with the role of a victim who
wants to please the therapist. Here again the therapist has
offered the patient an opportunity to project responsibility for his discomfort onto the therapist, and the patient
has halfheartedly accepted.*

T: And yet you felt relief when you were able to break out
of that—having to react to my demands. [*long pause*] Do
you feel more connected to me when you're talking and
reacting to me?

*The therapist asks a good question here and might have
asked it earlier in response to the patient's comment about
"quiet segments."*

P: No.

T: Do you feel connected to me at all?

P: I think so. Uh, it's real scary though, um, for me to feel
that. I think it's on a level that's real hard for me to get
past. I'm kinda thinking that the quiet segments are un-

comfortable because, during the quiet time, I think, uh, my mind is trying to go deeper, and that's scary. It's like, if I can keep talking, then, um, it keeps me from thinking too much and from going deeper, so I can stay at that level, and it's more comfortable . . . I'm not sure about that, it's just, you know, just a few minutes ago when I was looking at the wall here, I was a little more quiet and, uh, it was almost like a struggle where my mind wanted to go deeper and to feel things and, and I wouldn't let it. I'm not sure.

T: So words are like a lifeline that I can hold you above water with.

This comment seems to reflect a misunderstanding of what the patient has just said. Words are not a lifeline for this patient but a resistance against deeper feelings. It is to the patient's credit that he was able to resist agreeing with the therapist—this is hard for an as-if type of patient.

P: Hmm.

T: That's the image I got.

P: Hmm.

T: Reacting and talking with me keep you out of something scary. [*long pause*] How do you feel now?

P: I sorta went off someplace else. I guess I feel alone is what I feel. Because I did go off someplace and left you. I don't even remember what the last thing you said was.

This revelation must be anxiety-producing for the patient, who will probably expect the other person to be upset at having been "abandoned."

T: Uh-huh. What's it like being alone?

This is a central question and is linked to much of what the patient has said earlier, for example, the comment about "quiet segments."

P: [*pause*] I don't think I really like it. It's, um, what, uh . . . Where I went is, I was thinking about this dream I had the other night. And, um, but at the same time, I was thinking that I would like to share that with you. But . . . something was keeping me from just saying it. I think it's because I didn't want you to know that I went someplace and left you.

This is crucial. It goes to the patient's expectation that his independence will lead the therapist to feel left behind and in turn bring about some sort of retaliation. The patient expects the therapist to want him to remain dependent and compliant to ward off the therapist's imagined inability to tolerate aloneness.

T: What would happen if I knew that?

P: Hmm. [*pause*] You might feel alone, too. And you might feel like I wasn't interested in what you were saying and that we're not connected.

T: And what would that mean, for me and for you? [*pause*] I guess the question is, "Who's holding up the stable end of this lifeline?"

Again, this image brings no response from the patient.

P: Umm.

T: Are you protecting me, or am I protecting you?

The idea of who is being protected does not seem related to the patient's fear of exposing his occasional indifference to what the therapist is saying. The patient finds a way to return to the subject, which is the patient's need to hide his independence from the therapist out of fear that the therapist will abandon him if he seems too separate.

P: It's like I want you to be protecting me. And so, if I can, uh . . . It's like if I can fool you into thinking that I'm with you, then that's more likely to happen. But if you think that I left you and I'm not that interested, then, you could go and then, uh, I would have to be alone. But the other way I can kind of, you know, pretend like we're together and, you know, be alone when I feel like being alone—but as long as you don't know that. I don't know.

T: Because I can't tolerate your being alone when you're with me?

The therapist apparently knows Winnicott and hears an important theme.

P: Yeah, I think I have a hard time seeing that, that it can just be, uh, you know, it seems like it has to be all or nothing in any relationship with me.

This statement is an excellent example of the borderline patient's dilemma in relationships.

T: All or nothing how?

P: Well, it's like I have a hard time giving people credit that, um, or understanding that people are, are tolerant, that other people tolerate certain things and, um, they tolerate imperfection, they tolerate, uh, other people's feelings. I have a hard time giving people that credit, I think.

T: You haven't had much experience with that.

P: Hmm. [*pause*]

T: That's interesting. I'm struck by your saying that you're trying to fool me into thinking that we're connected.

The therapist has heard an important theme: The patient's need to fool the therapist into believing there is a connection between them is exactly what the as-if patient does in intimate relationships. This leads directly to the other issue, that if the patient shows too much independence, the other person may leave.

P: Yeah. [*pause*] Maybe that it's because I don't know that you'd be there, you know, if I were to say, "Well, [therapist's name], I wasn't gonna listen to what you were saying because I was thinking about something else." So I, I don't trust that you're gonna still be there, you know.

T: Um-hmm. Makes a lot of sense. [*long pause*] You're not sure that someone can maintain a reliable and consistent caring for you.

This intervention seems unnecessary. While correct in content, it is really much broader than the issues that have actually come up.

P: Hm-hmm.

T: So in your desperation you're willing to settle for faking it . . . or to withdraw completely.

P: Yeah, even though faking it is real uncomfortable.

T: It's a lot of work. You have to watch very carefully for what the other person's thinking and doing. [*pause*] Leaves you very little time for feeling comfortable and knowing who you are within yourself.

P: Um-hmm. I would like to turn around. [*turns chair to face therapist*]

The patient appears to hear the therapist's remark as a subtle command to turn back around. The patient's compliance with this "demand" comes after the patient has demonstrated a fair amount of independence. It is likely that the patient is uneasy about this and now wants to show that he can once more be what he imagines the therapist expects him to be. The patient's smile at the end of the session reflects a masochistic submission and is a way of again being the therapist's "good little boy."

T: I'm still here.

P: [*beaming*] Yeah, I'm glad.

Part III

THE MOMENTS
OF CONSTANCY

Introduction

Most of the preconstancy stage of treatment will be taken up with the topics discussed in the preceding three chapters. It goes without saying that there is no way to judge exactly how long those themes should be expected to dominate treatment, but we think it is fair to expect them to be prominent for at least the first year. At some point, however, the therapist will begin to sense that things are changing. The overall feel to the change is that the patient seems to be less intense about the therapeutic relationship, that the patient is starting to take it for granted that the therapist is there and will stay there. In short, the relationship is starting to feel more reliable.

This is the start of object constancy, of course. Treatment is moving into a new phase, one in which constancy is being established. We believe there are three recognizable stages to this phase and that these three stages occur in a fairly predictable sequence. Each stage centers around one important aspect of what it means to have a stable, constant attachment. We have labeled these stages:

- adaptive matrix constancy
- differentiating constancy
- reparation constancy

It would be wrong to regard these stages as goals to be targeted. Whether or not it is even possible to address them in such a way, it is not necessary to do so. These are features of constant attachment that will unfold naturally over the course of treatment. The therapist does not need to do anything to evoke them; they will simply be there eventually.

When these forms of constancy begin to arise, therapists should alter their treatment stance. For most of the preconstancy phase of treatment, therapists must "stand still" and let attachment develop. However, therapists should gradually become more active as these later stages of constancy begin to become noticeable. Thus we have devoted a fair amount of attention to these moments of constancy, even though they may occupy a relatively brief period of time compared to the rest of the preconstancy stage.

As these moments of constancy appear in treatment, therapy gradually takes on a more normal character. In place of the fairly specialized approach we have described throughout this book, therapists will find themselves behaving more and more as they might with nonborderline patients. By the conclusion of the reparation constancy stage, treatment is essentially proceeding as would the treatment of a neurotic patient. This should not be surprising; a specialized approach was called for in the first place because there was so little coherence or integrity to the borderline patient's experience of self and other. Object constancy, however, is a principal organizing force in the personality, and by the time it is achieved, patients are reachable by the interventions and techniques taught by the major schools of psychotherapy. In the first chapter we wrote that therapists would have to surrender these interventions for a time, but by the conclusion of the reparation constancy stage, they may reclaim them.

In each chapter we take pains to point out the changes that are needed in the therapist's approach compared to the basic approach of standing still. We have not used transcripts in these chapters, largely because it is so hard to capture the essence of these moments of constancy in the exchanges of a single session. We do, however, use more clinical vignettes, since these can often give a better feel of the flow of a case over time and thereby better capture the gradually developing nature of each stage.

7

Adaptive Matrix Constancy

The Adaptive Matrix

Long before the therapist as a person becomes important to the borderline patient, therapy itself becomes important, the overall atmosphere and the experience of being invited to feel at home in the world. It is the responsibility of the therapist to provide such a setting, an atmosphere free of demands, in which patients can gradually become confident the therapist is glad to see them regardless of what they are feeling or what they need at any given moment. The therapist's continuing, reliable interest must be independent of who the patient is. The patient should not have to do anything to create it; the therapist's attentive interest is not contingent on the quality (or quantity) of the therapist–patient interaction. It is simply there, as the context of treatment.

Patients come to depend on this atmosphere, and it influences them many months before the therapist's interventions influence them. The atmosphere gradually evokes in borderline patients the rough beginnings of hope that the world may be more receptive to them than they have hitherto found it to be, that their needs, wants, and demands might be tolerated or even acknowledged without resentment. It is not that these patients come to therapy seeking the therapist's interest in them; if borderline patients begin therapy seeking anything in particular it is probably tension reduction they primarily want. But the therapist's continuing, dependable interest in them serves much as Winnicott's (1963a) "environment mother," who meets the child's needs in such a way that the baby comes to need just what the mother offers. Similarly, borderline patients come to need the atmosphere of the therapy session. The therapist's calm, continuing interest sets a tone that makes the world seem increasingly safe and reliable. Adaptive matrix constancy refers primarily to the way in which therapy begins to make the world seem reliable.

What we call the adaptive matrix includes both the sense that the world is predictable and also confidence that we can master it. There is an interaction here between experience of self and experience of the world; on the one hand, the world must seem predictable enough to be relied on, and on the other hand, the individual must feel competent to move into the unknown. The result is a kind of confidence that becomes the backdrop of life and fuels the individual's efforts at mastery. When the adaptive matrix is not established, both the experience of self and of the world are affected. In such a case, the self is unstable, changing with each change in circumstance; therapists may sense that their patients are merely reacting to events with no overarching integrity or continuity from within, and patients, too, may speak of feeling wishy-washy and fragmented. In turn, the world then appears unsafe, a place that cannot be counted on.

There are several consequences to living in an unsafe world. First, one can never afford to *wait*. The unreliability of the world means that events must be responded to immediately, since the future cannot be trusted. If the world is not safe, it must be watched carefully and reacted to quickly. There is little chance of being able to relax, to be patient, or to see what might happen next; the individual tends to live in a constant crisis, poised for action. Additionally, if the self changes with every change in the world, there is no basis for waiting. When the world changes, the individual must react to the change.

Second, it is hard to have faith in the durability of relationships when the world is unsafe. Those living in an unsafe world are oppressed with the tentative nature of things. Relationships must either be checked constantly or else they seem virtually lost already. In the first case, individuals become possessive and unduly jealous, oppressing loved ones with their constant wish to control the other. In the second case relationships become colored with depressive and fearful themes—for example, a dread that one's children will be kidnapped or killed nearly every time they are out of sight. In either case, there is no sense of confident belonging to another person; rather, there is perpetual fear of loss.

Third, if the world is unsafe, it is difficult to feel that one has the right to *want*, to make demands for oneself, with any confidence that these are in keeping with what the world is willing to offer. To make appropriate demands, there must be a sense that my presence in the world is not questionable, that the world is able to provide what I need. Without such a sense, individuals must do one of two things: Either they experience an oppressive sense of guilt whenever they want something for themselves, and consequently back away from what they want in a masochistic fashion, or else they resort to entitlement as the only way to have their wants responded to. In either event, it is truly confusing to know what demands can be made on an unreliable world.

To move from the experience of the world as an unsafe place, and the consequent sense that who I am is utterly contingent on whatever response the world makes at any given moment, there must be some "home base," or emotional sanctuary, that is both safe and can be counted on. Of course, the problem is that the world cannot be counted on by the borderline patient. Splitting, or part object relations, keep the world unstable; the world shifts with the patient's moods, as these moods are projected onto the environment: The frustrated patient lives in an angry world, the happy patient in an exciting and wonderful world, and the speed and frequency with which these can change lend the world an unreliable and tentative character, even in the happy times. The world is unstable because the self is fragmented; however, the self will not be able to attain more integration without some help from the world.

For the growing child this help comes from the "good enough mother" for the most part, particularly the mother of rapprochement, who largely tolerates the child's many, often unpleasant, changes—allowing times of exuberant independence and mastery while remaining available for the inevitable regressions, the times of ambivalent neediness and sudden dependency. When the mother and other caretakers do this well enough over time, the world assumes a more stable appearance, but more importantly, the child also seems more stable. By accepting the child's right to make different demands at different times and to have changing needs and wishes, the mother communicates that the child is more than whatever he or she feels, demands, or wants at any given moment. The mother provides a stable and predictable setting in which the child can change and be different; paradoxically, by reliably accepting the child's changes, the mother promotes sameness. The child arrives at a more integrated experience of self when different and changing aspects of the child are all reliably acknowledged over time.

This emotional sanctuary is simply given to the child by the mother. The child need not create it or imagine it. It is simply provided, independent of the child's actual wants or wishes. This home base becomes the stuff out of which the child goes on to create the illusion of the constant object, and it is this illusion that makes it possible to experience the world as safe and predictable. The borderline patient, however, has not been able to create this illusion, presumably because early caretakers have not offered the sanctuary or home base the growing child needed, or have not offered it in a way the child could make use of. For the borderline patient, therefore, the therapy session must be this sanctuary.

Borderline patients do not begin therapy with the capacity to use the session as a home base. They will feel only the most tenuous connection with the therapist in the early stages of treatment and will be afraid to think in terms of "my" therapist. Even the demandingness and aggressive entitlement often shown by patients merely cover over their sense of being only tentatively welcome and their belief that they could be dismissed by the therapist at a moment's notice. In short, they do not feel any more at home in the therapy session than in the rest of the world, and, as earlier chapters have described, they will bring to the session the same problems and experiences they have elsewhere.

All of this gradually changes, however, and with it the patient's experience of the world gradually changes. Therapists will usually see two signs that this first stage of constancy is under way: First, therapy itself begins to seem important to the patient, and second, the patient begins to make discriminations in daily life between situations requiring a response and those that do not. The first sign implies a change from the experience of therapy as something that is supposed to make the patient "feel good" to something that is valuable in its own right. This change implies a budding capacity of the patient to value something for itself and not simply because it meets a need or reduces tension; this is the first step in becoming capable of a lasting attachment. The second sign reveals growing confidence both that the world can be managed and also that the self can endure whatever problem confronts it.

We emphasize that these changes occur before the patient is able to experience the therapist as a constant object. They are the early signs that constancy is unfolding, but the patient will continue to show unmodulated affect, fear of abandonment, and intolerance of separateness during sessions. We do not believe it is the therapist's verbal interventions that make this change possible, but something of the overall setting and atmosphere the therapist creates. To some extent, verbal interventions will be part of that setting, but more than anything else it is the therapist's ability to stay with the patient in a nonimpinging, nondemanding, yet empathic and interested manner that creates such a setting.

The Unfolding of Confidence in the World:
The Physical World

The first step in making the world reliable is to make the physical world predictable. The physical setting of therapy with borderline patients is therefore important. At the outset of treatment the office is experienced as if it were part of the therapist, and so the inanimate world must be as constant as the therapist is going to be. The office must reflect the same kind of predictability the therapist strives to present. It is antitherapeutic when borderline patients are shunted from one office to another in clinics or in other settings where limited space makes it necessary for therapists to rotate offices. We believe this shifting of offices will make it much more difficult for a constant attachment to unfold.

The therapy office gives the patient the chance to become connected to something before it is possible to feel connected to the therapist. Patients speak of "my chair" or "my couch";

this is one way for patients to appropriate some part of the inanimate environment and make it their own. Such claiming of some part of the office is not the same thing as making that item a transitional object. The patient's chair or couch is a given, something from the outside, not the patient's creation or illusion (cf. Searles 1960). While the function of a transitional object is to negotiate the move from purely subjective, magical thinking to objective, reality-oriented thinking, the function of "my chair" is to provide stability or reliability. No transition is taking place; the patient is simply trying to learn whether there is "room for me here."

It is therefore important that the physical setting of therapy be reliable. Paranoid fears or depression and outrage may unexpectedly emerge when the physical setting of therapy suddenly disappoints borderline patients in the early stage of treatment. One woman accused her therapist of trying to humiliate her when he moved his office. She complained, "You must assume I'll just follow you around!" While she completed the move to his new office building, she continued to rebuke her therapist and clearly felt vulnerable and exposed from having been placed in what she experienced as a purely passive position. She even threatened to seek out a new therapist so as to be able to return to the old building—even though the new building was actually more convenient for her.

Another therapist moved to a larger office and found that one of his borderline patients became angry and despondent. In the therapist's old office this patient had always sat on the couch, clutching one of the end pillows over her lap. When the patient entered the new office, she went to the couch and said, "Oh, you still have my old couch!" She then picked up all the pillows on the couch and held them on her lap, exclaiming, "Yep, they're the same ones!" The therapist then asked if she had been afraid they would be different, and the patient blew up, bitterly protesting, "What reason would I have to think you kept anything the same around here!"

In these cases we can see how sensitive borderline patients can be to instability in the physical world. The stability of the physical world plays a role in self-definition. Prior to being able to make consistent self-other discriminations, individuals learn to make self-world discriminations. When the physical world cannot be counted on, feels unsafe, or becomes unpredictable, the individual does not fully differentiate between self and the physical world, but overidentifies with aspects of the physical environment, clinging emotionally to physical items as sources of security. In adulthood this leads to excessive sentimentality and nostalgia, as places, items, and sometimes dates become loaded with emotional significance, replacing stable attachments as sources of emotional equilibrium. Borderline patients tend to do this, failing to differentiate fully between the inner world and the outer world. As a result, these patients will require a stable physical setting for therapy. The stable setting first gives them physical items to attach to at a time when they cannot allow themselves to feel that the therapist is "mine." Later, a stable setting provides enough predictability that they can begin to distinguish the therapist from the therapeutic setting. The predictable office becomes a backdrop of stability that allows the patient to begin to differentiate between self and world.

For many borderline patients, the physical world was chaotic, marked by a kind of instability during the growing-up years. One patient described going to scout camp when she was 13 and finding on her return that the family had moved to a new house on the other side of town during her absence. While she had known that a move was going to take place sometime that summer, she had not known it would occur while she was gone, and she was traumatized. Her parents explained that they had known the move would be hard for her and that they had sought to spare her the upset of the actual move (and presumably spare themselves having to deal with the upset). In this case, of course, it is the truly remarkable insensitivity of the parents that actually led the patient to feel that the world could not be counted on, but it is easy to see how the predictability of the physical world became important to her. As an adult in therapy, for example, she had a strong negative reaction when her therapist mentioned that he was thinking of buying a new couch. Additionally, throughout therapy she tended to be un- usually upset whenever an appointment had to be rescheduled. In short, she was always on the watch for a sign the world was not reliable, since her gut feeling was that it was not.

For other borderline patients, the physical world was stable enough, but they lacked any sense that they "owned" their part of it. Some borderline patients report that as children and adolescents they could not keep siblings or parents from com- ing into their rooms unannounced. One patient described his parents' having bought him a very nice bedroom suite for his birthday as an early adolescent. He was able to recognize that it was a generous gift, but he remembered feeling depressed about it, though at the time he did not know why. In treatment he realized he was offended that his parents essentially redeco- rated his room with no opportunity for him to have a say in it. He had felt infantilized—which was characteristic of the way he and his parents interacted—and alienated from his own space, while also feeling there must be something wrong with him for not being grateful. As an adult this particular patient had a great deal of trouble buying furnishings for his apart- ment; even when he could afford decent furniture, he tended to put up with run-down, shabby possessions.

These sorts of issues might not be especially troublesome for individuals suffering less extreme forms of pathology, and to some extent such problems of privacy and ownership of one's room are part and parcel of growing up. Yet borderline patients typically feel they have no right to be present in the world and that their wants and wishes are, at best, tolerated. In such a context, these issues take on exaggerated significance. When patients grow up without feeling they have control over their private physical space, they remain on shaky terms with the world. Since they are not in control, their sense of vulnerability is heightened, and the world seems correspondingly unsafe. Even if they live with the same people throughout their childhood, there remains the fear that if the physical world can change, so can the people. The physical world is the backdrop of life: When there is not enough reliability to the world for the patient to count on it, the individual cannot relax and be fully separate from the world.

The Unfolding of Confidence in the World: The Psychophysical Setting

The setting of therapy therefore plays a role, offering the patient the chance to become attached to something before it is possible to feel comfortable with or possessive of the therapist. Of course, it is not really the actual physical setting that makes this possible. While the stability of the physical setting allows the patient to become attached to features of the therapist's office, it is actually what goes on in the office that makes it seem like a haven or sanctuary to the patient. In particular, the therapist's ability to show patience and restraint creates a psychophysical setting for therapy. The patient will become attached first to the physical setting, but without a particular atmosphere (which the therapist must create), the office would seem forbidding to the patient.

The physical world will seem more reliable and stable when the therapist is able to remain attentive, yet calm. If the therapist becomes as reactive as the patient or agitated along with the patient, the physical setting of therapy will appear unstable and ominous. It may seem unnecessary to caution therapists to be calm with borderline patients, but these patients are actually quite good at stampeding therapists into premature action, prompting them to make verbal interventions long before these can be useful or even to propose action plans and solutions to problems.

As we have emphasized throughout this book, the essential ingredient in allowing the patient's attachment to unfold is the therapist's ability to wait. For example, at the start of a session the therapist may notice that the patient is anxious, depressed, angry, or otherwise upset. The therapist might well be tempted to probe with questions to learn why the patient is troubled or perhaps say something to let the patient know the therapist is aware of the mood, but we believe it is better to keep silent. A therapist who can wait in the face of the patient's evident distress communicates that the immediate situation is safe. The patient then has the chance to experience the therapist's calm interest and the stability of the psychophysical environment.

Borderline patients often describe a crisislike situation and either overtly demand or (more or less) subtly imply that the therapist should provide a solution. They may ask point-blank, "What should I do?" or even "What are you going to do?" Therapists make a mistake if they cave in to this pressure, proposing some action or even making a verbal intervention. Not only does this deprive patients of the chance to see that others can bear their tension (cf. Szasz 1959), but also the pressure to provide some help is frequently a setup for the therapist: Patients will usually reject whatever solution the therapist proposes or discount the helpfulness of a verbal intervention. The patient will then become more tense, since it appears the therapist has been stymied.

It is much more advisable for the therapist to listen with little interruption while the patient describes a crisis. As we have noted in earlier chapters, the final solution is generally to do nothing—it has been our experience that most of the "crises" experienced by borderline patients do not require a response. At most, the patient may be encouraged to come up with his or her own solution. It does not really matter whether any solution is generated; the important element in these interactions is that the patient has the chance to experience the therapist's continuing presence and ongoing, calm interest. The patient must be allowed to see that the world can maintain itself in the face of a storm that turns out to be transitory.

In taking this stance, therapists challenge the patient's assumptions about relationships. Therapists must not allow themselves to be saddled with the role of trying to make the patient feel better. Whenever therapists accept the role of problem-solver, or give an early interpretation in an effort to help, they are simply trying to reduce the patient's discomfort or alleviate tension (a posture more and more encouraged by third-party payers and others wishing to make change a rapid process). As we noted in earlier chapters, however, this is precisely the function borderline patients believe people are supposed to serve with one another, that relationships are founded on the capacity to make one another feel better. A major part of becoming a constant object for the borderline patient is allowing the patient to discover that relationships can in fact be governed by an attachment that endures even when neither party is trying to make the other feel better. The relationship becomes important for its own sake, not because one person is meeting the other's needs.

It is important for borderline patients to find that their relationship with the therapist is based on something beyond tension reduction or need satisfaction, and this is what gradually happens as adaptive matrix constancy becomes established. This is, however, something of a moment of truth for therapy. Borderline patients may not tolerate a relationship that fails to make them feel better, and they may leave treatment if they are too disappointed with the therapist's restraint. Those who remain discover that therapy becomes important for its own sake, that they may somehow feel better even though they have not had their tensions relieved or their crises resolved. These patients become attached to therapy, to the setting and its atmosphere, prior to becoming attached to the therapist.

There are three elements to this atmosphere that can be further defined in addition to the importance of the physical setting and the therapist's ability to show restraint. These are: the proper use of empathy, the creation of a "holding environment," and the therapist's tolerance for banal and tedious material. Each will be discussed in turn.

Empathy and the Adaptive Matrix

It would be hard to find anyone, particularly these days, who would deny the importance of the therapist's ability to empathize with the borderline patient. Unfortunately, for all that has been written about empathy, it remains a difficult process, requiring sensitivity to the other person's feelings, the courage not to shield one's own sensibilities from the intensity of those feelings, and yet also the separateness to avoid making the other person's burdens one's own. Although many writers have stressed its importance, the process of empathy remains like the meaning of life itself, a perpetual mystery and discovery.

Certainly one aspect of empathy is the capacity to adopt temporarily the viewpoint of the other. Szalita (1976) has noted, "The test of one's empathy is the capacity to relate to the sensitivity of the sufferer rather than to the magnitude of the misfortune" (p. 151). It is not clear what mechanism allows us to enter, as it were, the subjective world of the other person.

Freud (1921) spoke of empathy as a "resonance" between the therapist's unconscious and that of the patient. Fromm-Reich-mann (1950) and Sullivan (1953) recognized it as a mysterious, intuitive discovery that produced spontaneous, positive emotions in patients, who found that they felt understood. Chessick (1965) has noted, "All of us, sick and well . . . very much need the empathy of other people. We are reassured when we feel that someone has succeeded in feeling himself into our own state of mind" (p. 211).

In a process that is so hard to define and yet carries such a powerful effect on both the person empathizing and the person empathized with, there are occasions for problems. For instance, transference and countertransference distortions are certain to take their toll in any process that blurs boundaries in the way empathy does, even if the blurring is temporary. To some extent these distortions must be expected, tolerated, and worked through. We believe a greater cause for concern is the way the concept of empathy is used today. Current use of the term does not always carry the thoughtfulness or attempt at rigor shown by Freud, Fromm-Reichmann, Sullivan, or Ches-sick. For example, we suspect that many clinicians would be hard pressed to differentiate Kohut's concept of empathy from Rogers' notion of unconditional positive regard. We believe that many clinicians believe that being empathic is the same thing as offering the patient a kind of Rogerian supportiveness and clarification of feelings. If so, this is a conceptual sloppi-ness that cannot avoid degrading the quality of the therapy being done, especially with borderline patients. Even such re-spected authors as Adler and Buie (1979) seem to use the term rather loosely as they describe the creation of holding and soothing introjects. While we agree with Fromm-Reichmann's well-known position (cf. Szalita 1976) that training and consul-tation can certainly help elaborate the therapist's capacity for empathy, we do not believe empathy is a technique that can be learned or a tool that can be available for use whenever the situation calls for it. Rather, empathy is a subjective involve-ment with the inner experience of the patient, alternating with an ability to become objectively detached and communicate on the basis of one's understanding.

The capacity for detachment is especially important, for, as Szalita (1976) puts it, "It is good to be able to put yourself in someone else's shoes, but you have to remember that you don't wear them" (p. 145). When clinicians forget to detach them-selves from the patient's experience, they tend to make overly sympathetic interventions, as though an intervention informed by empathy should not upset the patient or be discordant with the patient's way of seeing things. We believe this essentially confuses empathy with an intervention. By contrast, we view empathy as simply one means by which therapists gather information about the patient: What intervention is subse-quently made, if any, is separate from the empathic process.

This means that empathizing with patients does not commit therapists to a mirroring, supportive, or sympathetic remark. At the risk of stating the obvious, being empathic is not a matter of being "nice" or of saying to the patient, "I know what you mean" or "I hear you." Finally, empathy does not mean reframing what the patient has expressed and reflecting back some underlying affect. It is one thing for the therapist em-pathically to grasp the patient's experience; whatever response is made, if any, is a separate matter. It may well be that no intervention is called for; if a response is needed, that interven-tion must be determined by the therapist's experience and understanding of the case, not by the desire to be empathic.

The importance of empathy is that it contributes to an atmosphere, a context or backdrop, by allowing the therapist to forge a connection with the patient before the patient knows how to connect with the therapist. While borderline patients expect connectedness to depend on tension relief or need satis-faction, the therapist's empathy offers the chance to form an attachment on the basis of interest, openness, and receptivity to inner feelings and thoughts. To the extent that patients can "hear" this—and it may take quite a while before they can—they may grow hopeful. This hopefulness is part of the patient's coming to value the therapy session.

Empathy depends on life experience and the capacity to draw on a combination of stored memories, along with imagination and openness to new experiences. One of the more unpleasant things this means for therapists is that they must manage to remain open, or in touch with, their own conflicts, problems, and pathology. We fully agree with Searles' (1978) point: "Particularly in work with borderline patients . . . it is essential that the analyst become as open as possible to acknowledging to himself that even the patient's most severe psychopathology has some counterpart, perhaps relatively small by comparison but by no means insignificant, in his own *real* personality functioning" (pp. 61–62).

The following case example may illustrate the point. The patient was a 30-year-old woman functioning in a management position. She had a history of short, intense sexual relationships, all of which terminated quickly, as soon as she felt the man had betrayed her in some manner. This feeling of betrayal invariably confirmed her feeling that she was alone in the world and forever misunderstood. When she started therapy, she was between relationships and felt depressed and angry with the world. In the third month of treatment she began a session by describing how insecure she had felt as a child. She had grown up in a home where rules were ambiguous and with a mother who drank heavily and became violent with the children. At one point she described her experience by saying, "It was like being in a London fog." When the therapist spontaneously added, "with Jack the Ripper out there somewhere," she began to giggle and cry at the same time. Thereafter she often referred to this exchange as a time when she felt that her terror and uncertainty were understood. In this case it had been necessary for the therapist to be attuned to his own paranoid fears as a child; this allowed him more fully to grasp the patient's feeling of vulnerability and illustrates the way therapists may draw even on their problematic experiences to understand those of the patient.

To our mind, this is the proper use of empathy. It may lead to an intervention—as in the case above, where empathy allowed the therapist to describe something of the patient's experience that she had not dared to expose—or there may be no direct intervention. In either case empathy allows the therapist to gather information about the world the patient lives in and to use the information to build connectedness with the patient.

Empathy and the Holding Environment

Winnicott (1960) coined the phrase "holding environment" to describe a particular aspect of mother–infant interaction. As reviewed in Chapter 2, this phrase refers to ways in which the mother screens out and protects her infant from factors that might disrupt the child—such as overstimulation—and provides other functions that allow the baby to feel the world is reliable and safe. She creates a world in which the baby can "go on being," to use Winnicott's poetic phrase. Winnicott and others have applied this concept to therapy, where the holding environment refers to a particular ambience or process that unfolds over time. The most critical feature is that the patient can feel confident or secure in the presence of the therapist.

Winnicott stressed the importance of the mother's avoiding intrusiveness with her infant. He saw unwanted maternal impingement as the critical factor in the development of severe psychopathology—in contrast to other theorists who have stressed the role of maternal unavailability. Winnicott was highly sensitive to the question of how much help normal infants need to grow in a healthy direction. At the risk of oversimplification, Winnicott taught that normal children know how to develop, and the role for caretakers is to provide just enough direction and help to allow the child to do what he or she knows to do—the idea of good-enough parenting.

Of course, different infants require differing levels of help or support from the parents, and it is perhaps a matter of accident whether infants and parents are well matched in terms of whether the parent is prepared to give just the help the infant needs. Chess and colleagues (1959), for example, found that it is best if the mother's temperament is congruent with the baby's need for stimulation. There should be a kind of fit between mother and infant such that the mother can sense when to interact, when to offer help, and when to leave the child alone. This fit or match between the mother's and the infant's temperament is what makes the holding environment possible. When the mother is not able to stay attuned to the infant's changing affects and needs, she is liable to be unfortunately unresponsive part of the time and disruptingly intrusive at other times. Infants have less chance to feel that the world is a place that can be trusted to "hold" them, to sustain and contain them. (Of course, it is an irony that the parents who did not fit emotionally with their infants might have done so with others of differing temperaments.)

Winnicott felt that maternal intrusiveness was the most destructive factor in emotional development. A hovering or impinging mother can destroy the child's drive toward independence. During the early months of life the mother must intuit what, if anything, her child needs and then make some response out of that intuition, knowing, too, when the best response is to let the baby alone. As every parent knows too well, the infant has few ways to communicate the details of what is needed, and the mother is, to a large extent, left to her imagination. She must try to identify with the infant to gauge what the child feels or wants, and then she behaves with the infant as though her identification were accurate. Of course, this is projective identification, only in a healthy and normal form.

The mother never simply picks up what the baby needs. She partially picks up the baby's feelings and partially attributes her own feelings to the baby. That is, the mother never merely reflects what is in the baby; she always adds a little of her own way of seeing things. There is a healthy mix between what the baby contributes and what the mother projects onto the baby. When the mother's projections are fairly consistent with the baby's moods, and she imagines her infant's needs in a way that helps her provide for them, she has built a holding environment. However, when the mother's projections are typically out of sync with the baby, a holding environment cannot be created; the mother is simply imposing her own state of mind onto the child, forcing the child to become empathic to her feelings rather than vice versa. In this case the mother's moods and needs hover over the child, impinging on the child's ability to grow and develop. Eventually the child is forced to deny or suppress his or her own expressions of liveliness, joy, and anger in favor of what the mother can acknowledge.

When we talk about the therapist's empathy with the borderline patient, we are describing something of the same process that occurs between mother and infant (the differences will be discussed below). The therapist tries to identify with the patient for a time. The key is that the therapist try to imagine the patient's state of mind, using that as a basis for creating an atmosphere that will allow the patient to go on being with the therapist. Of course, it is unavoidable that there be some projection on the therapist's part, and the danger is that therapists will impose too much of their own wishes or needs onto the patient. In this case they, like the mothers of most of their borderline patients, will be experienced as intrusive, as impinging on the patient's own needs and wishes.

With borderline patients, therapists are most likely to project their own desire for tension relief onto the patient, mixing up their wish that the session were less difficult with the patient's need to have the therapist tolerate the tension. When therapists make verbal interventions designed to ease the tension, whether by trying to show they empathize with the patient's difficulties or by interpreting the causes of those difficulties, they are impinging in a potentially destructive way. They are asking, as it were, that patients be less upset.

In therapy the patient must be able to express different needs and feelings as these arise and discover that they can be tolerated. This discovery allows patients to begin to recover their own feelings, no longer suppressing painful or "bad" feelings for fear that these will not be accepted by the other person. The therapist's chief means of showing tolerance for the borderline patient's often intense and always changing feelings is restraint; standing still implies the safety of the session and the therapist's confidence that the tensions of the moment will pass, or in any event will not destroy anything. The therapist's calm restraint starts to create the holding environment in therapy. There is no need to say or do anything special to make this happen; the therapist's attempts to identify with the patient and to avoid destructive projections onto the patient are enough to begin the process.

It is important to realize, however, that therapists are not trying to do the same thing with the borderline patient that mothers do with their infants. Most infants can develop properly if given adequate help, if the match between mother and child is even good enough. The borderline patient, by contrast, comes to treatment already having been burned by life, already set in maladaptive and pathological patterns of experiencing self and others. There is no question, then, of the therapist's being able to take care of the patient as a mother would a child or of the therapist's being able through empathy to create an atmosphere in which the patient simply grows and develops. Rather, the therapeutic holding environment above all else must take into account the patient's inability to make use of human relationships to feel secure in the world. While normal infants are able to use the empathic mother to feel emotionally held and secure, borderline patients certainly cannot use the therapist in the same way.

In fact, it might be said that what is being held at first in the holding environment is *the therapist!* The most important task in the early months of therapy is for the therapist's self-confidence to remain intact. Borderline patients, especially noisy patients, already believe that the therapist cannot stand being with them, that they will be repulsive and eventually drive the therapist away. In the course of the first months of treatment these patients will try to demonstrate these truths. The task for therapists during this time is to preserve some faith in their own capacity to hold meaning for another person. The patient's attacks are a serious challenge to the therapist's own sense of constancy, and before anything else can happen, therapists must be able to retain their faith in their ability to offer something of value to the patient—in the future if not now.

In effect the therapeutic holding environment involves an appreciation that the patient comes with a history of negative experiences and that the first task is to provide a sanctuary, while also displaying a tolerance—within limits—for the patient's aggression and expressions of fear. The holding environment may be said to be forming when the therapist demonstrates both the capacity to preserve self-confidence against the patient's attacks and failure to improve and also the ability to preserve an attentive interest in the patient. In its simplest form it means that the therapist is glad to see the patient, that the therapist's interest has not died away, that the therapist remembers the patient, and that the relationship may continue no matter what has transpired in the past session. From the patient's point of view there is a dawning sense of safety and reliability, a conviction that "I have a right to be here." Surely it goes without saying that this takes time and many repetitions before patients actually feel confident that therapy offers the ongoing concern and understanding of a competent caretaker.

Banal and Tedious Material
with Borderline Patients

The third critical feature of the adaptive matrix is allowing the borderline patient to relate nonemotionally laden material. Entire sessions may well be taken up with the patient's filling in the therapist on the events of the past week. Therapists may (correctly) feel that there is nothing special or remarkable about the patient's productions, that the same information could just as easily be shared with a spouse or best friend. This raises a problem: Most therapists are trained to listen for the interplay between resistance and material related to the patient's pathology. When borderline patients want to tell the therapist about their daily lives following the last session, the therapist may jump to the conclusion that this is resistance, that the patient is avoiding deeper, emotionally important themes. The time used here may well seem wasteful (i.e., nontherapeutic) to the therapist, who then seeks to interpret the resistance in an attempt to get the patient to produce more workable material.

It is not usually resistance, however, for borderline patients to share the events of their week, generally beginning near the end of the first year of treatment (although with many patients it may well take several months beyond the first year). In fact, this sharing is something of an accomplishment: The patient is sharing aspects of his or her life, fully expecting the therapist to be interested, and not wanting anything from the therapist in return. Sharing of such banal material is comparable to the child or teenager who returns from school eager to relate the events of the day to an interested parent. It is therefore generally a good sign when patients are able to do this. It suggests the therapist is experienced as interested and available, and the therapist is well advised simply to sit back and listen attentively, with as much curiosity as a parent would show a child in similar circumstances. Of course, the patience of the therapist can be sorely tested, since much of this sort of material may sound inane and possibly even be boring. However, it is important for the patient to find a setting that allows for such giving and that an interested listener be present.

The therapist here must be able to distinguish when such behavior by the patient is a healthy sharing, rather than what would usually be termed resistance to anxiety-laden material. There is no easy or hard-and-fast way to make this distinction. In general, the therapist should suspect resistance only if the patient begins to relate daily events too early in treatment or if the patient appears either unusually flat emotionally or unusually agitated, like someone trying to stay distracted. If the patient begins to share daily events near the end of the first year of therapy and if the patient relates such events with his or her usual affect and in the patient's typical interpersonal style, the material is probably not in the service of resistance.

The relating of ordinary, day-to-day life events suggests that therapy is being experienced as valuable for its own sake, that the patient no longer approaches therapy with the idea that the therapist will meet his or her needs. In turn, this is one of the signs that adaptive matrix constancy is being achieved. Sessions often seem less urgent and intense, especially with noisy patients. The therapist begins to notice that the patient seems to feel more at home during sessions, and the office constitutes a world that feels predictable or reliable.

Differentiating Situations That Require Action from Events That Do Not

Earlier we spoke of the adaptive matrix as the creation of an ongoing, secure psychophysical environment. With growing confidence in the reliable continuity of a secure attachment, the borderline patient learns to experience frustration within a caring context. This is turn makes possible the binding of time, and the patient can gradually alter his or her "now is forever" orientation. As this change occurs, patients can begin to differentiate between those situations calling for action on their part and those events that do not. In Chapter 4 we discussed the borderline patient's tendency to come to therapy experiencing most problems as crises, as matters requiring immediate action. The restraint of the therapist across many such "crises" gradually broadens the patient's experience of time. Events that would have been experienced as imminent disasters earlier in treatment take on a new context; they are seen as part of much larger means–end sequences that can be endured. The patient learns to wait as the world begins to appear safer and more reliable.

Therapists may first notice this change when they observe that the patient has handled a situation differently, more calmly, than would have been the case earlier. Patients themselves may comment on this, calling it to the therapist's attention, particularly if this has been a subject of discussion in sessions over the months. Therapists may also feel less pressured or pushed by patients to come up with solutions or to provide tension relief; such a change indicates the patient's growing ability to wait out a problem. These sorts of changes indicate that adaptive matrix constancy is becoming established. Patients can learn to wait only when their time sense has been broadened, and this can happen only when the world seems more reliable.

Paradoxically, therapists may find that patients who seem to want to react to almost everything often do not know when it really is time to take action, failing to recognize genuine crises when they arise. It is part of the therapeutic task to help patients with this discrimination. Of course, the basic therapeutic posture remains one of restraint, and the basic intervention remains silence. However, there are circumstances in which the therapist must intervene. When there is a "real" crisis—one in which someone is in danger or in which there are potential long-term, adverse consequences—the therapist must respond. These fairly infrequent occasions during which the therapist intervenes stand out in contrast to the vast majority of "crises," when the therapist makes no intervention. The contrast begins to build up a system of memories that the patient can later use to distinguish situations calling for response from those that do not.

The therapist's reaction to situations that require action should be different early in treatment from what it will be after adaptive matrix constancy begins to be established. In the early months of treatment therapists should simply try to focus the patient's attention on the problem he or she is overlooking. The therapist should use questions, clarifications, and confrontations to make the patient look at the problem, avoiding directly telling the patient what to do. The reason for avoiding direct advice even in a genuine crisis is the likelihood the patient will not comply with that advice; it is therefore preferable to point the patient toward a solution, avoiding a power struggle. Only in the event that someone's physical well-being appears to be in jeopardy should the therapist directly tell the patient what to do. Even then the therapist should try to put the intervention in if-then terms, pointing out to patients the likely consequences of their actions. In essence this amounts to putting interventions in an ego psychology framework, focusing on what will be needed if the patient is to cope with reality; such a focus enables the therapist to sidestep the patient's attempts to enter a power struggle.

For example, one teenage mother told her therapist of spanking her child so hard that it left marks. Part of the problem was that the mother tended to discipline the child when she was so angry that she could barely control herself, rather than sending the child to his room and waiting until she calmed down somewhat. Her therapist told her she had to stop spanking her son while she was so angry "or else [her caseworker] will have to press charges against you. You could wind up in jail, and they will certainly take the boy away from you." When the patient became angry and defiant, virtually inviting the therapist to "make me stop spanking him," the therapist avoided an unfruitful struggle by repeatedly returning to the unwanted consequence of the patient's behavior: "You know what the deal is. You can spank the kid while you're furious, or you can wait to calm down. If you don't calm down, you will lose the child and probably wind up in jail. However, it's your choice."

Another patient complained to her therapist that her husband had resumed using hard drugs. The therapist asked if the husband was using drugs intravenously, and the woman replied that he was. When the therapist asked if she had any thoughts about the possibility of getting AIDS if she had sexual relations with him, the patient minimized the danger and clearly did not want to think about the matter. When it became clear the woman was unwilling to face the issue, the therapist told her directly that she should not have sexual relations with the husband until he had stopped IV drug use and had obtained a negative HIV test, pointing out that if she contracted the disease and could no longer care for her children, they would undoubtedly be placed in the care of her mother, who was a brutal and sadistic woman. The patient, who hated her mother, was able to consider the problem when it was placed in this context, and she took appropriate steps.

When the therapeutic relationship is further advanced, therapists can actually be more direct with the patient when a genuine crisis arises, occasionally even insisting on what response they believe the patient should make. There are several reasons why therapists can get away with being direct later in treatment but cannot afford to do it earlier. First, therapists cannot afford to suggest a course of action until it is clear to the patient that they can bear the patient's tension, that they are not being stampeded into action by the patient's sense of urgency. Second, therapists cannot directly recommend courses of action at the start of therapy without gratifying the patient's sense of entitlement; the patient, after all, demands a response from the therapist early in treatment, and a response simply reinforces the demandingness. Paradoxically, the therapist should make a direct response only after the patient no longer demands it.

An example of a situation in which the therapist directly intervened, insisting on a course of action, was that of a 37-year-old divorcée who had been seen for over a year and who had gradually come to learn that the crises in her life were usually quite manageable once she no longer experienced them as requiring urgent action. In the course of one session she had been describing in a rather flat, resigned tone how her relationship with a teenage daughter was becoming destructive physically and emotionally for both of them. She related that the night before the session her daughter had threatened her with a knife, and it was plain the patient expected more physically dangerous altercations. The patient's depressed resignation in this session was in marked contrast with the way she presented material at the outset of therapy. At that time she had come into the room dramatically holding her stomach, complaining loudly that she was "sick from worry." At that time the worry concerned meeting "someone wonderful" who "took my number and promised to call." She would then spend the session worrying if she should have "gone to bed with the guy" or in other instances whether she should not have done so. She was forever wondering if she was "getting a line," and while she tried to sound cynical and wary, there was an equally strong urge to believe that each man was "Mr. Right." At these times she demanded the therapist advise her what she should do, feeling panicked and desperate when he would not.

In the session under discussion, the tone was entirely different. The patient sounded discouraged and resigned, and there was a sense that she felt trapped. In many previous sessions the patient had bitterly complained about the daughter's behavior and the arguments that ensued. Noteworthy even then was the fact that she did not ask the therapist to resolve the situation. In this session she sounded as if she had reached the exhaustion stage described by Selye (1956) in his studies of stress and formulation of the general adaptation syndrome. In her flat-toned discussion of the situation she was able to articulate that she felt "stuck" with the child and, more importantly, felt guilty for wanting to be separated from her.

The therapist grew concerned at the physical danger to the patient and also at the patient's obvious inability to handle the problem. Accordingly, the therapist decided to insist that the daughter move to her father's home. This stance came as a surprise and initially evoked much ambivalence. Gradually, over a period of four weeks, this ambivalence was resolved: the patient came to see the therapist as concerned with her well-being; as aware of the pros and cons of the child's father as a parent; and, most critical, as not judging her as an inadequate or "bad" mother. In turn this relieved her exaggerated sense of guilt, since the therapist as an authority on parent–child relationships was taking responsibility for the proposed action; furthermore, it offered the patient some armor against the anticipated criticism from her parents and ex-husband.

Once the daughter moved, the patient found they (mother and daughter) each could feel more relaxed, both when they were together and apart. It should be noted that the therapist considered having the daughter join her mother for a joint session, but this option was rejected because it was felt that one or both might feel they were being punished if a final decision still resulted in the daughter leaving home. In this case example, the feature to be noted is that the patient learned that the therapist had the ability to discriminate between what might require action as distinct from what doesn't. This allowed the patient to see how perspectives might develop, thereby alleviating the pressure of an all-or-none response, learning in effect that one is not automatically trapped and that options do exist.

It may seem odd for us to suggest that there are times when the therapist should try to direct the borderline patient's behavior, whether through the ego-supportive interventions we recommend for the earliest months of treatment or through the overt directions we recommend for use later in the preconstancy stage. After all, we have repeatedly counseled the therapist to stand still and show restraint when working with this patient population. It may be helpful to say, then, that the purpose of standing still with the borderline patient is to create an atmosphere in which a lasting attachment can unfold, correcting the patient's assumption that tension reduction is the sole basis for relationships. The gradual creation of such an attachment in itself begins to broaden the patient's time sense and allows for many more gradations of experience than were previously possible. Thus the purpose of directing the patient's behavior in a real crisis is not to reduce the therapist's tension, nor even to reduce the patient's tensions. It is, rather, to create further gradations or discriminations for the patient and is therefore not at odds with the basic, restrained stance we advocate.

When borderline patients begin to value therapy for its own sake and no longer see the therapist as someone whose job is to make them feel better, and when they begin to lose their earlier sense of urgency when faced with a problem, therapists should realize that adaptive matrix constancy is being established. At this point therapists should begin to listen for themes associated with the next stage of constancy, the task of differentiating self from other.

8

Differentiating Constancy

The Desire to Eliminate Differences

Kierkegaard once wrote that the early days of romance were the finest, the days when feelings were most intense, when lovers felt most alive and pathos was at its peak. Most persons can grasp his meaning and conjure an image (or a memory) of young lovers gazing adoringly into one another's eyes, intensely interested in and excited by one another and thrilled beyond words. Of course, these days do not last forever, and most couples move on to something more mundane but also more durable. This movement from the ardent pursuit of emotional union evolves into a gradual acceptance of the other's freedom and independence. In the process couples accept variability in the intensity and content of the relationship and may even find that these enrich the relationship.

Borderline patients seem to struggle against this evolutionary process. They are forever trying to maintain *throughout* a relationship what young lovers experience at the *outset*. Hav-

239

ing once felt a sense of magical unity, the borderline patient seeks to maintain the feeling and finds variability and differences to be threatening. This is not to say that borderline patients have no capacity for boundaries or that they always deny the separateness of others. In most situations—for example, work or casual social interactions—these patients are able to recognize and accept that those around them have separate interests, wishes, and intentions. It is only in intimate relationships that they are driven to intense closeness and seek to maintain it without a letup. Or as one therapist said of borderline patients, "When they first meet you, of course they know you're different from them, but by the end of the first date they may well have forgotten."

The literature often refers to the borderline patient's loss of boundaries, and one might assume (mistakenly, from our point of view) that this process occurs without the patient's consent or intent, that it just happens to the patient. We do not believe this is an accurate way to describe the matter. Rather, we believe that borderline patients may be more properly said to will an elimination of boundaries. This is not to say that there is a conscious, preplanned, deliberate decision, only that borderline individuals are ever open to the possibility: In potentially intimate relationships they interact with others in ways that blur boundaries, thereby producing, for a while, the illusion of closeness.

By remaining so intensely focused on obtaining a magical unity, borderline patients close themselves off to other possibilities. Ironically, some of these ignored possibilities are among those that would in fact cement and further genuine closeness, such as appreciating the other's uniqueness or discovering that time spent away from the other person can heighten the pleasure of reunion. While borderline patients can certainly accept that loved ones have different interests or that they must spend time away from them—for instance, at work—they tend to view these differences and absences as intrusions into the unity they might otherwise be enjoying or even as occasions for doubting whether the loved one will return. This undermines their confidence in the relationship, while it could just as easily have increased the joy of coming back together.

In their quest for timeless harmony in intimate relationships, borderline individuals tend to operate with a kind of tunnel vision. What they see at the end of the tunnel is an idealized image of the other person, an image they have created, of course. They expect the other person to welcome this idealization, thereby providing the opportunity for merger. Idealization restricts the range of emotion that can be experienced with loved ones (thereby contributing to the patient's all-or-none tendencies); chiefly, there are two options, euphoria and despair. Euphoria occurs when the loved one appears to accept the idealization—the patient then feels special, having attained merger with a flawless object. Despair, by contrast, follows the other's failure to accept or live up to the idealization.

The loss of idealization and the merger fantasies associated with it are traumatic for borderline patients, returning them to a state of terrifying aloneness. Idealizations are often lost when patients are forced into the awareness that the other person feels differently than they do or even that the other's feelings are not as intense as their own. One patient, for example, felt rejected whenever his wife was not as turned on during sex as he was. It was not enough for her to be receptive and loving; if she failed to experience an orgasm he felt "the magic's gone," and truly believed it must only be a matter of time until his wife began to have affairs and eventually divorce him. He would go so far as to begin to seek jobs in other parts of the country whenever he failed to make her come. He experienced her occasional disinterest in sex as a betrayal and was determined to "get out before she does." His tunnel vision kept him from seeing the affection implied by her being receptive even when she wasn't as aroused as he was.

When forced to recognize differences from significant others, borderline patients display a curious paradox. On the one hand, they can become remarkably hypersensitive to any sign that the other feels differently than they do, and they seem to go out of their way to uncover such signs for fear of being surprised and betrayed. At other times, however, they can be quite insensitive to differences, or even to the possibility that there might be differences. In this state of mind they simply deny or avoid seeing differences that are obvious to everyone else, in an apparent effort to preserve their idealization. It is our impression that insensitivity and hypersensitivity to differences appear to be opposite sides of the same coin, the former coming from the desire for merger and the latter coming from the patient's fear/expectation of abandonment. Either can be figural at any time, and certainly both will be prominently displayed during relationships. The important point to keep in mind is that both come from an unrealistic desire to maintain closeness without a break once such closeness has been experienced and from an equally unrealistic fear that any difference is a threat to closeness.

Individuals who feel this way suffer two problems. First, they cannot be comfortable with any sign that the other person fails to share their intentions, wishes, and feelings, and second, they never get the chance to experience moderate, middle-range affect. They are faced with the impossible task of preserving a degree of closeness that is more illusory than real, more built on their own wishes than on actuality, and therefore unstable. When the relationship settles down and enters a period of less intensity (as relationships normally do), borderline patients feel they are losing the other person and are gripped with fears of abandonment. Thus they can never relax with the other person or with themselves; their feelings are extreme no matter what the state of the relationship: If there is conflict, borderline patients are in despair; if there is closeness, they are euphoric; if there is some middle state between intimacy and distance, they see only the loss of closeness and either feel abandoned or become painfully bored and impatient for someone to excite them.

The task of therapy, therefore, is to teach borderline patients various discriminations, including both self-other differentiation and discrimination among different feelings. This task cannot be deliberately addressed before the later stages of the preconstancy phase of treatment. When dealing with differentiation issues, therapists should adhere to the basic approach of standing still until they see evidence that adaptive matrix constancy is being established. Only then should they modify this basic stance and begin deliberately to address what might be termed boundary setting and maintenance (Federn 1952).

The therapist's restraint has in fact already begun to address the borderline patient's unstable boundaries and lack of discriminations. When therapists refuse to panic, give advice, or try to ease patients' distress in the first months of treatment, they lay a foundation for differentiating between those events that might call for extreme emotional responses and those that do not. This experience gradually builds up some capacity for more modulated affect. The basic approach of standing still during this time also helps establish boundaries; whenever it is clear that the therapist feels differently than the patient, it also becomes clearer that these two people *are* different. After all, many of the tense periods experienced in the first months of therapy stem from patients' anger and sadness at feeling distant from the therapist when they had hoped to eliminate distance. This happens even though the therapist has really done nothing to emphasize separateness during the first months of treatment. Therefore, the basic approach of standing still establishes a foundation for further work on differentiation; in the later periods of the preconstancy stage it is time to build on this foundation.

Teaching Patients a Differentiating Language

To tolerate separateness, borderline patients must first be helped to grasp and retain their own unique and individual experience of the world. They cannot be expected to embrace separateness until they are able to represent, and therefore preserve and place in perspective, their own distinct experience of self and other. Language is the means by which we do this. In contrast to the momentary and ever-changing nature of moods and feelings, language provides an enduring structure for experience. Consequently a language that acknowledges—and thereby creates—gradations of feelings allows patients to bind time and transcend the feelings of the moment. In turn, transcendence allows patients to develop a sense of what is transitory and also what continues: In contrast to their shifting and changing feelings, they are able to experience an abiding core of sameness, or a center of intention and observation that is constant across the changing emotional landscape. Of course, this is part of what we mean by the term "self."

The self may be conceived in part as a linguistic device through which we define and delineate ourselves. Borderline patients tend to use a language that reflects an inner world filled with tension and urgency. Noisy borderline patients in particular typically use evocative language (Stierlin 1969) comprised of superlatives and affectively charged images. By necessity, this is a dramatic language and tends to be loose and circumstantial. The patient does not simply apprehend affect when using evocative language; rather, this language leads the patient to feel swept away. Overreliance on such extreme terms as "horrible," "never," and "miserable" can lead patients to experience situations as crises when in fact they are merely troublesome.

If we imagine ourselves in the place of the patient, we can see how easily impulsive action can follow when the patient is upset. A language that, as Stierlin (1969) says, must "lose in precision what it wins in color" (p. 67), leads every problem to seem awesome. Patients are simply captured by a global feeling of urgency and distress, and details that might mitigate this sense remain unrepresented. As patients develop a vocabulary that provides for precision and gradation, action becomes less an automatic and imperative response and more a matter for deliberation. Interestingly, patients tend to change their fantasy life as this process develops. For example, as one woman became able to assess and label her feelings more carefully, she found herself less prone to think of others as magical answers to her needs and also less anxious that she might displease someone and be abandoned.

In contrast to the evocative language of the noisy patient, the quiet, as-if type of patient tends to use a propositional language based on abstraction. Such an overly controlled, affectively arid language is designed to gain distance from particular types of experience. Even though the abstract nature of such language can make it appear that these patients are able to make appropriate distinctions, or even that they differentiate themselves from others, the actual intent of their language is to become detached from the shared world of other persons. They do not differentiate self from other as much as they isolate themselves from the impact of others.

In this case, language is being used to allay anxiety, especially the anxiety of object loss, separation, and abandonment. A high price is paid for this form of adaptation: The patient splits off everything that is potentially disappointing, frustrating, or disillusioning, and so a great part of the emotional life is jettisoned. Such patients typically complain, as did one young woman who had taken care of a psychotic mother, alcoholic father, and four siblings since age six, "I'm just going through the motions; I don't feel like I'm really 'there' no matter who I'm with or what I'm doing." Such patients frequently have a stiff, wooden appearance—like their language. Their attempt at not needing anyone entails a self-image that is not solidly embodied and gives them an automaton or robotlike appearance.

The task of therapy is similar with both the noisy and the as-if borderline patient. In both cases the therapist must teach the patient a new, differentiating language. Borderline patients need to grasp and develop many more varieties of affective experience than they bring to treatment, distinguishing among related but different affect states. This does not mean that therapists simply teach patients new words to describe their feelings. Noisy borderline patients will not be impressed by a therapist who tries to effect gradations of feelings by pointing out that the patient is using the wrong word, that the patient is perhaps irritated rather than angry, for example. Such an effort by the therapist would lead, at best, to an attack by the patient for not understanding and, at worst, might lead the patient to see the therapist as superficial and irrelevant. Quieter, as-if types of patients might very well try to accommodate the therapist by learning new words and rigorously applying the new terms as they think the therapist applies them. But the effort is, like as-if patients themselves, an act, a matter of going through the motions to conform with what the other (in this case, the therapist) seems to expect. It is not at all adequate, then, simply to suggest new words as a means of teaching the varieties of emotional experience.

The means by which patients will learn a differentiating language is experiential: patients learn to differentiate affects by seeing the therapist do it in their presence. As mentioned, the therapeutic posture of standing still accomplishes much of this. Patients slowly learn to distinguish crises from mere problems by seeing that the therapist usually does not respond with any urgency or tension to the patient's complaints, and also by noting that there are some exceptions. Occasional re-marks to the effect that the patient has overreacted or that the patient panics too quickly also contribute. As one patient put it, "I used to panic whenever I got scared about something. Now I think of you telling me it's natural for people to feel uneasy or frustrated at times and that I should save my panic for an earthquake." The key, however, is not *what* the therapist says to the patient but that the emotions being discussed are or have been present in the session. The key part of teaching grada-tions among different affect states is that therapists confront a troublesome situation with the patient and show—often merely by their restraint—that they experience the matter differently from the patient.

Therapists may challenge the patient's overreliance on evoc-ative language through questioning what the patient says. If patients, for instance, say they feel just terrible, the therapist may ask what that means and continue to ask until the patient begins to compare and contrast what is felt with other expe-riences. Borderline patients often become irritated by such questions and hope to blur distinctions implied by the therapist's inquiries. When pressed, they may complain that the therapist is treating them like kindergarten children, to which therapists may legitimately reply that kindergarten children usually already know the distinctions they are trying to teach the patient.

One patient began a session by saying a job interview had been "just horrible—I never ever want to go through that again" but seemed unable or unwilling to describe what had actually occurred, simply repeating that it was horrible. The therapist then asked her to hold her arm behind her back, and when she said that was uncomfortable, he asked whether that was the same as how the interview felt. The patient was not sure but thought it felt different, and this led to further distinctions. Eventually the patient realized that she had apparently applied for a job that was beyond her training and had felt exposed and humiliated in the interview; she had almost felt raped during the interview, in fact, which in turn reminded her of sexual abuse she had experienced as a child. Her reliance on evocative language helped her avoid having to struggle with such uncomfortable recollections and associated feelings of helplessness.

The therapist is basically trying to draw on the patient's own memory, creating distinctions and gradations in the process. Therapists should help patients compare and contrast current experiences with similar experiences in the past, effecting a framework for more closely defining and evaluating what is happening. This process draws on evocative memory, so it is not a process that can be begun early in therapy. Until object constancy is beginning to become established, evocative memory will not be reliably available to borderline patients. Even in the late stages of the preconstancy phase of treatment, therapists must be prepared to supplement the patient's memory with their own, offering examples from the patient's own behavior that can be used for comparison.

For example, a patient often described arguments with her

husband by saying, with obvious guilt and embarrassment, "I lost control." At the start of treatment, this meant that she grew intensely angry, began to scream hysterically at her husband, and often that she physically attacked him. Even though the patient's behavior during arguments became much less extreme and intense near the end of the first year of treatment, she continued to refer to arguments by saying that she had lost control of herself. It was clear that she experienced these conflicts as though she had screamed hysterically and fought with her husband, even though in fact she seldom did that anymore. The therapist began to explore what actually went on, pointing out the differences with earlier, more violent arguments. At first the patient had trouble seeing that there were differences and needed the therapist to point them out. Gradually, however, the patient was able spontaneously to contrast her behavior with earlier conflicts. As she grew able to see the differences between her earlier and present behaviors, she became correspondingly less guilt-ridden about arguments; in turn this made it easier for her to take them in stride and experience these conflicts more moderately.

Therapists must focus on their own use of language if they are to change the language of their as-if patients. In particular, therapists should go out of their way to use words related to the body, to bodily needs and functions. Therapists should be comfortable using emotionally laden terms, phrases that shock and arouse. The idea is to demonstrate controlled spontaneity, and this can take the form of using slang or "dirty" words, clapping hands together for emphasis, and using body movements. These interventions typically surprise the as-if patient and make some impact by virtue of their very intrusiveness. For a long time these patients may not quite know what to make of the therapist's language, but they do seem to notice.

For example, one patient described his experience: "I used to think your language was crude and vulgar. Then one day when I was talking with my mother and she was going on as usual about what was wrong with me, I could hear that expression you use with me, 'That's a crock of shit,' and I smiled at the thought of saying that to my mother and you laughing in approval." For another example, one as-if patient was having trouble with the therapist's description of her mother as intrusive and controlling, in spite of the fact that she felt trapped and uncomfortable every time she was with her mother. As the patient defended her mother against the charge of intrusiveness, the therapist gradually leaned toward her until he was only a few inches from her face. The patient was agitated, and the therapist asked if she were uncomfortable. Not wanting to complain, the patient replied that she felt confused, and the therapist asked if she had ever felt confused like that before. There was a smile of recognition and a spontaneous laugh (unusual for this patient) as she said, "Maybe last night," and added that she had been at her mother's house the previous evening. In this case body movements had helped the patient make a connection she had been resisting.

There are times when therapists will need to teach patients to label their feelings more appropriately—though again we want to emphasize that it is never sufficient for therapists simply to suggest new words for differing affect states. Nonetheless, therapists will notice that patients sometimes show one emotion when in fact they seem to be feeling another, and it can be helpful to point this out. One patient, for instance, became angry with his wife whenever he was worried. The therapist pointed this out and found that he had to teach the patient the difference between anxiety (a global fear), worry (a focused fear), and anger (a symbolic form of action designed to hide the feeling of impotence). Once it became established that "real men" could have fears and not always be "on top of things," the patient became better able to acknowledge these feelings and express them both more clearly and more appropriately. The same principle applies to positive feelings. The therapist must sometimes help patients establish criteria for applying different labels to different feelings. This process can be useful when it takes place late in the preconstancy stage, in the context of other tasks associated with differentiating constancy.

Differentiation among feeling states remains difficult for borderline patients throughout therapy. Nevertheless, the process does unfold, and we see patients gradually replace their earlier, all-or-none mode of affect. As a result, patients begin to display an inner world that is more enriched, and the interpersonal world, too, comes to be experienced with more options and variations. These changes contribute to the capacity to differentiate self from other. As with the task of differentiating among separate feelings, self–other distinctions are likely to be troublesome for borderline patients throughout treatment. But the fact is that elaboration of the inner world begins to modify the secret hope for oneness. Fusion fantasies tend to rest on the sense that the self is empty and needs merger with an other to be filled. As the patient feels more substantial, as it were, fantasies of oneness become harder to maintain.

Differentiating Self from Other

In dealing with the patient's projections and projective identifications, it falls to the therapist to establish the differentiation between "me" and "not me" and yet remain sensitive to when and how differentiating interventions are most appropriate. As discussed in Chapter 6, separateness is threatening to borderline patients, who do not easily tolerate the differences that distinguish them from loved ones. Even when therapists are not trying to emphasize boundaries but are merely behaving with restraint, patients will often feel rejected and abandoned. Consequently, therapists must use good judgment in deciding when to emphasize boundaries; if delayed too long, patients may become more firmly enmeshed in still another fused relationship, but if done too early, the patient may be too threatened to tolerate separateness. There is probably no time when borderline patients will welcome the subject; there are simply some times that are better than others. Certainly there must be a fairly solid therapeutic relationship, which means that these interventions should not be attempted until late in the preconstancy phase.

Borderline patients typically respond to these interventions with perplexity at first and then with either anger and depression or relief. Patients will probably become angry and withdrawn when they have idealized the therapist and find that their idealization does not lead to pleasure on the therapist's part or to heightened closeness. If, on the other hand, patients have engaged in projective identification, the response may well be one of relief. For example, patients who have identified with an angry, disappointed, or critical attitude they have projected onto the therapist may experience themselves as deserving objects of these attitudes. They may then be relieved to discover that the therapist does not feel what they had imagined and that no punishment is in the offing. The exact form of the patient's response, then, depends on whether the therapist's intervention was in reaction to a projective identification or to an idealization.

The key to handling such interactions is to focus on what patients are doing to themselves in their projective identifications and idealizations. For example, patients may devalue themselves to put the therapist on a pedestal, thus attributing an omnipotence with which they can identify. Clearly this is a difficult situation to untangle, and the therapist must find some way to sort out the realities of the matter in a way the patient can "hear." Borderline patients are primed to experience the therapist's refusal of their idealization as a personal rejection. They will feel that they have offered something to the therapist and that this gift was rebuffed.

In this situation, therapists sometimes resort to self-disclosures about their actual limitations, apparently hoping that the patient will be better able to accept this way of refusing the idealization. That approach is a mistake. The emphasis should remain on what patients imply about themselves, in this case on the denial of their own capacities and the way in which this denial avoids the experience of separateness and maintains the magical hope for oneness. In addressing idealizations and projective identifications, therapists must remember the lessons taught us by the object relations theorists (e.g., Dorpat 1981): there is no image of the other without a corresponding image of the self. When therapists hope to undermine how the patient sees them, they should start by articulating the patient's corresponding self-image.

For example, one borderline patient well into her second year of treatment had been furious with her therapist for over a month after he tried to place a limit on potentially self-destructive behavior. For six sessions the patient spent most of her time in vicious attacks, degrading him in every way she could think of, questioning his technique and even his ethics. The therapist found that his most useful intervention as this conflict was gradually resolved was to point out that the patient made herself into a thoroughly righteous, wounded victim, hopelessly trying to fight off an omnipotent oppressor, which he referred to as an "Antigone complex." He observed that this kept the patient from even having to examine whether her behavior had been dangerous, much less change it. As long as this patient could see herself as powerless, she had no responsibility for what she did and could experience herself as an extension of the therapist's actions.

The same principles should guide therapists when they examine the patient's relationships outside therapy. They ought not focus on whether a patient's image of a lover, child, or boss is accurate but rather on what patients imply about themselves when they idealize a lover or experience their boss as "out to get me." One patient consistently experienced all authorities as about to turn on her and punish her, and she badly distorted many experiences as a result. A dramatic instance of this occurred when her child had been kidnapped by a relative; the patient actually believed that the police who came to help her would probably help the kidnapper instead because "they would see that my house was so messy." For weeks after her child had been returned, she fully expected the police to come back suddenly and snatch the child away from her. The therapist repeatedly pointed out to her the way she distorted policemen, supervisors, and even bank tellers, but these confrontations made no discernible impact. The patient was not able to modify her distortions until the therapist began to point out that the patient experienced herself as helpless, misunderstood, and about to be taken advantage of by all of these people, entirely forgetting her very real competencies. It seemed to surprise the patient that others might in fact be able to see her competencies (she feared all they could see was her messes), and she felt relieved even to consider the possibility.

These interventions may not appear directly related to creating boundaries or establishing self-other differentiations, but they are. These interventions try to replace rigid, inflexible idealizations and projective identifications with more realistic self-other images. Whenever patients experience themselves in more adaptive and realistic ways, they automatically differentiate themselves from other people—they are better defined and more substantial, and this in itself makes it more difficult to feel empty enough to fuse with an other.

Another important avenue for differentiation is any issue related to the body and to gender identity. Many borderline patients have no sense of "owning" a body and so do not experience their body as "mine." These patients may engage in reckless and dangerous sexual liaisons or destructive drug use and yet not feel alarmed. There is no anxiety, because there is little sense that the body that is having these experiences is "me" or "mine." One young woman repeatedly picked up strangers in bars and had been raped and beaten on more than one occasion; she was, however, relatively unconcerned with this and seemed detached from the whole experience, as if it had happened to someone else. In a way, it had—she was trying, like many borderline patients—to disown her body, viewing it as a concrete symbol of her "badness." Borderline patients often use dissociation and/or psychosomatic ailments in their efforts to avoid the experience of being embodied.

Thus a critical part of differentiating constancy becomes helping patients recognize their ambivalence over the value of the body and their reluctance to stake a claim to it. The latter is necessary for identity formation. After all, one must establish "that I am" before proceeding to the question of "who I am" (Lichtenstein 1976). One patient with a history of sexual and alcohol excesses described her dilemma: "People are only interested in my body and how they can get at it. I think a lot about what would happen if I didn't have it." This woman tried to make herself into a kind of sexual robot: She was orgasmic, demonstrated a wide variety of sexual techniques, and to all appearances was completely uninhibited; yet she never experienced herself as personally involved and said, "It is just my body that gets excited." Often she would add, "Maybe I should be one of those women who make films for Masters and Johnson, because I know how to get 'lubed up' real good."

Early in her second year of treatment, this patient raised the question of whether she would become more inhibited during sex if she ever believed that a man really cared for her. The timing of this question was significant; the patient was in the midst of developing a separate sense of self, and with her dawning sense of separateness she was beginning to feel that "this body is mine." As she felt more physically real, she gradually became disenchanted with her various sexual experiences and began to present a series of physical complaints to the therapist. The issue was quite clear: "Can someone care about me when my body hurts and isn't performing?"

In addition to addressing patients' idealizations, projective identifications, and issues related to bodily reality, therapists may also emphasize differentiation by simply pointing out that they see things differently than the patient. Borderline patients often become angry at such remarks, even if the therapist's differing perspective is complimentary to the patient! In such cases, the patient is clearly responding to what might be called the metalevel of the therapist's intervention. Even though the content of the remark seems favorable to the patient, the underlying implication is that "You and I are separate," a communication that is threatening to the patient.

Therapists are not always sensitive to the fact that they have imposed a genuine frustration on the patient when they highlight differentiation. There is a kind of existential guilt that therapists must accept, the guilt of having caused the patient's distress, even though the distress was necessary. Thus therapists should reflect back to patients that their rage or depressive withdrawal is *legitimate* and that the frustration felt by the patient is in fact universal. Without such an acknowledgment, borderline patients will be tempted to experience their frustration as a punishment for some unacceptable wish or action. Therapists must accept responsibility for being the "bearer of bad news"; this helps patients discover that they have the right to feel bad when life has frustrated them.

For example, one patient in the latter stages of the preconstancy phase started a session by complaining that she had tried all weekend to call the therapist but had been unable to reach him (apparently due to problems with his answering service). She said she had had no one to be with Saturday evening and that this had made her lonely and about to panic. As it happened, the therapist had also been alone that Saturday night and was not sure that the patient's plight was any worse than his own. He thought about telling the patient to read a magazine, watch some television, or take a shower—to pass the time like that, but decided such a response came more from his own resentments of the patient's complaining than an interest in confronting her unnecessary panic.

The therapist therefore decided to explore the merger fantasy the patient had probably been acting on and asked what she had expected to happen when she tried to call. She replied that she thought they would spend the evening just talking together and that way she would not have to be alone. The therapist replied that he would not have done this, that it would have intruded too much into his private life. The patient was visibly taken aback at this indication of boundaries where she had expected none. She became saddened and withdrawn, and this depressive tone hovered over treatment for many sessions. The therapist acknowledged the patient's right to feel depressed and did not try to interpret or remedy her sadness, simply accepting it as a natural part of giving up a cherished illusion.

This example illustrates the way in which differentiating interventions cause distress to patients. Such distress occurs in normal development, of course, when parents demonstrate to the young child that their wishes and interests differ from the child's. The best-known example of this is probably the parents' refusal to indulge the young child's oedipal wishes and the child's corresponding "grand disillusionment" (Cameron 1963), a healthy depression that creates appropriate generational boundaries. Such distress and depression seem worse, however, when patients must accomplish in adulthood what they were not able to do in childhood, and therapists must realize that they are engaged in a necessary but painful process when they use differentiating interventions.

The Problem of Pseudoindividuation

One of the most difficult tasks for the therapist arises when borderline patients first begin to make use of a differentiating language. The therapist must decide whether patients are actually accepting a greater degree of individuation or whether they are making use of an as-if adaptation. In the latter case, the apparently more differentiating language represents a pseudo-individuation that is essentially withdrawal into an autistic-like state. Blanck and Blanck (1974) have described this as "precocious ego development," a premature attempt at self-sufficiency designed to replace a symbiotic attachment that has proven too frustrating or threatening. Stierlin (1969) describes the process in some detail, observing that precocious individuation is a highly specialized structure with little flexibility for change, expansion, or adaptation to any sort of relationship except a symbiotic one. Premature self-sufficiency creates an emotional climate of "silent despair, frustration and autistic unconcern. It

259

results in a living parallel to, but not with, one another"
(p. 28). As-if patients bring this form of adaptation with them
into therapy, of course, but noisy patients may resort to it when
they fear loss of closeness with the therapist.

Dealing with patients who show a pseudoindividuation can
be taxing. These patients have usually received considerable
praise for the appearance of self-sufficiency and will expect the
therapist also to encourage them to take care of themselves.
Additionally, such patients will be wary of depending on someone and being cut off again before they are ready to let loose of
the dependency. Most such patients grew up with parents who
either did not want to bother with the child's neediness or were
themselves so needy that the child had to take care of them. In
either case, dependency and neediness came to feel dangerous
and eventually ego-alien to these patients, who mastered the
fine art of looking much better than they felt.

One patient described this issue in poignant terms. "All my
life I've tried to take care of myself. When I was little, it was
like there was a younger kid I had to take care of because no one
else wanted to, and my mother was too sick to do it. It was like
it was my job to keep this kid quiet so we wouldn't bother
people and get into trouble. I hated needing to go to anyone for
anything—like I should have known how to take care of things
by myself. Until I came here I never thought I'd be able to say
out loud, 'I don't know how' or ask someone for a favor without
the sky falling down." This statement was made after almost
two years of therapy. The patient had gradually come to recognize how premature development of certain skills was a neces-
ary solution at that time of his life but created certain problems
for him as an adult. He had earlier tearfully described his
growing attachment to the therapist and the anger he felt at
himself for being so dependent. This was shortly followed by
growing anxiety and by a projective identification that the
therapist saw him as a bother. In turn this led to paranoid
accusations that the therapist was trying to "cloud my mind"

and leave him in a state in which "I won't be able to take care of myself." The therapist was careful not to react in a defensive manner to these accusations. It can be tempting in such a situation to disclaim responsibility for what is happening or, as would be appropriate with a neurotic patient, to offer an interpretation. However, the therapist patiently provided feedback that he did not see the situation as dangerous, even though the patient did, and this helped eventually to firm up appropriate boundaries.

Patients showing precocious ego development tend to believe they will have value for other persons to the extent that they do not want anything. There is, thus, a paradox to be confronted when dealing with these patients: They hope the other will love them if they want nothing from them; therefore their seeming independence masks the hope that they will please the other person and be accepted. Whereas many patients appear dependent on the therapist early in treatment and must gradually be weaned away from such a stance, patients suffering premature self-sufficiency must be led to genuine dependency, and this will not occur early. A painful part of therapy comes when the therapist confronts the patient on this point. The patient must come to see that his or her premature self-sufficiency is a very limited way of coping with the world, an adaptation designed to confront a situation encountered in childhood but not very well able to adapt to the larger, adult world. The painful part of the process is the therapist's highlighting the patient's limitations. Whereas these patients present themselves as able to take care of themselves, the therapist must expose this as inaccurate; they can care for themselves only in a very limited fashion. Patients must come to see that in their limited self-sufficiency, there are many areas in which they need help.

This approach will run counter to the patient's narcissism. Patients showing premature self-sufficiency generally completed childhood without losing infantile omnipotence. Most children have many frustrations and disappointments that disabuse them early of the notion that they already know all they need to know or have mastered all the tasks of living. Part of this disillusionment, of course, is the discovery that there are others (the parents) who seem to know more and who are willing both to teach and to care for the child as maturity is reached. By contrast, children who become precociously independent are hardly encouraged to look to the parents for support and guidance; rather, they are praised for not needing these things, and they are therefore allowed to retain the grandiose illusion that they already can manage life on their own.

As a result, patients who show premature self-sufficiency overvalue their abilities and accomplishments. They are not fully in touch with reality in this regard and may wonder, for example, at a spouse's complaints against their limitations. Faced with a contradiction between what they consider to be their own abilities and the way others experience them, they are truly confused and virtually impotent to make changes. Denying their limitations, or, at best, the significance of those limitations, they cannot learn from their mistakes or make the changes others request. The therapist's task is to throw a spotlight on the limits of the patient's competence, emphasizing that the patient's abilities are not at all as profound as the patient, under the influence of infantile omnipotence, had thought. This will be difficult for patients, of course, who fear abandonment whenever their "weaknesses" are exposed.

These patients not only overvalue their abilities but also tend to hold themselves to overly high standards. They have a very hard time asking for help, admitting they cannot accomplish an assigned task, or doing anything else that reveals an inability to care for themselves. Therapists may feel sad for patients who are unaware that others are willing to lend a hand, that relationships can be mutual, or that they do not have to carry the load by themselves. In effect these patients must learn to expect less of themselves, not to gauge their success by unrealistically high standards. Paradoxically, they cannot learn to accomplish more until they learn first to accept less from themselves. (All of this, of course, is in sharp contrast to borderline patients who avoid the experience of competence to coerce others to be responsible for them [Kroll 1988].)

One patient showing premature self-sufficiency had managed to surround himself with people who were excessively clinging and dependent. This sad fact came home to him when he suffered a serious illness and was hospitalized; he was upset to find that his family, one after another, came to visit and seemed preoccupied with how hard a time *they* were having without him to care for them. His wife collapsed weeping and plaintively asked when he would be able to come back home to provide for her. Similarly his sister told him he must "get out of here soon and get back home—the whole family is collapsing without you." While the patient did not let his family know that these demands bothered him, he complained to his therapist, saying that everyone expected him to carry the whole load, as always.

The therapist tried to make plain that the patient was himself "buying into" the family's demands. He pointed out that being needed provided his only sure means of being connected to others. The patient could not imagine anyone's not needing him and believed they could not manage for long without his money or emotional support. The therapist asked what the patient imagined he (the therapist) would need from him. When the patient could not imagine anything, the therapist pointed out that he had surrounded himself with people who matched his expectations. The therapist went on to ask what the patient would do with a wife who was able to support herself financially and who was comfortable being by herself. As the therapist described a hypothetical scene in which the wife was comfortable sitting quietly in the evening, reading a book, the patient began to weep. Exploration of the patient's sadness revealed that he thought such a scene was not attainable for him, that others could only want to be with him if he took care of them.

This patient then entered a period of treatment in which he was keenly aware of being lonely and uncertain that anyone could care for him. During this time he came to feel increasingly dependent on the therapist, which was both new and problematic for him. Such a scenario is typical of patients showing precocious ego development. The therapeutic task is to help the patient experience emotional dependency in the context of a reliable relationship. Paradoxically, this very dependency itself implies differentiation; in contrast to a dependency based on fusion, a healthy dependency entails one separate person needing another separate person. As precociously self-reliant patients begin to need and count on the therapist, they are also aware that the therapist is free of their control and could possibly reject or betray them. Thus a necessary part of healthy dependency is paranoidlike anxiety, the fear that the therapist may yet despise the patient's dependency or may otherwise fail the patient. Whenever a patient who has shown premature self-sufficiency begins to develop a genuine dependency on the therapist, there will be a concurrent heightening of paranoid fears.

Healthy Strains on the Therapeutic Relationship

During the differentiating constancy stage of treatment, the therapeutic relationship is exposed to a number of stresses. For example, patients will feel angry and depressed when the therapist begins to refuse their idealizations. Similarly, interventions aimed at self-other differentiation are upsetting to the patient, who must give up fantasies of special closeness with the therapist. Finally, those patients showing premature self-sufficiency will find themselves fearful and ambivalent as they grow dependent on the therapist. While potentially unpleasant, these are healthy stresses. Eventually they give patients the chance to discover that the therapeutic relationship can be buffeted and yet endure. An important part of this process is finding that conflicts in the relationship are not fatal, that repairs can be made when ruptures occur.

Of course, there have been tensions and stresses throughout the course of therapy; the difference at this point is that adaptive matrix constancy is well established, so there is a growing confidence in the reliability of the relationship. This confidence serves as the context for the strains experienced during the differentiating constancy phase and places the patient in a position to discover that relationships can often be restored and repaired when they are strained. The capacity to make reparation after a break in a relationship is the final piece of the constancy puzzle.

9

Reparation Constancy

The Problem of Repairing Relationships

Most human beings face the task of repairing breaches in intimate relationships. Only the most detached and isolated individual avoids experiencing disruptions with important others from time to time and the tension, sadness, and fear these disruptions entail. Repairing relationships can be a difficult process for the most adaptive and resilient person, and it is exceptionally tortured for the borderline patient. We do not expect to see progress in this area during the first year of treatment generally. The patient will need to feel a secure attachment to the therapist and also be able to make distinctions among different feeling states before being able to effect reparation in therapy. Consequently we believe it will become a focus of treatment only near the end of the preconstancy stage of therapy.

Reparation requires skills and adaptive capacities that borderline patients typically lack. Individuals must be able to tolerate sudden emotional distance and endure the accompanying tensions. Additionally, there must be some ability to see the matter in a larger context than the immediate disruption in the relationship; the disruption must be seen in light of the overall relationship and its history. Finally, individuals must be willing to engage in painstaking "negotiations," including a willingness to see things from the other person's point of view before a feeling of reconciliation can be achieved. When closeness is threatened, borderline patients usually feel too much urgency and pressure to accomplish any of these tasks.

Several other factors make disruptions in intimate relationships more of a problem for borderline patients than for other persons. First, as we discussed in Chapter 4, borderline patients tend to create crises in relationships as a means of evoking reassurance that they will not be abandoned; additionally, many other minor or ordinary problems are blown up to crisis proportion by the patient's inability to modulate effect. The result is that relationships never fully get the chance to unfold or develop naturally. Instead of a gradual building of confidence and security, there is a kind of lurching from one intense and fear-ridden incident to another. Reparation cannot occur in such a situation. There must be some backdrop of secure attachment to the other person against which the present break in the relationship can be seen, and this simply cannot develop in an atmosphere of constant crisis.

Second, reconciliation takes time, at least enough for each person to hear the other out and weigh a response. Borderline patients, however, cannot take time in the face of conflict. Pressed by fear of abandonment, they attribute to the other person the intention of breaking off the relationship. Rather than wait long enough to judge how serious the problem is and what could and should be done about it, borderline patients rush to do something before the other person can carry out the assumed intent. They tend to make a precipitous submission in hopes of immediately restoring the relationship, or they as-

sume it's all over and promptly abandon the relationship themselves. In either event, the tension produced by the rift in the
relationship feels unbearable and evokes some urgent reaction,
thereby cutting off the reparation process.

Finally, borderline patients have had little or no experience
repairing ruptured relationships in a manner that allows both
parties to preserve their self-respect. When there is a break
with another person, they assume that someone will have to
surrender before there can be a return to closeness. Working
with such an assumption, the borderline patient will distort
what the other person tries to communicate, usually not even
hearing the real issues at stake. The more the problem is heard
in terms of who has to give in, the less the actual problem can
even be recognized, much less resolved.

As we have noted in earlier chapters, borderline patients
tend to experience relationships in terms of a cycle of idealization and devaluation. The initial desire in a relationship is
typically to dissolve the boundaries that mark each person as a
separate individual; the loved one is idealized so that an emotional merger can take place. Of course, disappointments and
frustrations are inevitable, and these can lead to devaluations
and emotional storms that are as intense as the idealizations
that preceded them. Just as quickly as it began, the devaluation
process can end, and idealizations are resumed.

Such a cycle keeps the borderline patient from ever seeing
the simple fact that human relationships are imperfect and
invariably entail conflict, disappointment, and hurt. Healthy
intimate relationships would be impossible if there were no
process to address and resolve the breaches that normally occur
and no ability to remember the positive aspects of the relationship prior to the breach. The borderline patient, however, does
not see conflicts as inherent in human relationships but rather
as bitter betrayals of the patient's desire to idealize and merge
with the other. Needless to say, this leads the patient to experience such disruptions in exaggerated forms bordering on the

chaotic, precluding all but the most pathological means of restoring the relationship.

These factors illustrate the reason borderline patients cannot successfully learn to repair relationships early in their treatment. Reparation is not an isolated skill to be worked on and mastered. Rather, the capacity to effect reparation depends on the capacity to develop lasting attachments. Those factors that undermine the borderline patient's ability to enjoy healthy relationships also interfere with the ability to repair broken relationships. Consequently, healthy reparation cannot occur before the patient begins to develop a healthier relationship.

Patients should not be expected to begin to repair relationships in a healthier way until after they start to feel more confident of themselves and secure in the world (adaptive matrix constancy) and until after they come to differentiate self from other, showing more tolerance of their own separateness (differentiating constancy). It does not make sense even to discuss the matter with borderline patients earlier in treatment; while some patients may be able to grasp the subject intellectually, it will not affect them emotionally and will certainly have no impact on their relationships.

The Psychology of Reparation

Relatively little has been written about reparation. Within the field of psychoanalysis, Klein and also Winnicott, who studied under her, have had the most to say on the subject. Klein (1975a) eloquently says, "Side by side with the destructive impulses in the unconscious mind both of the child and of the adult, there exists a profound urge to make sacrifices, in order to help and put right loved people who in phantasy have been harmed or destroyed" (p. 311). Following Klein's ideas, Winnicott has spoken of developing the "capacity for concern," which is his term for the desire to restore a connection that has been broken through aggressive fantasies. Winnicott (1963b) describes concern: "The word 'concern' is used to cover in a positive way a phenomenon that is covered in a negative way by the word 'guilt'. . . . Concern refers to the fact that the individual *cares* or *minds*, and both feels and accepts responsibility" (p. 112).

Klein and Winnicott are discussing the matter from the standpoint of psychoanalytic drive theory, focusing on the way aggressive energies may at times sweep away feelings of affection and—in fantasy, at least—do harm to the other person. Concern develops after there has been some differentiation of self and other; with the recognition of the other's separateness comes concern for preserving the loved one. This is the dawn of depressive anxiety, of the capacity to feel responsibility, and, in addition to the desire to destroy, there now runs alongside the wish to preserve. We come to accept our own contribution to a conflict and learn to feel sorry for the distance we have helped to create. The development of evocative memory helps us to realize that the person with whom we are now angry is also the person we need and love. There is thus a basis for moderating our anger and, later, for wanting to bridge the distance we experience between ourselves and the other person. The other side of the coin is recognizing that we ourselves are the very ones who both love and hate; when anger runs its course, and we remember our affection for the person with whom we were angry, we may then feel concerned that we could have hurt the relationship or the other person, and want to repair the damage.

Prior to developing the capacity for concern (and being able to experience the concern of the other), we must keep love and hate apart so that attachments cannot be eroded by anger. In this situation we experience all-or-none attitudes toward loved ones, either fully hating and devaluing them or fully loving and idealizing them, usually alternating between these extremes. This, of course, is the position of the borderline patient, who must split positively and negatively colored experiences off from each other to preserve the positive experiences. Anger can run unchecked by love, then, and take extreme, primitive forms, awakening fears of retaliation in turn. In any conflict with a loved one, therefore, borderline patients must struggle with paranoid anxieties that distort and exaggerate the conflict and make concern or the desire for reparation impossible.

We can also consider the desire for reparation from an interpersonal point of view in addition to the intrapsychic perspective given us by Klein and Winnicott. In a phenomenological study of the experience of reparation, Hawthorne (1988) noted that "the urge to do something to mend relationships seems to be as normal and universal as our tendency to damage them" (p. 9). He described "a mutual acceptance of the desire and opportunity to reconcile that defines the experience of forgiveness" (p. 51). It is precisely this mutuality and acceptance of the desire to reconcile that have been absent in the borderline patient's life. Throughout the growing-up years, the borderline patient's experience tended to be that any breach in relationships with important others, especially the mother, could only be healed in self-defeating, often humiliating ways, that the mother was typically not emotionally available after angry or even merely tense exchanges. These patients found that even though they desperately wanted a reconciliation, there did not seem to be the same desire on the part of the other person, leaving them wondering how long the rift would last and having no good way to bring reconciliation about. The mother would not accept their wish to reconcile; they were left helplessly wanting it by themselves.

In part this is the situation Masterson and Rinsley (1975) described when they wrote of the mother's "withdrawal of libidinal availability" during the rapprochement subphase of development, and many other authors have picked up the theme. We want to emphasize, however, that this pattern of interaction is not specific to only one period of life. When we speak of there being no mutuality in efforts to effect reconciliation and of the child's having to hold to this wish on his or her own, we do not mean that this occurred only or even chiefly between the eighteenth and thirty-sixth months. Rather, we believe our borderline patients found this pattern of interaction throughout their childhood years and came to behave in ways that served to perpetuate it. Parent–child interactions during rapprochement should be seen as an early model that comes to characterize the overall relationship. The model is that conflict between the mother and the child leads the mother to distance herself in anger, withholding acceptance when the child seeks to end the conflict. By the time such a child reaches adulthood, he or she harbors a generalized expectation that a breach in a relationship means rejection and humiliation.

It is not simply the mother's problems that cause this situation. It is important to note that the father also makes a contribution, although it is a harder one to describe. In healthy families there will be times when the mother is too angry to be available to the child, but the father is there, bridging the gap or mediating between the mother and the child. With borderline patients, however, it is more likely that the father was oblivious to the mood of the home or was for other reasons ineffectual in mediating a reconciliation. Additionally, of course, the very problems between the mother and the child may grow from the mother's frustrations with her husband, or the mother may even be acting out the husband's own frustrations and anger. Whatever the precise role the father plays, we should remember that all family members contribute to the failure to achieve reparation after conflict.

There are three predictable psychological and interpersonal consequences to the child's finding the parents unavailable for reparation. First, the capacity for concern, which naturally unfolds in healthy development, slowly dwindles into an emotional detachment. The *appearance* of concern replaces the capacity for concern, and an as-if style may develop. These individuals develop a false self that allows them to maintain the appearance of being in a relationship while at the same time being well insulated from any real engagement that might lead to hurt. The patient all the while stands back, as it were, and watches interactions from a psychological distance. Even the most demanding and apparently needy borderline patient is quite practiced at appearing to be much more involved and trusting than in fact he or she is.

Noisy borderline patients typically express their diminished capacity for concern differently from the quiet, as-if patient. Noisy patients project their own detachment onto the important people in their lives, including the therapist, complaining, for example, "You don't care about me" or "You're just doing this for the money." These complaints suggest that the noisy patient experiences others as remote and indifferent, which more accurately reflects the patient's own stance.

Second, experiences of estrangement from a love object occasion extreme anxiety on the child's part. Since reunion is not in the child's power and waits on the caprice of the angry parent, the child has no way to endure the period of estrangement. Tension can be tolerated when it is time-limited, when its beginning is clear and its ending can be confidently anticipated, but the more open-ended tension is, the less easily it can be endured. Of course, to the young child waiting on a withdrawn parent to change moods, it seems as though the estrangement could go on forever, and the accompanying tension rapidly grows to anxiety and desperation.

The child, in turn (and later the adult borderline patient), begins to make exaggerated and stilted efforts to become attached again, even if only on a fragmented and unsatisfying basis. The quiet, as-if type of borderline patient seeks attachments (or, rather, pseudoattachments) through an automaton-like compliance with the other person. Interpersonally, there is a compulsive desire to please the other through mimicry or projective identification (for example, the patient discussed in Chapter 6 who reported masturbating with her brother's sports trophy when she thought the therapist wanted some self-disclosure). Attempts at attachment by noisy borderline patients tend to have a tempestuous and engulfing quality, usually beginning with fierce idealizations followed by attempts to provoke guilt when frustrated. Good judgment seems to be missing with both types of patient, as desperation to join with someone repeatedly overrides the ability to sort out what is in the patient's own best interests. It is sad to see these patients, so hungry for lasting attachments, consistently moving into the least promising relationships imaginable.

Borderline patients have not been able to develop competency in intimate relationships (Kroll 1988). There is a cognitive component as well as an emotional capacity in effecting lasting attachments. Without the opportunity to learn ways of making up, saying that one is sorry, or negotiating an end to a conflict, an individual is at a loss during times when these skills are needed. Growing up in a home where reparation does not consistently take place, borderline patients lack the social skills needed for maintaining intimacy. Unfortunately, this further predisposes them toward maladaptive ways of creating and maintaining relationships.

Third, an unrelieved sense of guilt, focused on the loss of relationships, comes to permeate the individual's total existence. Such guilt stems from experiences with a mother who either does not appear capable of withstanding or surviving the child's aggressive activities and anger or who provides no opportunity to repair breaks in the relationship. The first situation is most likely to come about with an enmeshing mother, who experiences the child's anger and/or desires for independence as a rejection of her. Normal anger and healthy strivings toward autonomy thereby make the child guilty of damaging the mother, a subtle kind of guilt that hangs over the child's life and yet also proves very difficult to identify or describe. The second situation often occurs when the mother resents the child's separateness and, in effect, acts on this resentment with a vengeance by creating barriers to the child's regaining closeness with her once the child has moved away.

In either case, the mother is communicating that the child's existence is solely for *her* needs to be met. Children are placed in an impossible situation by such a message, for it leaves them guilty for wanting lives of their own. Attempts to meet their own needs, pursue independent interests, or express their own feelings come to be defined as attacks on the mother, as though they were the results of hostile intent when in fact they were part of expectable development. Children may be quite confused to find their normal urges and wishes defined by the other as aggressive when this was not usually their conscious intent. As a result, borderline patients suffer an abiding and oppressive sense of guilt at wanting anything for themselves. When they seek their own best interests or, more simply, selfishly want something, they may feel in danger, although they will not know why.

In fact they may be in danger. When the mother is not available for reparation after a rift, her lack of concern for the child as a separate person may be exposed. Ferenczi (1929) long ago noted that children who observe conscious and unconscious signs of the mother's aversion to them or impatience with their needs may suffer a breaking of the desire to live. In later life, even slight frustrations may then awaken a desire to die. Presumably, intuitively perceived maternal hostility becomes incorporated into the personality, perhaps explaining why so many borderline patients have histories of suicide attempts and self-mutilation.

We believe that the mother's lack of concern for the child is most visible in instances of conflict and the resulting difficulty in restoring connectedness (consequently, self-destructive urges are most likely to occur with adult borderline patients in the context of a falling out with a loved one or other object loss). In Hawthorne's (1988) study we find a statement by Hannah Arendt (1958) that is relevant here. She notes that human beings need two intertwined capabilities to sustain meaningful relationships: the capacity to promise and the capacity to forgive. As Hawthorne puts it, "The first is the remedy for 'unpredictability' and represents the possibility of anchoring a secure future; the latter is the remedy for 'irreversibility' and represents the possibility of redemption from one's past" (1988, p. 254).

The borderline patient certainly does not experience a "redemption from one's past." Consequently the patient lives with a pervasive sense of primitive guilt and yet with no clear understanding of the basis for such a feeling. There are several consequences. First, relationships are excessively built on idealizations; recognizing a flaw or failing threatens the seamless unity borderline patients seek as a support to their sense of self. Honest appraisal of the other's failings comes too close to declaring that one has independent wants and wishes, an unacceptable declaration of autonomy. Second, since primitive idealizations cannot be preserved when the other person's good and bad qualities are both acknowledged, these must be split off from one another. Finally, this prevents the experience of continuity in a relationship, which instead moves jarringly from good to bad and back to good perhaps, but in any event the relationship is not constant across time. Thus the guilt that pervades the borderline patient's relationships indirectly supports the tendency to move between idealizations and devaluations and undermines a sense of continuity about the relationship. In this context there is no way to heal a breach without someone having to pay for it.

Masochistic Rapprochement

Since borderline patients typically grew up with the sense that they were alive chiefly to meet the other person's needs, they could gain no feeling of mutuality in relationships. Relationships were not matters of shared commitments and meanings but rather matters of one person's being needy and the other person's meeting the need. Such relationships are unbalanced, or unilateral: At any given time, the person who is the needy member of the duo has the responsibility of keeping the relationship going. Even if in fact the other person feels invested in the relationship, too, borderline patients will usually not realize this but will feel the entire burden on their shoulders.

As a result, borderline patients do not expect reparations to be a two-way street. Rather, either the patient or the other person is expected to make some sacrifice (or be coerced into making one) as a way of bridging the gulf between them. Other options simply are not available; for example, it makes no sense to the borderline patient to let the passage of time soothe hurt feelings, for there is no expectation that both people could care whether the relationship is repaired and therefore no hope that the other person might allow feelings to be soothed. Someone must therefore accept responsibility for the conflict and also the burden of making up.

Accepting (or inflicting) responsibility for the breach has an exaggerated, desperate quality. Borderline patients are not trying to reestablish a sense of connectedness with the other person as much as a sense of union. The desire for fusion in itself exaggerates these patients' experience of the conflict. Their efforts are intensified by the fear that comes with aloneness—faced with the terror of being left alone, they feel that reunion outweighs all else. Borderline patients are willing to sacrifice their own best interests for the relief of reconciling with the other person.

For example, near the end of his first year of treatment, a 36-year-old man commented on the contrast between his poise and self-assurance with people who were not emotionally significant to him versus the constant tension and fear he experienced around his parents, wife, and children. To all appearances this man was simply an attentive son, devoted husband, and indulgent father, but in fact he was driven by the ever-present fear that he would lose all meaningful relationships if he stood up for himself. His anxiety was greatest when two people made conflicting demands simultaneously. Then he would run to his bedroom, where he would have a tantrumlike rage reaction, breaking various objects. He would, however, quickly be overwhelmed with guilt and return seeking rapprochement by offering to give more than was originally requested, feeling ashamed of himself and taken advantage of afterward.

This patient illustrates how borderline individuals are vulnerable to emotional blackmail. These patients are remarkably naive about their rights and responsibilities in a relation-

ship. It can be sad to hear borderline patients complain repeatedly about how they are taken advantage of by loved ones and
yet remain unable to impose corrective limits. This situation is
not surprising, however, when seen in light of the patient's
desperate desire to fuse again with the loved one. The other
person seems to hold all the cards. As long as the tension
between the patient and the other person lasts, the other
appears to be an omnipotent, wrathful judge who must be
appeased. Similarly, the patient is on trial, a supplicant hoping
to escape the guilty verdict that is felt to be inevitable.

Borderline patients typically offer this omnipotent other
some proof of submission. Humiliation becomes the price of
reconciliation, and the patient does something to indicate
that he or she would rather be close to the other person than
retain a sense of pride. This is the masochistic submission
discussed in Chapter 4, and it is virtually the borderline patient's only means of reparation, a pattern usually laid down in
childhood.

> The patient mentioned in Chapter 4, who as a child promised
> his mother whatever she wanted even though he knew he was
> lying, remembered feeling ashamed while he was making the
> required promises. He in fact tried to please his mother by
> cleaning the house, shopping for groceries, and bringing home
> good grades from school. These efforts, however, were typically
> ignored or disparaged, and counted for little when the mother
> was angry. Playing the part of a wounded martyr, the mother
> required a period of crying and promising that it would never
> happen again before she would even consent to talk. The pa-
> tient remembered feeling humiliated and guilty over betraying
> his own integrity during these times. He had felt he must be a
> chronic liar and untrustworthy to make promises he knew he
> could not keep: "Even as I was promising (for example, never
> again to go out to play with friends), I knew it would happen
> again, and so I was asking for something I didn't really de-

serve." There was no way out, however; humiliation was the mother's price for regaining a feeling of connectedness.

In this case, the mother's sadism made the boy's humiliation necessary. Borderline patients as adults, however, are not necessarily involved with sadistic others. Although they may experience the other person as sadistic and may behave to "pull" sadism from the other, this is a pattern of interaction they will create on their own even if the other person does not. For instance, one homosexual patient in his early thirties frequently picked up men at a gay bar, idealizing them quickly, and inviting them to move in with him. In a short time—usually within two weeks—he found himself feeling very possessive and suspicious whenever his lover spent any time at all away from him. A series of accusations that the lover was spending time with someone else would then follow, leading to angry exchanges, and then to the patient's tearful apologies for having been so suspicious. These interactions usually resulted in pseudoreconciliations, and the patient gained a sense of euphoria that lasted several days. Soon, however, the accusations would start again; eventually the patient would accuse his lover of exploiting his generosity and threaten to evict him. When the lover would agree to go, the patient would reverse field, profess his love, and tearfully express regret over having been so unreasonable, often offering money if only the other would stay. Finally the relationship would end with the other person's leaving, often complaining, "I've had enough. You're too suffocating."

In the course of therapy it became apparent that this man felt no one could possibly like him and that all relationships had to be tested. Eventually the patient came to see that he could never please his father—a stern, authoritarian military officer who kept aloof from the family and only checked in periodically to see how the children were progressing. That left his mother as his sole means of emotional support within the family, and since the family moved frequently, the patient never developed lasting friendships. The mother was a docile woman who tended to be overly protective of the patient and virtually insisted on seeing him as a victim.

Borderline patients have few options in the face of conflict apart from masochistic submission. Generally the alternative is the loss of the relationship. This may occur if the relationship has been through so many crises that it has become too unstable to continue, and one or the other party has had enough, deciding to leave. Borderline patients are most likely to abandon a relationship if they have already secured a replacement for the person they leave. Since the terror of aloneness keeps borderline individuals motivated to effect a masochistic rapprochement, they lose this motivation only after they find someone else to buffer them from aloneness. However, things are not likely to be that much different in the new relationship, and so a new cycle of conflict and masochistic submission will probably begin.

Curiously, the borderline patient's relationships very rarely end with any sense of closure. There seem to be two reasons for this. First, boundaries were ambiguous in the relationship from the beginning. The structure of the relationship was such that the patient could not cleanly leave because it was not comprised of two "real" people. Overly contaminated by fantasy and by need satisfaction, the relationship continues "in the patient's head" and even becomes confused with following relationships. Second, there is a dynamic factor, that the borderline patient has trouble separating from anyone who was once an idealized source of satisfaction (a good example of this can be seen in the behavior of the woman protagonist in the movie *Fatal Attraction*). Thus borderline patients may find themselves strongly attracted to persons they encounter after many years and may several times reconcile and decide to try again with people they have broken up with previously.

What is missing, of course, is any means of reconciling in a way that allows both parties to retain their integrity and pride. This would entail a mutual commitment to the relationship and the intention by both people to work through a hard time. The borderline patient cannot easily imagine such a thing. It presupposes constancy on the part of the other person to believe that he or she will remain interested when frustrated or when there is tension. Constancy, of course, is something the patient is only beginning to experience at this point, certainly not something the patient counts on.

Therapy Implications

The issue of reparation is most likely to arise in therapy around the patient's growing sense of differentiation from the therapist. As we noted in the previous chapter, patients begin to experience both positive and negative feelings toward the therapist as they grow aware of the therapist's separateness from them. The patient will want to have exclusive possession of the now separate therapist and also to destroy this object of frustration. When patients come to experience these contradictory wishes as aimed at the same person, they feel much ambivalence, as though it is dangerous to expose the same object to these differing impulses. The strength of their attachment leads them to feel guilty for wanting to attack the therapist, and they become concerned with preserving the relationship from their own ability to destroy.

Of course, conflict between patient and therapist is bound to arise before the patient begins to accept the therapist's separateness. As noted many times in this book, borderline patients are repeatedly made angry with the therapist in the course of treatment, and it goes without saying that therapists will often be angry or even infuriated with borderline patients during their conflicts. There can be no question of reparation, however, because the patient cannot experience ambivalence until late in the preconstancy stage. Before the patient begins to accept the therapist's separateness, experiences of anger are simply split off from periods of idealization and love, and the two types of emotional experience are kept apart from each other. As long as anger is split off from attachment, the patient simply moves between the two states, and there is no need to repair the relationship, only the need to move again to a period of attachment, usually through masochistic rapprochement. Reparation becomes possible when patients begin to differentiate their feelings from those of their therapist. Differentiation makes it possible to have mixed feelings, to feel ambivalent, and therefore to grow anxious over the possibility of destroying the relationship.

At this point in treatment, patients may venture to offer something to the therapist. What is offered is the modifying of guilt and anxiety over aggression into concern. If the therapist is perceived as someone who will accept destructive and loving intentions, there is opportunity for the patient to try to learn to live with these conflicting desires. Care involves the attempt to preserve relationships in the face of aggressive impulses toward the loved one. It really is not possible to love someone without becoming angry with that person at times—love implies intense involvement, and it is impossible to be closely involved with another person without occasionally being frustrated and disappointed. Love therefore implies the capacity to hate, and so concern and anger (preservation and destruction) are not as exclusive of one another as they may in fact sound. The task for all individuals is to learn to tolerate hatred toward loved ones and to preserve meaningful relationships in the face of that hate.

It is critical for therapists to realize that loving and destructive desires are never far from one another. At any given time one may be figural while the other is in the background, while at other times the situation is reversed, but both are constantly present in any lively or "real" relationship. They are especially present in therapy. After all, patients who have gradually learned to accept without undue guilt the fact that they have their own wants and desires may be quite shocked to find that one of those wants is to destroy the very therapist who had helped them to their newfound acceptance. Or patients who have come to experience themselves as centers of autonomy without at the same time feeling they have abandoned their loved ones may be frightened when they find that they are also more independent of the therapist who helped them to their autonomous stance. In either case patients may fear that their love for the therapist cannot survive destructive impulses or independence, and it will be crucial for the therapist to realize that these troublesome wishes were present all along, that the patients who love them must also hate them at times, and that the patients who need them must also be free of them.

By this late point in the preconstancy stage, the patient's destructive urges toward the therapist are different from those that arose early in treatment. The chief difference, of course, is that they are no longer being split off from loving feelings but are being experienced as part of an overall flow of affects that are directed toward *this* therapist. In a sense it is probably not correct to speak of feelings being split off from one another; what is split in splitting may be the person experiencing the feelings (Pruyser 1975). Thus, as splitting declines, we are mostly saying that the patient "owns" or acknowledges and takes responsibility for the entire range of his or her affect. At first this phenomenon will frighten borderline patients, who are unaccustomed to opposing feelings toward the same person and who may need reassurance that love can—and in fact always does—coexist with hate.

For example, a patient presented a dream to his therapist during the last period of the preconstancy stage of treatment. In the dream the therapist's spouse had died and the patient was taking care of all funeral arrangements, making sure "the spouse was buried good." After some exploration of the dream and the patient's current feelings toward the therapist, it became clear that the patient wanted to make sure the spouse was "good and buried." This discovery initially produced considerable anxiety in the patient, who vehemently denied any hostile intent and who pointed out that in the dream he announces that he will personally be responsible for taking over the care of the therapist. The patient could acknowledge his desire to take exclusive responsibility for (and therefore exclusive possession of) the therapist, but he could not easily accept that hostile intentions were involved in the scenario. With the therapist's acceptance of both desires, however, and reassurances that both were normal, the patient felt a great sense of relief and a stronger faith in the durability and solidity of the relationship.

Reparation issues will be visible to therapists early in treatment, but as we have already noted, it is impossible to address such issues effectively for a long time, and probably not in the first year of treatment. Thus therapists ought not look too early for signs that borderline patients are able to work with reparation issues. Often some signs will begin to appear late in the preconstancy stage of therapy—clues, as it were, that patients may be ready to begin struggling with the notion that they can not only create distance in relationships but also bridge it. Such signs are merely suggestive; there are no hard-and-fast rules therapists can follow to know when reparation becomes a possibility for the patient. These are, in general, signs that the patient is beginning to master tasks associated with adaptive matrix constancy and differentiating constancy. First, the tendency to act precipitously is much diminished; there is, in turn, a heightened capacity to contain problems in thought. Second, there is likely to be a certain toning down of intensity of affect and less shifting back and forth rapidly between contrary affect states. Third, the patient may seem less self-absorbed, more capable of noticing the reactions and even the needs of others.

These sorts of changes in the patient (often referred to in the psychoanalytic literature as changes in the transference) indicate that it is time for therapists to alter their stance somewhat. During the reparation constancy stage of treatment, therapists should begin to become more active. Verbal interventions should take on more of the character of confrontations and interpretations, whereas earlier in treatment verbal interventions carried a more simple purpose, that of staying in touch with the patient and creating the sense that the therapist was attentive and interested. By the reparation constancy stage, verbal interventions can become more focused on content, and themes related to early parent–child interaction can be addressed. In brief, treatment begins to take on more of the character of a normal case, with fewer modifications aimed at establishing constancy.

There are two general areas for therapist and patient to explore during this time. Both will be visible in most treatments with borderline patients near the end of the preconstancy stage. The areas are: first, therapists may have occasion to make reparation with the patient, modeling the process; second, patients must acknowledge and accept the bitterly disappointing nature of their relationship with the mother, often facing the mother's actual sadism and self-centeredness toward them. This eventually leads to what might be termed a healthy depression.

The Therapist as a Model

Therapists will need to communicate a desire for reparation when they have failed in some fashion and experience guilt toward the patient. We want to emphasize that this must not occur in the early months of therapy; during that period, borderline patients spend much of their time accusing the therapist of having failed them, and it is important for the therapist simply to survive these attacks—no apology is necessary at that time, and one would probably scuttle the treatment. Late in the preconstancy stage, however, there may be times when the therapist becomes aware of having been harsh or unfair, or even of having simply slighted the patient in a small way, such as beginning a session late. It is appropriate for an apology to be offered, one that will undoubtedly surprise the patient.

This may be thought of as modeling a socially acceptable way of behaving. It is not, however, a planned therapeutic technique, such as the modeling described in some behavior therapies. Rather, it simply reflects the humanness of the therapist and will inevitably arise in the course of treatment, even as there will be need for reparation in any significant relationship. Therapists do, after all, make mistakes or otherwise fail their patients in large or, more likely, small ways. For instance, they may lose critical distance due to countertransference issues and misunderstand a patient on some important point, or respond out of a wrestling with their own unresolved problems rather than out of a sense of what would be best for the patient. These countertransference errors and failures of empathy must first, of course, be looked at in light of the overall treatment relationship to see if the errors reflect or give information on the patient's pathology. Often the matter will end there, but from time to time therapists may find that they feel guilty at their mistake and that the guilt reflects something appropriate to human relationships, not the patient's pathology. In such a case

an apology may be made, and if it is made at the right time—
late in the preconstancy stage—the effect can be highly beneficial.

Borderline patients will usually be surprised and perplexed
when the therapist assumes responsibility, acknowledges guilt,
and indicates a desire for reconciliation. It is quite alien, of
course, to the patient's experiences with significant others and
violates their expectation of what happens when there is conflict in a relationship. What often surprises the patient most is
the therapist's having taken the lead. In spite of the borderline
patient's characteristic feeling of entitlement, they are not
prepared for the therapist's saying to them, in effect, "You're
entitled to an apology."

More often than not, patients eventually become uneasy with
the therapist's apology. This may be due to the way the apology
challenges the patient's own constant sense of guiltiness, and,
of course, it may challenge the patient's desire to idealize the
therapist. Additionally, there is a novelty effect: Patients may
remark that it is the first time anyone has ever apologized to
them without their having to coerce it or behave masochisti-
cally to induce it.

The therapist's making an apology to the borderline patient
is very often the way the issue enters treatment for the first
time. Certainly it is a mistake to wait until the patient brings up
the subject of reparation if it is appropriate for the therapist to
make an apology and if the treatment is far enough along to
warrant it. Many patients simply have never seen important
others try to make reparation, so they do not know how it is
done, and they may not even know that most people do in fact
try to repair damage to relationships when such damage occurs.
Thus the therapist's apology creates the possibility that the
patient may be able to attempt reparation on his or her own.

The therapist's attempts at reparation, then, may be among
the first such attempts in the patient's entire life. These experiences suggest to the patient that relationships can have more

flexibility and consequently more durability than previously imagined. The therapist's apologies communicate that both parties may have an interest in continuing a relationship and that damage can therefore be repaired. Thus mutuality enters the picture as a factor in relationships that the patient had not counted on. Patients may gain a sense that there are actually two people in a relationship, that matters do not simply rest on whomever feels needier at any given moment. A foundation is laid for teaching the patient that it is possible to be separate and yet connected, that separateness does not necessarily mean the other person is indifferent to the relationship.

Patients vary, of course, in how they react to their therapist's attempts at reparation. Patients sometimes respond by crying and have difficulty expressing the feelings of warmth generated by this display of concern by the therapist. Most patients at least feel that the therapeutic relationship is sturdier than they had believed. We do not believe such responses to the therapist's efforts at reparation should be regarded as transference reactions, requiring analysis and working through. It is more as though the patient has begun to glimpse new options or possibilities; the world looks more receptive than before, less rigid and more forgiving. In turn this takes self-imposed pressure off the patient. If forgiveness is possible between people, patients need not be so hard on themselves: Their errors are not fatal.

Facing the Mother's Rejection of the Patient

Once the borderline patient finds that the therapist is capable of making reparation when there is a rift, it eventually raises the question of why the patient's parents, and especially the mother, were not. This will be a difficult question for the patient. Borderline patients may complain about the treatment they received from their mothers throughout treatment and yet secretly hold to the expectation that this will one day change, that the mother will eventually love and cherish them. Thus therapists should not assume that patients have given up on a parent simply because the patient complains of the parent's failings, even if the complaints are bitter, intense, and convincing. The complaints may be real enough and probably reflect— in part—the patient's conscious feelings. But the complaints probably also mask a split-off, idealized fantasy that one day the mother will return to the patient's life and establish the blissful, sustaining closeness the patient has always yearned for, a fantasy the patient may or may not be fully aware of.

For example, one paranoid, borderline patient scathingly denounced her mother, who had physically brutalized her as a child. Yet this patient also made frequent visits to her parents' home, even though the journey was a long and difficult one and even though the visits never went well. Additionally, the patient often expressed a terrific fear of her mother's dying, saying she did not know whether she could endure the pain. Had the patient been functioning at a higher level, this fear could be understood as a reaction formation against a desire to kill the mother; however, it is unlikely that a higher-level defense would occur in such an emotionally immature individual. The therapist believed the patient fantasized that the mother would one day change and would accept and praise the patient in place of the brutal beatings and devastating rebuffs that had characterized their interactions. The patient's concern with her mother's death undoubtedly reflected her fear that the mother would die before this change occurred.

In spite of treatment, the patient never surrendered that hope and merely displaced it onto her children. As soon as one child would grow big enough to make movements toward autonomy, the patient found herself wanting another baby, even voicing that she didn't get enough closeness from the previous one. She exchanged the desire to be her mother's idealized infant for the desire to enjoy idyllic closeness with her own children: Through the process of identifying with her babies, she could, on the one hand, experience the ideal mothering she yearned for and, on the other hand, feel that she was in fact being the ideal mother she had fantasized.

As long as the borderline patient harbors the secret hope that a "bad" parent will change and become the yearned-for "good" parent, the patient must also harbor a sense of his or her own inherent badness. Patients must nurture the belief that there is something wrong with them and that this accounts for why the parents did not seem to take pleasure in their existence. Without such an explanation, patients would have to surrender a cherished fantasy, confronting the futile nature of their hope that the good parent will magically appear when their own badness goes away. Borderline patients will typically react with deep depression whenever this fantasy is undermined; it is preferable to many patients to feel that they are somehow bad or wrong, for the alternative is to feel utterly alone.

It is easy to see, then, that borderline patients will enter treatment with two intertwined cores of resistance: their unrealistic expectations of their parents and their own longstanding sense of inherent badness. Patients will not be willing to examine the limitations of their relationship with the mother, often including their mother's actual indifference or even sadism toward them, until they have some sense that the therapist can be counted on—until, in other words, the therapist begins to become a constant object. They need to count on the therapist to face the depression that accompanies giving up their hope that the mother will one day change. Giving up such a hope hits patients from two sides at once. On the one hand, there is the loss of the hoped-for mother; the future can seem empty and flat without this sustaining fantasy, devoid of a conceivable replacement.

Second, patients have secretly maintained a grandiose self-image through believing their badness was the cause of maternal inadequacy. They have, that is, believed that they were themselves the cause of what happened to them, that some of their traits or behaviors controlled and directed the mother's activities toward them. It is depressing to give up this power through guilt posture. Not only is it deflating to surrender a grandiose experience of self, but, perhaps more importantly, patients must also give up magical thinking in this area. They have clung to the expectation that what is most desired will somehow, against all evidence, magically come. Patients are left with reality in place of the lost magic: Others will not read their minds, see how utterly important it is that they be cherished, and suddenly change to satisfy the patient's hope.

In effect the reality is now that patients must openly acknowledge that they want something for themselves. Earlier in this chapter we described how the mother's refusal to acknowledge the patient's separateness left the patient guilty for wanting a life of his or her own. In its most basic form this means that borderline patients suffer a primitive sense of guilt whenever they want something for themselves. Thus they try to avoid the experience of wanting, of taking the risk that others will attack them for wanting or even the disappointment of finding that what they want may not be available. We find that borderline patients use such maneuvers as magical thinking, entitlement, and projective identification as ways of bypassing any open acknowledgment *that* they want, much less *what* they want.

In general we may view the desire to fuse or eliminate boundaries as related to this issue. The experience of wanting implies a gap between what one has versus what is desired. To escape awareness that something is wanted, borderline patients avoid anything that would confront them with this gap. They therefore tend to eliminate differences or boundaries between self and other, merging their wishes with those of the other person to avoid separate, guilt-provoking wants of their own.

There is a kind of boldness to openly, freely admitting what is wanted, a boldness that defines and highlights the self, as it were, and implies separateness. None of this is welcome to an individual whose existence has remained built around trying to satisfy the mother's needs. It is impossible to maintain the illusion of closeness with the mother and at the same time define oneself through boldly wanting something that may be different from what she seeks. Wanting something for oneself amounts to a declaration of independence, exposing patients to terrible fears of abandonment and guilt over having placed the relationship in jeopardy. These fears of abandonment can, however, be bypassed by assuming one's own inherent badness; this keeps control in one's own hands and preserves the hope that abiding, satisfying closeness with the mother is indeed possible.

With the discovery that rifts in relationships can often be repaired, however, the entire borderline solution breaks down. It becomes clear that it is not necessary to surrender independence to have a reliable relationship. Rather, it is quite possible to overcome the times when people feel differently and often even the times when one person may have hurt the other. Thus it is not necessary to assume one's own inherent badness as the explanation for why a relationship is unstable.

Now patients can see the relationship with the mother in a new light, seeing that the relationship may have been troubled by problems not of their own making. This is not to say that every patient will discover that his or her mother was sadistic, indifferent, or deeply pathological. We believe this will very often be the case, but therapists should also be alert for other factors that made the mother–child relationship precarious. The emotional match may have been unfortunate, for example, making it truly difficult for either party to stay affectively attuned (Stern 1985) with the other. The mother's health may have played a role, as well as the nature of the mother–father interaction, and socioeconomic circumstances could have influenced the atmosphere of the home. As we noted earlier in this book, some writers (e.g., Chessick 1977, Rinsley 1982) have even pointed to cultural factors as crucial in the formation of borderline dynamics. Whatever the actual causal factors, the crucial thing is that patients discover they were not themselves the cause. They certainly played a role, and their behaviors later in life undoubtedly kept pathological patterns of interaction alive and well, but patients must give up the notion that their badness controlled the mother's behavior toward them or that they can now control loved ones.

The Patient's Disillusionment
and the Therapeutic Aftermath

When the patient has experienced reparation of some conflict with the therapist and has subsequently begun to see that there will probably not be such experiences with the mother, disillusionment sets in. The patient, as noted, is surrendering the grandiose presumption that his or her badness controlled and determined the nature of the mother–child interaction, and this has a deflating, depressing effect. Additionally, the patient has to give up an idealized fantasy of special closeness with the mother. It is hardly surprising, then, that patients often begin a period of healthy mourning for "the mother who will never be." These events have consequences for treatment.

Therapists may notice that patients again become overly dependent on them during this period of mourning, a dependency that may be in contrast to the increased separateness and competence noticeable when adaptive matrix constancy and differentiating constancy were being established. We do not believe this renewed dependency should be viewed as a regression; rather, a reorganization is taking place. The patient is forming new images and experiences of self, trying to jettison the power to control others as well as the flip side of the coin, the tendency to project all power onto the other person and become an incompetent victim. The therapist is being used as a transitional object during this phase, the first time during the preconstancy stage that it is appropriate to describe the therapist's role with this term. This is the first time in treatment, however, when the patient is trying to move from an egocentric, magical experience of self and other to a more objective, reality-based experience. The therapist serves the same function as the young child's transitional object, as a representative and container of the patient's self, or personal reality, so that this fragile self will not be lost during the storm and stress of the transition.

Consequently the therapist should tolerate the patient's renewed dependency. It sometimes happens that therapists feel disappointed, taking the dependency as a sign that they have failed or not done their job well, when in fact the renewed dependency is a sign that the treatment is going as well as could be hoped for. Patients may begin calling the therapist during this phase. These phone calls tend to be brief and often involve some scheduling or logistical problem that is easily seen through as merely an excuse for contact with the therapist. We believe the patient is simply seeking reassurance to see if the therapist, as someone who "holds" the patient's reality, is still there. These calls fade out with time and should probably be tolerated.

Another consequence of the patient's mourning is a lessening of harsh and critical attitudes toward others and also toward the self. When patients give up feelings of omnipotence and magical control, they become less likely to project such feelings onto others. This leads to heightened tolerance and patience. As less omnipotence is expected of self and other, there is less tendency to blame someone for the average, ordinary, or expectable problems of life. The illusion of omnipotence causes even typical, daily frustrations to be taken personally, as evidence of one's own failings or signs that others do not care as much as they might. But if no one is all-powerful, then no one need be blamed for everything unpleasant, and there can be some measure of understanding even when someone is clearly at fault. These are changes that may begin to be visible during the healthy mourning process.

One patient, for example, would become so angry at slow traffic, a poorly done car repair, a bad phone connection, or a loss by his favorite football team that he behaved irrationally. He suffered temper fits, often damaging his own possessions in the process, and occasionally got into fights with strangers or relatives over these everyday sorts of troubles. Even though he was not paranoid, he felt "they're doing it just to me," explaining that "they wouldn't do it to me if I was really somebody" and often adding that he figured that sort of thing never happened to the therapist. It was over a year into treatment before he would consider the possibility that these problems happened to everyone and was able to encounter even slight frustrations without becoming enraged or depressed.

A final possible consequence of the patient's mourning is a sudden, heightened competitiveness with other persons in the therapist's work or life. Often this takes the form of questions about other patients, especially those who have the therapy hour preceding or following the patient's. It may also take the form of paranoidlike anxieties on whether the therapist talks to others about the patient. Jealousy, envy, and fantasies of betrayal typically dominate this competitive period.

It may appear at first that these patients are entering an oedipal type of interaction, since the apparent pattern of interaction is triangular and features competition for a fantasied special place in the therapist's life. We do not believe that competitiveness is actually the central feature of this type of concern, however. Rather, we believe that these patients are trying to deal with the anxiety of wanting to swallow up the therapist and the attendant fear of being rejected on account of such a wish. Thus these patients *are* possessive. Yet the patient is not actually competing with other persons for possession of the therapist; their struggle is more with the therapist and is therefore a two-party interaction. The attempt to make the interaction appear triangular is a displacement that tries to dilute the struggle by directing it to a more socially acceptable, less primitive situation.

When such a pseudocompetition arises in treatment, the therapist is well advised to look for parallels in the patient's childhood. Therapists will often find that the patient felt similar competition with the same-sex parent during childhood. Investigation generally reveals, however, that this was not oedipally determined but was driven by the child's ongoing frustrations with the mother. For example, boys may compete with the father as a reaction formation to the desire to grow close to him. This may occur when the boy has been thwarted in his efforts to be close to his mother and views the father as potentially more accepting and loving than the mother. Competitiveness with the father becomes a counterphobic response to the strong desire to merge with him.

An alternative scenario occurs when the son notices that the mother devalues the father. The son may then compete with his father in order to endear himself to the mother. This pattern often undermines the boy's sexual identity. He can feel compelled to devalue or even deny his masculinity if rejection of masculinity is perceived to be what the mother wants. Again, the boy's competitiveness at first appears to be oedipal in nature, but it is in fact a screen for the desire to be accepted by or even to fuse with the mother.

Female children may compete with their mothers to gain from the father what the mother has failed to provide. Girls may also compete with their mothers in an attempt to deny the importance of what the mother failed to be and give. In this case the girl may develop a tomboy style, rejecting femininity in hopes of pleasing the father by being different from the mother. Girls may also sacrifice gender identity if they perceive that the father devalues the mother.

It is important for treatment that therapists realize they are dealing with a two-party interaction and not with an oedipally determined sequence. Thus no limits need be set and no reality-based interpretations need be made. Rather, therapists should simply allow the situation to unfold and let patients express their desires. Patients will come to see the limits of the situation on their own without being told, and this will bring them to the real issue, reparation. It is not important that patients be confronted on their desires to possess and incorporate the therapist. It is, however, important that patients be allowed to transform the desire to swallow up the therapist into love and then into concern, eventually making reparation for the aggressive overtones of their desire to incorporate.

Patients will learn by themselves that they cannot share the therapist's daily life and be a special part of his or her existence. Eventually patients will feel guilty for having wanted such a thing, and they will grow concerned that they may have hurt the relationship with their possessiveness or with the intensity of their feelings. If therapists allow the patient to make reparation, they will have helped the patient; if, by contrast, they make an oedipal interpretation, patients may feel criticized and rebuffed, and the issue will fade from therapy without resolution.

The Remainder of Treatment

By the time the therapist hears the issues just discussed, the treatment has really ended the preconstancy stage. The patient's mourning for the ideal mother, renewed dependency on the therapist, reduced criticisms of self and other, and guilt over the desire to consume and control the therapist are all signs that the therapist has become a constant object. The nature of treatment therefore changes. The therapist may begin to leave the basic approach of standing still and again rely on those interventions that are useful with most nonborderline patients. Indeed, in exploring the patient's relationship with the mother, therapists have already begun to conduct the case more along the lines of business as usual, and this is appropriate. At this point therapists may begin to work with the patient without too much concern for the special issues posed by the patient's borderline features; the patient may be looked on as a normal patient for the most part and engaged as such.

References

Adler, G. (1979). The myth of the alliance with borderline patients. *American Journal of Psychiatry* 136:642-645.
—— (1985). *Borderline Psychopathology and Its Treatment*. Northvale, NJ: Jason Aronson.
Adler, G., and Buie, D. H. (1979). The psychotherapeutic approach to aloneness in borderline patients. In *Advances in Psychotherapy of the Borderline Patient*, ed. J. LeBoit and A. Capponi, pp. 433-448. New York: Jason Aronson.
Angyal, A. (1965). *Neurosis and Treatment: A Holistic Theory*. New York: John Wiley.
Arendt, H. (1958). *The Human Condition*. Chicago: University of Chicago Press.
Bakan, D. (1966). *The Duality of Human Existence*. Chicago: Rand McNally.
Basch, M. (1980). *Doing Psychotherapy*. New York: Basic Books.
Bergman, A. Personal communication to V. Sherwood, June 1, 1988.
Blanck, G., and Blanck, R. (1974). *Ego Psychology: Theory and Practice*. New York: Columbia University Press.
Breuer, J., and Freud, S. (1895). Studies in hysteria. *Standard Edition* 2.
Buber, M. (1970). *I and Thou*. New York: Scribner.
Buie, D. H., and Adler, G. (1972). The uses of confrontation with borderline patients. *International Journal of Psychoanalytic Psychotherapy* 1:90-108.
—— (1982). The definitive treatment of the borderline patient. *International Journal of Psychoanalytic Psychotherapy* 9:51-87.
Burgner, M., and Edgcumbe, R. (1972). Some problems in the conceptuali-

zation of early object relationships. Part II: The concept of object constancy. *The Psychoanalytic Study of the Child* 27:315-333. New Haven, CT: Yale University Press.

Cameron, N. (1963). *Personality Development and Psychopathology.* Boston: Houghton Mifflin.

Chatham, P. (1985). *Treatment of the Borderline Personality.* New York: Jason Aronson.

Chess, S., Thomas, A., and Birch, H. (1959). Characteristics of the individual child's behavioral responses to the environment. *American Journal of Orthopsychiatry* 29:719-802.

Chessick, R. (1965). Empathy and love in psychotherapy. *American Journal of Psychotherapy* 19:205-219.

——— (1977). *Intensive Psychotherapy of the Borderline Patient.* New York: Jason Aronson.

——— (1979). A practical approach to the psychotherapy of the borderline patient. *American Journal of Psychotherapy* 33:531-546.

——— (1982). Intensive psychotherapy of a borderline patient. *Archives of General Psychiatry* 39:413-419.

Cohen, C., and Sherwood, V. (1989). Becoming a constant object for the borderline patient. *Bulletin of the Menninger Clinic* 53:287-299.

Cushman, P. (1990). Why the self is empty: toward a historically situated psychology. *American Psychologist* 45:599-611.

Deutsch, H. (1942). Some forms of emotional disturbance and their relationship to schizophrenia. *Psychoanalytic Quarterly* 11:301-321.

Dorpat, T. (1981). Basic concepts and terms in object relations theory. In *Object and Self: A Developmental Approach,* ed. S. Tuttman, C. Kaye, and M. Zimmerman, pp. 149-178. New York: International Universities Press.

Dorr, D., Barley, W., Gard, B., and Webb, C. (1983). Understanding and treating borderline personality organization. *Psychotherapy: Theory, Research and Practice* 20:397-404.

Druck, A. (1989). *Four Therapeutic Approaches to the Borderline Patient.* Northvale, NJ: Jason Aronson.

Fairbairn, W. D. (1952). *Psychoanalytic Studies of Personality.* London: Tavistock.

Federn, P. (1952). *Ego Psychology and the Psychoses.* New York: Basic Books.

Ferenczi, S. (1929). The unwelcome child and his death-instinct. *International Journal of Psycho-Analysis* 10:125.

Freud, A. (1952). The mutual influence in the development of ego and id: introduction to the discussion. *The Psychoanalytic Study of the Child* 7:42–50. New York: International Universities Press.

——— (1965). *Normality and Pathology in Childhood: Assessments of Development.* New York: International Universities Press.

Freud, S. (1921). Group psychology and the analysis of the ego. *Standard Edition* 18.

Fromm-Reichmann, F. (1950). *Principles of Intensive Psychotherapy.* Chicago: University of Chicago Press.

Gay, P. (1988). *Freud: A Life for Our Time.* New York: Norton.

Grinker, R., Werble, B., and Drye, R. (1968). *The Borderline Syndrome: A Behavioral Study of Ego-Functions.* New York: Basic Books.

Gunderson, J. (1984). *Borderline Personality Disorder.* Washington, DC: American Psychiatric Press.

Gunderson, J., and Singer, M. (1975). Defining borderline patients: an overview. *American Journal of Psychiatry* 132:1–10.

Guntrip, H. (1968). *Schizoid Phenomena, Object Relations, and the Self.* New York: International Universities Press.

Hartmann, H. (1952). The mutual influence in the development of ego and id. In *Essays in Ego Psychology: Selected Problems in Psychoanalytic Theory*, pp. 155–181. New York: International Universities Press, 1964.

Hawthorne, M. (1988). *The human experience of reparation: a phenomenological investigation.* Unpublished doctoral dissertation. Knoxville, TN: University of Tennessee.

Hoch, P., and Polatin, P. (1949). Pseudoneurotic forms of schizophrenia. *Psychiatric Quarterly* 23:248–276.

Kahn, M. (1969). Vicissitudes of being, knowing, and experiencing in the therapeutic situation. In *The Privacy of the Self*, pp. 203–218. New York: International Universities Press, 1974.

Kaplan, L. (1978). *Oneness and Separateness: From Infant to Individual.* New York: Simon & Schuster.

Kernberg, O. (1967). Borderline personality organization. *Journal of the American Psychoanalytic Association* 15:641–685.

——— (1968). The treatment of patients with borderline personality organization. *International Journal of Psycho-Analysis* 49:600–619.

——— (1975). *Borderline Conditions and Pathological Narcissism.* New York: Jason Aronson.

——— (1976). *Object Relations Theory and Clinical Psychoanalysis.* New York: Jason Aronson.

—— (1977). Structural change and its impediments. In *Borderline Personality Disorders: The Concept, the Syndrome, the Patient*, ed. P. Hartocollis, pp. 275–306. New York: International Universities Press.

—— (1980). *Internal World and External Reality*. New York: Jason Aronson.

—— (1984). *Severe Personality Disorders*. New Haven, CT: Yale University Press.

—— (1987). Projection and projective identification: development and clinical aspects. *Journal of the American Psychoanalytic Association* 35:795–819.

Kernberg, O., Selzer, M., Koenigsburg, H., et al. (1989). *Psychodynamic Psychotherapy of Borderline Patients*. New York: Basic Books.

Klein, M. (1975a). *Love, Guilt, and Reparation and Other Works: 1921–1945*. New York: Delacorte Press.

—— (1975b). *Envy and Gratitude and Other Works: 1946–1963*. New York: Delacorte Press.

Knight, R. (1953). Borderline states. *Bulletin of the Menninger Clinic* 17:1–12.

Kohut, H. (1971). *The Analysis of the Self*. New York: International Universities Press.

Kroll, J. (1988). *The Challenge of the Borderline Patient: Competency in Diagnosis and Treatment*. New York: W. W. Norton.

Langs, R. (1973). *The Technique of Psychoanalytic Psychotherapy*, vol. 1. New York: Jason Aronson.

Leichtman, M. (1989). Evolving concepts of borderline personality disorders. *Bulletin of the Menninger Clinic* 53:229–249.

Leon, I. (1984). Psychoanalysis, Piaget, and attachment: the construction of the human object in the first year of life. *International Review of Psycho-Analysis* 11:255–278.

—— (1987). Object constancy as a developmental line. *Bulletin of the Menninger Clinic* 51:144–157.

Lichtenstein, H. (1976). *The Dilemma of Human Identity*. New York: Jason Aronson.

Mahler, M. (1968). *On Human Symbiosis and the Vicissitudes of Individuation*. New York: International Universities Press.

—— (1971). A study of the separation-individuation process and its possible application to borderline phenomena in the psychoanalytic situation. *The Psychoanalytic Study of the Child* 26:403–424. New Haven, CT: Yale University Press.

Mahler, M., and Furer, M. (1968). *On Human Symbiosis and the Vicissitudes of Individuation*, vol. II, *Infantile Psychosis*. New York: International Universities Press.

Mahler, M., Pine, F., and Bergman, A. (1970). The mother's reaction to her toddler's drive for individuation. In *Parenthood: Its Psychology and Psychopathology*, ed. E. J. Anthony and T. Benedeck, pp. 257–274. Boston: Little, Brown.

—— (1975). *The Psychological Birth of the Human Infant: Symbiosis and Individuation*. New York: Basic Books.

Masterson, J. (1972). *Treatment of the Borderline Adolescent: A Developmental Approach*. New York: John Wiley.

—— (1976). *Psychotherapy of the Borderline Adult: A Developmental Approach*. New York: Brunner/Mazel.

—— (1978). The borderline adult: transference acting-out and working-through. In *New Perspectives on Psychotherapy of the Borderline Adult*, ed. J. Masterson, pp. 121–147. New York: Brunner/Mazel.

—— (1981). *Narcissistic and Borderline Disorders: An Integrated Developmental Approach*. New York: Brunner/Mazel.

Masterson, J., and Rinsley, D. (1975). The borderline syndrome: the role of the mother in the genesis and psychic structure of the borderline personality. *International Journal of Psycho-Analysis* 56:163–177.

McDevitt, J. (1975). Separation-individuation and object constancy. *Journal of the American Psychoanalytic Association* 23:713–742.

Meissner, W. (1984). *The Borderline Spectrum*. New York: Jason Aronson.

Modell, A. (1976). The "holding environment" and the therapeutic action of psychoanalysis. *Journal of the American Psychoanalytic Association* 24:285–307.

Ogden, T. (1982). *Projective Identification and Psychotherapeutic Technique*. New York: Jason Aronson.

Pruyser, P. (1975). What splits in "splitting"? *Bulletin of the Menninger Clinic* 39:1–46.

Rinsley, D. (1982). *Borderline and Other Self Disorders*. New York: Jason Aronson.

Schachtel, E. (1959). *Metamorphosis: On the Development of Affect, Perception, Attention, and Memory*. New York: Basic Books.

Schmideberg, M. (1959). The borderline patient. In *American Handbook of Psychiatry*, vol. 1, ed. S. Arieti, pp. 398–416. New York: Basic Books.

Searles, H. (1960). *The Nonhuman Environment*. New York: International Universities Press.

—— (1978). Psychoanalytic therapy with the borderline adult: some principles concerning technique. In *New Perspectives on Psychotherapy of the Borderline Adult*, ed. J. Masterson, pp. 43–65. New York: Brunner/Mazel.

—— (1979). The countertransference with the borderline patient. In *Advances in Psychotherapy of the Borderline Patient*, ed. J. LeBoit and A. Capponi, pp. 309–346. New York: Jason Aronson.

—— (1986). *My Work with Borderline Patients*. New York: Jason Aronson.

Selye, H. (1956). *The Stress of Life*. New York: McGraw-Hill.

Selzer, M., Koenigsberg, H., and Kernberg, O. (1987). The initial contract in the treatment of borderline patients. *American Journal of Psychiatry* 144:927–930.

Shapiro, E. (1978). The psychodynamics and developmental psychology of the borderline patient: a review of the literature. *American Journal of Psychiatry* 135:1305–1315.

Shapiro, E., Zinner, J., and Shapiro, R. (1975). The influence of family experience on borderline personality development. *International Review of Psycho-Analysis* 2:399–411.

Sherwood, V. (1987). The schizoid personality in light of Camus's actor. *Bulletin of the Menninger Clinic* 51:158–169.

—— (1989). Object constancy: the illusion of being seen. *Psychoanalytic Psychology* 6:15–30.

Singer, M. (1977). The borderline diagnosis and psychological tests. In *Borderline Personality Disorders*, ed. P. Hartocollis, pp. 193–212. New York: International Universities Press.

Spence, D. (1987). *The Freudian Metaphor: Toward Paradigm Change in Psychoanalysis*. New York: W. W. Norton.

Spitz, R. (1945). Hospitalism: an inquiry into the genesis of psychiatric conditions in early childhood. *The Psychoanalytic Study of the Child* 1:53–74. New York: International Universities Press.

Stern, A. (1938). Psychoanalytic investigation of and therapy in the borderline group of neuroses. *Psychoanalytic Quarterly* 7:467–489.

Stern, D. (1985). *The Interpersonal World of the Infant*. New York: Basic Books.

Stierlin, H. (1969). *Conflict and Reconciliation*. Garden City, NY: Doubleday Anchor Books.

Stolorow, R., and Lachmann, F. (1980). *Psychoanalysis of Developmental Arrests*. New York: International Universities Press.

Stone, M. (1987). Systems for defining a borderline case. In *The Borderline Patient: Emerging Concepts in Diagnosis, Psychodynamics, and Treatment*, vol. 1, ed. J. Grotstein, M. Solomon, and J. Lang, pp. 13–35. Hillsdale, NJ: Analytic Press.

Sullivan, H. (1953). *The Interpersonal Theory of Psychiatry*. New York: W. W. Norton.

Szalita, A. (1976). Some thoughts on empathy. *Psychiatry* 39:142–152.

Szasz, T. (1959). The communication of distress between child and parent. *British Journal of Medical Psychology* 32:161–170.

Van den Berg, J. (1961). *The Changing Nature of Man: Introduction to a Historical Psychology*. New York: W. W. Norton.

Wells, M., and Glickauf-Hughes, C. (1986). Techniques to develop object constancy with borderline clients. *Psychotherapy* 23:460–468.

Wheelis, A. (1958). *The Quest for Identity*. New York: W. W. Norton.

White, R. (1960). Competence and the psychosexual stages of development. In *Nebraska Symposium on Motivation*, ed. M. Jones, pp. 197–240. Lincoln, NE: University of Nebraska Press.

Winnicott, D. (1947). Hate in the countertransference. In *Collected Papers: Through Paediatrics to Psychoanalysis*, pp. 174–193. New York: Basic Books, 1958.

——— (1958). The capacity to be alone. In *The Maturational Processes and the Facilitating Environment: Studies in the Theory of Emotional Development*, pp. 29–36. New York: International Universities Press, 1965.

——— (1960). The theory of the parent-infant relationship. In *The Maturational Processes and the Facilitating Environment: Studies in the Theory of Emotional Development*, pp. 37–55. New York: International Universities Press, 1965.

——— (1963a). Communicating and not communicating leading to a study of certain opposites. In *The Maturational Processes and the Facilitating Environment: Studies in the Theory of Emotional Development*, pp. 179–192. New York: International Universities Press, 1965.

——— (1963b). The development of the capacity for concern. In *The Maturational Processes and the Facilitating Environment: Studies in the Theory of Emotional Development*, pp. 73–82. New York: International Universities Press, 1965.

Wong, N. (1980). Borderline and narcissistic disorders: a selective overview. *Bulletin of the Menninger Clinic* 44:101–126.

Zetzel, E. (1971). A developmental approach to the borderline patient. *American Journal of Psychiatry* 127:867–871.

Index